The Industrious
Child Worker

To Julie
With Best Wishes

Mary Nejedly
2021

The Industrious Child Worker

Child Labour and Childhood in Birmingham and the West Midlands 1750 to 1900

Mary Nejedly

West Midlands Publications
an imprint of
University of Hertfordshire Press

First published in Great Britain in 2021 by
West Midlands Publications
an imprint of
University of Hertfordshire Press
College Lane
Hatfield
Hertfordshire
AL10 9AB

© Mary Nejedly 2021

British Library Cataloguing in Publication Data
A catalogue record for this book is available from the British Library

ISBN 978-1-912260-43-0

Design by Arthouse Publishing Solutions
Printed in Great Britain by Charlesworth Press, Wakefield

Contents

Illustrations

Abbreviations

BAH	Birmingham Archives and Heritage
BPP	British Parliamentary Papers
SCRO	Staffordshire County Record Office
TNA	The National Archives
VCH	Victoria County History
WALS	Wolverhampton Archives and Local Studies
WCRO	Warwickshire County Record Office
WoCRO	Worcestershire County Record Office

Acknowledgements

My greatest debt is to Dr Malcolm Dick of the University of Birmingham, for his expertise, support, guidance and encouragement. His insightful comments and enthusiasm for this subject have continued to inspire me. My thanks are also due to Professor Carl Chinn and Professor Jonathan Reinarz for their advice and helpful suggestions.

I would also like to thank the staff of the Record Offices of Staffordshire, Worcestershire and Warwickshire, together with staff at The National Archives, Wolverhampton Archives and Local Studies, and the British Library for their help and assistance with my research. The majority of my research for this study was undertaken at the Wolfson Centre for Archival Research at the Library of Birmingham, and I am particularly grateful to the archives staff for their valuable contributions.

I am grateful to the editor of *Family and Community History* for publishing an article based on aspects of the research in this book, and to the anonymous reviewers for their helpful comments.

Finally, I would like to thank my friends and family for their ongoing support and keen interest in my book, especially Steve, Rob and Kate.

1

Introduction

> My first job came when I was only a little over six years of age; it was turning a wheel for a
> rope and twine spinner at Rob's Rope Walk, Duddeston Mill Road, Vauxhall, Birmingham.
> I received 2s 6d per week, and worked from six in the morning until six at night.[1]

Will Thorne was very young when he began work in 1863, joining thousands of young child workers in Birmingham's factories and workshops. If he had arrived at the gates of a cotton mill in search of work, six-year-old Thorne would have been refused employment because he was too young, but legal restrictions on child labour in 1863 did not apply to all sectors of the economy. Government legislation aimed at regulating and restricting the employment of children was first introduced with the Health and Morals of Apprentices Act of 1802, followed by a series of Factory Acts during the nineteenth century. However, it was only in 1867 that employment of children below the age of eight was prohibited in all factories and workshops, despite the large numbers of children who worked in manufacturing industries other than textiles.[2] Studies of child labour have examined the experiences of child workers in agriculture, mining and textile mills, yet surprisingly little research has been concentrated on child labour in industrial towns that had quite different patterns of economic activity and organisation.[3] This book explores child labour in Birmingham and the West Midlands from the mid-eighteenth century to the end of the nineteenth century, focusing on the economic contributions of child workers under the age of 14 and their experiences of a childhood dominated by work. It offers insights into the relationship between child workers and their families, highlighting the extent to which children's education and health could be damaged for the economic benefit of families as well as employers. Furthermore, it enhances our current knowledge of childhood and child

---

1   Will Thorne, *My Life's Battles* (London, 1925), p. 15.

2   Peter Kirby, *Child Labour in Britain, 1750–1870* (Basingstoke, 2003), p. 94.

3   Joyce Burnette, 'Child Day-labourers in Agriculture: Evidence from Farm Accounts, 1740–1850', *Economic History Review*, 65/3 (2012), pp. 1077–99; Hugh Cunningham, 'The Employment and Unemployment of Children in England, c1680–1851', *Past and Present*, 126 (1990), pp. 115–50; Maxine Berg, *The Age of Manufactures, 1700–1820: Industry, Innovation and Work in Britain* (London, 1994); Eric Hopkins, *Childhood Transformed: Working Class Children in Nineteenth-Century England* (Manchester, 1994).

labour by illuminating this previously unexamined aspect of the Birmingham and West Midlands' economy, arguing that child labour was not a short-lived stage of the early Industrial Revolution but an integral part of industry in the region until towards the end of the nineteenth century.

The literature on child labour has expanded over the last three decades to include the significance of child workers' contribution to industrialisation and the relative importance of children's earnings to the family economy.[4] More recently, attention has turned towards the themes of child workers' health, diversity of employment and agency among child workers.[5] These studies have informed the arguments developed in this book, which examines the nature and extent of child labour in Birmingham and the West Midlands and the changes that took place in the levels of child labour between 1750 and 1900; the importance of children's earnings to the family economy; changes in the intensity of children's work and the impact of early work on children's education, health and life chances; and changes in attitudes to child labour and childhood over time, as well as evidence of children's agency as participants in historical change.

In the centuries before industrialisation approximately a third of households in early modern England contained servants, including children, who were housed, clothed and fed within the household in exchange for unpaid work.[6] A further one-third of households had older children who were living away from home: children from poor rural families were expected to leave home from the age of ten to live and work as farm servants until they were old enough to marry and set up their own household. Younger children still living at home earned small amounts for bird-scaring or watching sheep. When not working on the land, the entire family would be occupied with the sorting, carding and spinning of wool.[7] Most children lived in rural or semi-rural districts in the mid-eighteenth century, working at bird-scaring, picking stones or weeding and planting crops, and many continued in this rural way of life until much later in the nineteenth century. Roger Langdon, for example, began work as a farmer's boy in 1833 at the age of eight: 'For the princely sum of one shilling a week I had to mind sheep and pull up turnips in all winds and weathers,

---

4   Sara Horrell and Jane Humphries, '"The exploitation of little children": Child Labour and the Family Economy in the Industrial Revolution', *Explorations in Economic History*, 32 (1995), pp. 485–516; Jane Humphries, *Childhood and Child Labour in the British Industrial Revolution* (Cambridge, 2010).

5   Peter Kirby, *Child Workers and Industrial Health in Britain, 1780–1850* (Woodbridge, 2013); Nigel Goose and Katrina Honeyman (eds), *Childhood and Child Labour in Industrial England: Diversity and Agency, 1750–1914* (Farnham, 2013).

6   Peter Laslett, *The World We Have Lost* (London, 1971).

7   *Ibid.*, pp. 16–17.

starting at six o'clock in the morning'.[8] However, with enclosure and the move towards day-labour, the problem of seasonal employment in agriculture became more acute, as high levels of unemployment among adult agricultural workers became common from October to March.[9] The main period of enclosure in Warwickshire, from 1760 to 1790, may have been a significant factor in encouraging rural families to migrate to Birmingham and other nearby towns in search of industrial employment.

Peter Kirby has identified the important role of workshop-based industries in absorbing migrant labour as structural changes occurred in the agricultural labour market. Workshop production was relatively flexible, as employers relied on the use of hand tools rather than capital-intensive machinery and could lay off workers when trade was depressed.[10] Even in textiles, domestic production within small units remained important: more than half the employees in the silk industry in 1851 were employed in small firms of fewer than 20 employees. Boys and girls were employed in a wide variety of domestic workshop occupations, ranging from hose and stocking manufacture to gloving, printing and soap-boiling. In the late eighteenth and early nineteenth centuries regional specialisation developed based on established rural domestic industries, such as woollen textiles in the West Riding of Yorkshire.[11] Joseph Terry began work in 1823 at the age of seven in a Yorkshire woollen mill, later recalling the experience in his autobiography:

> some part of my time was spent Setting Cards, or inserting the Card Teeth into leaves and Garters as they were called to fit on the Scribbling Machines for Scribbling Wool etc. This was a most wearisome and dreary task … great numbers of children and young and grown-up families got their bread by this poor and unhealthy means; the very best hands never exceeding one shilling per day, and great numbers suffered much in their health from this, worse than slavish employment.[12]

In metal-working industries men and boys were employed in the production of machines and machine parts, whereas women workers and girls were found in the less-skilled work of chain-making, nail-making and pin-making.[13] Metal

---

8   John Burnett (ed.), *Destiny Obscure: Autobiographies of Childhood, Education and Family from the 1820s to the 1920s* (London, 1994), p. 46.

9   K.D.M. Snell, *Annals of the Labouring Poor: Social Change and Agrarian England, 1660–1900* (Cambridge, 1985), p. 144.

10 Kirby, *Child Labour*, p. 61.

11 Pat Hudson, *The Industrial Revolution* (Sevenoaks, 1992), p. 118.

12 Burnett, *Destiny Obscure*, pp. 57–8.

13 Kirby, *Child Labour*, pp. 63–4.

industries in Birmingham became specialised during the eighteenth century in brass-wares, jewellery-making, buttons, buckles, toys and the gun trade. Intermediate technologies, particularly the introduction of the stamp, press, draw-bench and lathe, encouraged small firms to meet the growing demand for a variety of goods. Pat Hudson and Eric Hopkins have argued that the increased division of labour and specialisation of Birmingham's metal trades in the late eighteenth century involved the expansion of female and child labour.[14] Skilled workmen employed child assistants, while young girls were employed to hand-paint buttons and buckles and in the manufacture of covered buttons and gilt jewellery. This book explores differing forms of children's industrial employment, including parish apprenticeships and non-apprenticed child labour in various occupations and work environments in the West Midlands, with a particular focus on Birmingham. E.P. Thompson famously referred to the 'exploitation of little children' as one of the most shameful aspects of industrialisation in Britain.[15] However, the experiences of non-apprenticed children employed in occupations such as pin-making and nail-making in manufacturing workshops or factories have been largely neglected. A comparison of these experiences with those from elsewhere illuminates and adds to the existing literature on child labour.

Studies of child employment in agriculture and rural industries by Helen Speechley, Joyce Burnette and Nicola Verdon found that children's earnings, however small, were important to their families.[16] The impact of enclosure may therefore have encouraged rural families to migrate to industrial towns, where work was available for women and children as well as men. Studies of parish apprenticeship by Katrina Honeyman and Alysa Levene suggest that parish apprenticeships were important in providing child workers to local craftsmen and women as well as to new textile manufacturing industries.[17] Research by Sara Horrell and Jane Humphries highlighted the significance to family incomes of the earnings of children of factory workers and outworkers, reflecting the

---

14   Hudson, *The Industrial Revolution*, pp. 122–5; Eric Hopkins, *Birmingham: The First Manufacturing Town in the World 1760–1840* (London, 1989), pp. 102–03.

15   E.P. Thompson, *The Making of the English Working Class* (London, 1991), p. 331.

16   Helen Speechley, 'Female and Child Agricultural Day Labourers in Somerset, *c.*1685–1870', PhD thesis (University of Exeter, 1999), pp. 19–48; Burnette, 'Child Day-labourers'; Nicola Verdon, 'The Rural Labour Market in the Early Nineteenth Century: Women's and Children's Employment, Family Income, and the 1834 Poor Law Report', *Economic History Review*, 55/2 (2002), pp. 299–323.

17   Katrina Honeyman, *Child Workers in England, 1780–1820: Parish Apprentices and the Making of the Early Industrial Labour Force* (Farnham, 2007); Alysa Levene, 'Parish Apprenticeship and the Old Poor Law in London', *Economic History Review*, 63/4 (2010), pp. 915–41 at 929–30.

situation in agricultural families.[18] These studies thus raise questions about the amount children could earn in particular industries or sectors of the economy, and at what age they typically began work. Furthermore, historians such as Hans-Joachim Voth, Jan de Vries and Nigel Goose have suggested there was an intensification of work between 1760 and 1850 that markedly impacted the life chances of working children in terms of educational attainment, levels of literacy, health and life expectancy.[19] These important themes and avenues of research are drawn together here to frame a new history of child labour in Birmingham and the West Midlands.

Children and childhood

One of the tasks confronting historians is identifying changes in attitudes towards children and concepts of childhood over time. During the eighteenth century new thinking emerged about the concept of childhood and how children should be raised and educated as future citizens. The Enlightenment philosopher John Locke set out his ideas for educating children based on scientific principles and rational thought. His *An Essay Concerning Human Understanding*, published in 1690, suggested that humans were born with a mind that was a *tabula rasa*, or 'blank slate', that could be moulded by careful attention to education.[20] He followed this in 1693 with *Some Thoughts Concerning Education*, which provided a detailed explanation of his educational theories.[21] Locke emphasised the importance of good physical health, self-denial and rational thinking in children. He advised parents to focus on their child's aptitudes and interests, enabling them to enjoy learning and develop critical-thinking skills. The recommendations in *Some Thoughts Concerning Education* were clearly aimed at parents from the elite and middling classes who wished to raise their sons as gentlemen, good citizens and potential leaders in society. In contrast, Locke's ideas about children of the labouring classes were

---

18   Horrell and Humphries, '"Exploitation of little children"'; Sara Horrell and Jane Humphries, 'Old Questions, New Data, and Alternative Perspectives: Families' Living Standards in the Industrial Revolution', *The Journal of Economic History*, 52/4 (1992), pp. 849–80 at 851–2.

19   Hans-Joachim Voth, 'Living Standards and the Urban Environment', in R. Floud and P. Johnson (eds), *The Cambridge Economic History of Modern Britain* (Cambridge, 2008), pp. 268–94 at 293; Jan de Vries, 'The Industrial Revolution and the Industrious Revolution', *The Journal of Economic History*, 54/2 (1994), pp. 249–70 at 255–76; Nigel Goose, 'Employment Prospects in Nineteenth-Century Hertfordshire in Perspective: Varieties of Childhood?' in Nigel Goose and Katrina Honeyman (eds), *Childhood and Child Labour in Industrial England: Diversity and Agency, 1750–1914* (Farnham, 2013), pp. 157–214 at 159–67.

20   John Locke, *An Essay Concerning Human Understanding* (London, 1690); Hugh Cunningham, *Children and Childhood in Western Society since 1500* (Harlow, 1995), p. 61.

21   John Locke, *Some Thoughts Concerning Education* (London, 1693).

focused on training for work so that they could become useful and productive members of society rather than a burden on the parish. He proposed that each parish should establish a school of industry to train all poor children from the age of three upwards, providing an income for the parish and instilling 'the habits of industry' at the earliest age.[22] At the end of the seventeenth century Locke thus identified education and vocational training for poor children as a way of dealing with the growing problem of poverty and dependence on the Poor Law. These were ideas that continued to appeal in later decades to political leaders, manufacturers and Poor Law officials concerned about the increasing numbers of poor children placing demands on local ratepayers. For example, in 1796 William Pitt emphasised the value of work done by young children employed in the new manufacturing industries.[23] At the same time, however, social reformers such as Jonas Hanway highlighted the exploitation of children by unscrupulous employers and campaigned for the improved treatment of children dispatched to mills from the London workhouses and against the use of climbing boys by chimney-sweeps.[24]

Locke's emphasis on moulding a child's character through strictly defined education and training was called into question by the ideas of the French philosopher Jean-Jacques Rousseau, whose treatise *Émile, ou De L'Éducation* was published in 1762.[25] Rousseau's theory was that because children are innately good and innocent they should be free to learn through experience in the natural world rather than be educated from books. Accordingly, a child's natural goodness should be preserved by encouraging them to learn through play and exploring nature. The role of parents was to protect a child from corrupting influences by removing them as far as possible from the world of adults until they reached adolescence. In Rousseau's example of an ideal childhood, Emile was allowed to learn from nature without any formal education or imposition of moral rules, thus offering an entirely new perspective on child-rearing.[26] In addition to the prominent philosophies of Locke and Rousseau, cultural historians have identified the spread of a 'cult of maternity' from early in the eighteenth century, in which the mother was placed at the centre of child welfare and the perceived value of motherhood

---

22 John Locke, *An Essay on the Poor Law* (London, 1697); Cunningham, *Children and Childhood*, p. 138; Alysa Levene, *The Childhood of the Poor: Welfare in Eighteenth-Century London* (Basingstoke, 2012), p. 3.

23 Honeyman, *Child Workers in England*, p. 4.

24 Cunningham, *Children and Childhood*, pp. 138–9.

25 Jean-Jacques Rousseau, *Émile, ou De L'Éducation* (Geneva, 1762); Levene, *Childhood of the Poor*, p. 4.

26 Cunningham, *Children and Childhood*, p. 67.

increased.[27] Joanne Bailey has argued that by the late eighteenth century children 'were imagined as the culmination of married love' and portrayed in newspapers and journals as bringing joy to parents of all social classes.[28] Consequently, parents were advised of the importance of raising happy children within a moral Christian family, as 'a happy child was a virtuous child'.[29] Middle-class parents were expected to educate their children to become independent gentlemen and accomplished gentlewomen. On the other hand, the advice given to lower-class families was to teach their children the virtues of industriousness, cleanliness and religiosity. The image of the rural cottage-dwelling family embodied the qualities of contented family life: they were hard-working, modest and uncomplaining. These 'cottage-door' images of the 1790s were circulated to urban residents in the form of 'cottage' songs that praised the virtues of domestic happiness among rural labouring families.[30]

Rousseau's concept of a childhood in which emotions and freedom of expression were inspired by the natural world influenced not only the child-rearing practices of middle-class parents but also the philosophy, art and literature of the Romantic Movement that emerged in the late eighteenth century.[31] Reynolds' popular painting (?1788), *The Age of Innocence*, presented the concept of a carefree childhood in a portrait of a simply dressed small child under a tree in a rural setting.[32] Children were perceived as emblems of truth and beauty by the Romantic poets, who condemned poverty, social deprivation and the exploitation of child workers. William Blake's illustrated poems *Songs of Innocence and of Experience*, published in 1794, contrasted the innocent world of childhood with the harsh adult world in which children were exploited and their innocence destroyed through early child labour. Blake championed the cause of climbing boys in the story of a poor young boy sold by his parents to a chimney-sweep. Similarly, Samuel Taylor Coleridge used his writing to draw attention to children working in the cotton factories, referring to them as 'white-slaves'.[33] Despite such attempts to highlight the plight of the poorest and most exploited children, it remained generally accepted that early work for children of the lower classes was both established and inevitable, although social reformers such as Sarah Trimmer argued that pauper children should be

---

27 Joanne Bailey, *Parenting in England 1760–1830: Emotion, Identity & Generation* (Oxford, 2012), pp. 5–7.

28 *Ibid.*, pp. 23–5.

29 *Ibid.*, p. 75.

30 *Ibid.*, p. 116.

31 Cunningham, *Children and Childhood*, p. 73; Levene, *Childhood of the Poor*, pp. 173–4.

32 Joshua Reynolds, *The Age of Innocence*, oil on canvas (London, ?1788).

33 Cunningham, *Children and Childhood*, pp. 139–40.

trained in traditional craft skills instead of new factory employment. But it was not until later in the nineteenth century that it became clear that a sharp divide existed between middle-class notions of an innocent and carefree childhood and the actual experiences of child workers.

Campaigns in the early decades of the nineteenth century aimed to reduce hours and improve working conditions for child workers, rather than to abolish child labour. Prominent supporters of the Ten Hours Movement, such as Lord Shaftesbury, were not opposed to child labour in principle, but were concerned that children should work part-time hours combined with part-time schooling.[34] Over the course of the nineteenth century new legislation gradually removed children from certain hazardous roles in mining and textile mills, notably working underground and cleaning moving machinery. The 1842 government report on children in mines and factories inspired Elizabeth Barrett Browning's poem 'The Cry of the Children', focusing further attention on the conditions endured by working children.[35] However, changes in employment legislation emerged only slowly over several decades, and school attendance for all children up to the age of 13 did not become compulsory until the passing of the Education Act of 1880. The extent to which changing ideologies about childhood filtered through society and impacted on the reality of child workers' lives in Birmingham and the West Midlands is one of the important issues explored in this study.

Methodology, sources and structure

This book takes a thematic approach to the study of child labour through a number of case studies, examining the extent and nature of child labour, the experiences of child workers and changes in attitudes towards children and childhood. Shining a spotlight on child labour allows insights into the attitudes of ordinary families towards everyday events, enhancing our understanding of their relationships, experiences and perceptions, not only as regards child labour but also in terms of the poor law, parenting, schooling, illness and family finances. John Tosh has suggested that the ultimate aim of historical research is to 'recapture human life in all its variety' – in other words, 'to write total history'. He points out, however, that this is problematic unless the research is limited to a local geographical area, which allows broad conclusions to be reached.[36] This book restricts its investigation to child labour in Birmingham and the West Midlands in order to illuminate a wider picture of social, economic and political change. In the case of education, for example, a focus

---

34   *Ibid.*, p. 142.

35   *Ibid.*, p. 143.

36   John Tosh, *The Pursuit of History* (Harlow, 2006), pp. 138–40.

on child labour reveals attitudes towards the type and length of schooling that working families deemed appropriate for their children, showing that parents were anxious for their children to learn basic skills in reading and possibly arithmetic, but only until they reached working age. Birmingham children, for example, typically began work at around the age of eight, although many child workers continued their schooling on Sundays or at evening schools. Parents thus adopted strategies for education that did not interfere with the child's ability to earn a living.

Small incidents involving child workers can also indicate the wider economic and social circumstances of families and their attitudes to parenting. In one case, a mother carried her child to work at a Birmingham pin manufactory each day because the child, at just four years old, was too young to walk the two miles to work.[37] Was the mother uncaring and interested only in the money her child could earn? Or was the family in dire straits and in desperate need of the child's small weekly wage? Alternatively, was it possible that the mother regarded the pin factory as a safe place to leave her child while she worked nearby? These details help to paint a larger picture of the lives of working families over the period, shedding light on the diversity of childhood experiences.

A study centred on the lives of working children faces the issue of a lack of direct evidence in the form of the child's voice. Children's experiences are often relayed through adults, as in the case of evidence given by child workers to the Children's Employment Commissions in the nineteenth century. Honeyman has emphasised that when child workers were questioned by officials they were likely to provide positive responses. For example, by expressing satisfaction with their conditions of work because they believed that was what the questioner expected, and because they feared reprisals if they answered otherwise.[38] Cultural differences in language, understanding and attitudes between middle-class inspectors and manual workers were also likely to create barriers, affecting the child workers' responses to queries. In addition, young children were probably nervous and apprehensive when questioned about educational standards and working conditions by these unfamiliar visitors. Nonetheless, the evidence given by child workers to the Commissions provides useful insights into the experiences of working children in the absence of alternative sources such as letters, diaries or school essays. These accounts also show some evidence of children's agency. One interview with a young boy revealed that he had chosen to go to work rather than attend school, even though his mother was willing and able to pay the school fees for him. On the other hand, there are numerous examples of children who had no choice other than to end

---

37   BPP, 1843, 431, XIV, *Children's Employment Commission, Second Report*, p. 326.

38   Honeyman, *Child Workers in England*, p. 201.

schooling at an early age because of their family's economic situation. Many of these children expressed a strong desire to continue their education, with some attending evening classes or Sunday school on top of their work commitments.

A wide range of sources are used in this study, including local poor law records, parliamentary papers, census reports, local business and institutional records, newspaper reports, autobiographies and memoirs. Parish apprenticeship records for the county of Warwickshire and the neighbouring counties of Worcestershire and Staffordshire are examined to establish whether Birmingham industries took advantage of the availability of cheap child labour in the form of pauper apprenticeship under the old Poor Law, as the cotton industry did. This raises questions about whether parish overseers were willing to place pauper children at a distance from their home parish, the types of occupation deemed suitable and the links overseers maintained with apprenticed children.[39] In view of the amount of data, three parishes were selected from each of the three counties, providing a sample size of 2,028 apprenticeship indentures of pauper children from nine parishes. One limitation of using apprenticeship records is the problem of incomplete or missing data, which may lead to a reliance on parishes where records have survived.[40] Parishes in this study were chosen based on their geographical proximity (within 20 miles) to Birmingham, the survival of parish apprenticeship records and diversity in economic activity.

The minute books of the Birmingham Guardians of the Poor provide details about the establishment and operation of a separate workhouse for children, the Birmingham Asylum for the Infant Poor, which was opened in 1797 to provide residential accommodation and industrial employment for pauper children. Difficulties with this type of source include a lack of information about the children or their families and incomplete or missing records. In this instance, admission registers and books detailing the day-to-day running of the infant asylum have not survived, so only the official viewpoint of the Board of Guardians is presented. Despite this, considerable information is revealed about the institution and the attitudes of guardians towards child labour, providing insights into their attempts to minimise poor law expenditure and maximise income from children's work.

Inspectors appointed by the Factories Inquiry Commission of 1833 and the Children's Employment Commissions of 1843 and 1862 visited industrial premises over a period of more than three decades.[41] During this time they interviewed employers, adult workers and supervisors, and child workers of

---

39   *Ibid.*, p. 11.
40   *Ibid.*, p. 56.
41   Kirby, *Child Labour*, p. 13.

varying ages and occupations. The reports of the commissions provide extensive information about the number of establishments and types of manufacturing industry in Birmingham and the West Midlands, the working conditions and the numbers of adults and children employed; in particular, the pin industry in the 1830s and the button industry in the 1860s were major employers of child labour. These extensive investigations offer numerous insights into the lives of child workers, including their experiences of early work and its impact on education and health. Additional evidence comes from local newspaper reports and business records that provide details of average weekly earnings.

An alternative perspective comes from first-hand accounts of child workers' experiences in autobiographies by George Jacob Holyoake and Will Thorne. These two men were from working-class Birmingham families and both were successful in adult life, but they had differing childhood experiences. Autobiographies by working-class authors usually include an account of the author's childhood experiences, providing valuable insights into family life, schooling and children's work, although there are few examples written by working-class women.[42] The two accounts used in this study shine a light on the different experiences of child labour encountered, despite the authors' similar backgrounds. A further perspective is offered by the records of the Middlemore Emigration Homes in Birmingham. These provide details of children admitted into the home and subsequently sent to live in Canada, including information about the children's lives before and after migration. They offer insights into both the perceived problem of so-called 'gutter children' or 'street arabs' in the 1870s and attitudes towards child migration as a solution for removing the poorest children from the streets of Victorian towns and cities. The inclusion of records relating to children sent as migrants to work in Canada adds a new dimension to the history of child labour in England.

By combining evidence from a wide range of primary sources, this study sheds light on the motivation and circumstances of poor families, exploring their interactions with the Poor Law and with the labour market. Chapter 2 examines the supply of child workers from a selection of parishes in the counties of Warwickshire, Worcestershire and Staffordshire, adopting a regional approach to the study of child labour and analysing the attitudes of parish overseers under the old Poor Law. The treatment of pauper children in the Birmingham workhouse is explored in Chapter 3, which also considers the changes in attitudes of Guardians of the Poor towards child labour in response to new legislation. Chapter 4 discusses whether there was an increase in demand for child workers at particular points during this period and whether there was any intensification in the pace of work. Chapter 5 analyses

---

42   Goose, 'Employment Prospects', p. 159.

the contribution of child workers to the family economy, considering the costs and benefits of early work and the notion of 'habits of industry' within working families. The opportunities for schooling available to children from the lower classes are discussed in Chapter 6, raising the issue of middle-class perceptions of education as a means of social control. Chapter 7 assesses the impact of work on the health of children in terms of exposure to accidental injuries, chronic ill-health and ill-treatment in the workplace. An international dimension to the research is added in Chapter 8 by considering the treatment of children admitted to the Middlemore Emigration Homes and sent to work as agricultural labourers and farm servants in Canada. Chapter 9 extends the discussion to include changes in attitudes to childhood and provision for children of the poor in the final decades of the nineteenth century. Finally, the concluding chapter draws together the main themes of the study, discussing the ways in which the research findings enhance our knowledge of the importance of child labour for industrialisation and the experience of being a child worker in Birmingham and the West Midlands.

2

Parish apprentices and the old Poor Law

Introduction

> Tender mother dry your tears
> hear is no cause for Greef or fears
> our brother is gon tho for the best
> whe hop is soule is gon to rest[1]

This verse, in memory of William Brittain from Knowle in Warwickshire, was pencilled onto the back of his parish apprenticeship certificate. It draws attention to early death as a frequent experience for poor families. William, who was bound by the parish in 1806 to Abraham Lee, a Birmingham carpenter and joiner, died during his service as an apprentice in Birmingham. The literature on child labour has frequently focused on parish apprentices as a major source of child workers in cotton mills and coal mines during industrialisation, but research has highlighted that parish apprentices were bound in various traditional crafts and trades, such as tailoring or cordwaining, often remaining in or close to their home parish.[2] This chapter examines and evaluates the supply of parish apprentices to Birmingham from a sample of parishes in the West Midlands counties of Warwickshire, Worcestershire and Staffordshire. During the eighteenth and nineteenth centuries Birmingham was an expanding industrial town that attracted migrants from the surrounding counties and further afield in search of employment. Birmingham's traditional metal industries were largely based around numerous small and medium-sized enterprises and the town enjoyed a reputation for attracting well-paid workers who were adaptable and innovative. It seems reasonable to suppose, therefore, that Birmingham was drawing in parish apprentices from the surrounding rural areas to meet the demand for child workers in its industries. But to what extent was this actually the case?

Formal apprenticeship began in England with the Statute of Artificers in 1563, which stated that a seven-year apprenticeship was required for entry into crafts and trades. The intention of the act was to control the training and

---

1 WCRO, DRB0056/143–144 Knowle Parish Apprenticeship Certificates.
2 Honeyman, *Child Workers*; Levene, 'Parish Apprenticeship'.

freedom of young people until the age of 21, placing them in the household of a master who was legally obliged to provide food, shelter and clothing while teaching the apprentice the 'arts and mysteries' of his (or her) trade.[3] A written indenture of apprenticeship was essential, both for private agreements between the master and the parents and for parish apprenticeships binding children of the poor. One of the most significant differences between private and parish apprenticeships was the age of starting work: for private apprentices the typical age of binding was 14 years, whereas pauper apprentices were bound from the age of seven years upwards, reflecting the pressure on parish officials to control the poor rate. Under the terms of the act, householders with a minimum of 'half a ploughland in tillage' were obliged to take in apprentices until at least 21 or 24 years old.[4] A pauper child with an agricultural apprenticeship might thus have an unwilling master. Boys apprenticed in husbandry were trained in cultivating the land and raising livestock, whereas girls apprenticed in housewifery were trained in the domestic skills required of a farmer's wife. A pauper child might also be placed in a trade with poor future employment prospects, such as nail-making, silk-ribbon-weaving or stocking-making. These were low-paid trades in which pauper children were frequently neglected or badly treated by masters who took on young apprentices in order to receive the apprenticeship premium paid by the parish. The child's family was unlikely to have any influence over the choice of trade because they were dependent on the parish for relief from poverty. As Alysa Levene points out, parish apprenticeship was perceived as a way of raising children and their families out of destitution by providing a future for the child and reduced dependency on the parish.[5]

The evidence in this chapter is drawn from 2,028 apprenticeship certificates from nine parishes in Warwickshire, Worcestershire and Staffordshire, which were selected for their proximity to Birmingham (within 20 miles) and diversity of economic background. The parishes of Coleshill, Knowle and Tanworth in Arden lie to the east and south-east of Birmingham; Northfield, Alvechurch and Bromsgrove to the south-west; and Harborne, Tamworth and Wednesbury to the north and north-west. A number of issues are addressed in the analysis: first, where were pauper children most likely to be apprenticed and how far were they sent from their home parish? Second, did the supply of pauper apprentices increase or decrease over the period, especially those sent to Birmingham? Third, did the trades open to parish apprenticeship change over time and did this reflect the expansion of Birmingham industries? Fourth, what were the characteristics of parish apprenticeship in terms of gender and

---

3   Joan Lane, *Apprenticeship in England 1600–1914* (London, 1996).

4   *Ibid.*

5   Levene, 'Parish Apprenticeship', p. 918.

the age of starting work? Finally, what were the attitudes of parish overseers of the poor towards pauper children and child labour?

Parish apprenticeship in rural and industrial parishes

The parishes of Coleshill, Knowle and Tanworth in Arden in Warwickshire were rural villages situated in the north of the county, whose inhabitants followed traditional occupations such as husbandman, yeoman farmer, tailor, sawer, saddler and maltster.[6] The parishes of Northfield, Alvechurch and Bromsgrove were located in the north of the county of Worcestershire. Although only six miles from Birmingham, Northfield was a rural parish largely populated by farmers who typically combined farming with other part-time occupations. For example, William Hinton was a farmer and blacksmith; Job Connup was a farmer and miller; George Fellows combined farming with nail-making; and William Brown was a farmer and innkeeper.[7] The village of Alvechurch, situated 11 miles south of Birmingham, was a rural parish supported by agriculture and occupations such as blacksmithing, and the economy of the parish of Bromsgrove, 16 miles south-west of Birmingham, was based largely on agriculture, supplemented by nail-making and needle-making.[8] A slightly different pattern emerges in Staffordshire: the parish of Harborne, only three miles from Birmingham, was inhabited by a mixture of farmers and nailers; on the other hand, the industrial parish of Wednesbury, situated eight miles north-west of Birmingham, was dominated by occupations in metal trades such as gunlock-filing and awl-blade-making. Finally, Tamworth, 16 miles to the north of Birmingham, was a small market town serving local coal-mining and textile villages in Staffordshire and Warwickshire.[9]

The breakdown of pauper apprentice numbers from the three Warwickshire parishes during the period 1750–1835 is shown in Table 2.1. The overseers of Coleshill and Knowle parishes bound almost 40 per cent of their parish apprentices to masters in Birmingham, whereas less than 20 per cent of Tanworth in Arden children were bound in Birmingham. In contrast to the other two parishes, Tanworth in Arden apprenticed more than 50 per cent of its pauper children (231) within the home parish, almost all of whom were bound in agricultural occupations of husbandry or housewifery to a husbandman or

---

6   WCRO, DRB0100/107–109 Coleshill Parish Apprenticeship Certificates; DRB0056/143–144; DRB0019/83–89 Tanworth in Arden Parish Apprenticeship Certificates.

7   BAH, EP 14/157 Northfield Parish Apprenticeship Certificates.

8   WoCRO, 5498/9 Alvechurch Parish Apprenticeship Certificates; 9135/38–41 Bromsgrove Parish Apprenticeship Certificates.

9   SCRO, D4383/6/5 Wednesbury Parish Apprenticeship Certificates; D3773/5/1059–1251 Tamworth Parish Apprenticeship Certificates.

Table 2.1 Comparison of destinations – three Warwickshire parishes, 1750–1835.

	Home parish	Birmingham & Aston	Other in Warks., Worcs., Staffs.	Other counties	Total no. of apprentices	% to Birmingham
Coleshill	24	80	100	12	216	37
Knowle	9	35	40	1	85	41
Tanworth in Arden	231	69	78	2	380	18
Totals	264	184	218	15	681	27

Source: WCRO, DRB0100/107–109 Coleshill Parish Apprenticeship Certificates; DRB0056/143–144 Knowle Parish Apprenticeship Certificates; DRB0019/83–89 Tanworth in Arden Parish Apprenticeship Certificates.

Table 2.2 Comparison of destinations – three Worcestershire parishes, 1750–1835.

	Home parish	Birmingham & Aston	Other in Warks., Worcs., Staffs.	Other counties	Total no. of apprentices	% to Birmingham
Northfield	111	15	44	0	170	8.8
Alvechurch	170	5	19	0	194	2.5
Bromsgrove	459	5	70	0	535	0.9
Totals	740	25	133	0	899	2.7

Source: BAH, EP 14/157 Northfield Parish Apprenticeship Certificates; WoCRO, 5498/9 Alvechurch Parish Apprenticeship Certificates; WoCRO, 9135/38–41 Bromsgrove Parish Apprenticeship Certificates.

Table 2.3 Comparison of destinations – three Staffordshire parishes, 1750–1835.

	Home parish	Birmingham & Aston	Other in Warks., Worcs., Staffs.	Other counties	Total no. of apprentices	% to Birmingham
Harborne	11	12	29	2	54	22.2
Tamworth	37	13	107	14	171	7.6
Wednesbury	101	4	113	6	224	1.8
Totals	149	29	249	22	449	6.5

Source: BAH, EP 61/7/8 Harborne Parish Apprenticeship Certificates; SCRO, D4383/6/5 Wednesbury Parish Apprenticeship Certificates; D3773/5/1059–1251 Tamworth Parish Apprenticeship Certificates.

yeoman of the parish.[10] A further 78 children were apprenticed to other parishes in Warwickshire, Worcestershire or Staffordshire. In addition, Tanworth in Arden sent nine children to silk-weavers in Coventry in 1757 and a further six in 1758, suggesting that there was an increase in demand for apprentices from the Coventry silk ribbon trade in the late 1750s, but no further apprentices were sent to Coventry silk-weavers after this date. Moreover, from 1802 onwards the Overseers of the Poor in Tanworth in Arden began to apprentice their pauper children to a range of occupations and trades in Birmingham as well as in parishes such as Redditch in Worcestershire and Darlaston in Staffordshire. Only two children from Tanworth in Arden were apprenticed beyond the West Midlands counties: Richard Leedom was bound in 1764 to Christopher Leedom, a husbandman in Hinckley, Leicestershire; and in 1806 Philip Leeson was bound at ten years old to Edmond Tibbotts, a tailor in Gloucester.[11] Pauper children from the parishes of Coleshill and Knowle were also apprenticed mainly within the counties of Warwickshire, Worcestershire and Staffordshire. Around 40 per cent of these children were bound to Birmingham masters and a further 40 per cent to masters in Wolverhampton, Bilston and Walsall in Staffordshire, or Alcester, Solihull and Coventry in Warwickshire. In addition, a small number of children from Coleshill were bound to framework knitters in the neighbouring county of Leicestershire.[12] This analysis of parish apprenticeship certificates in Warwickshire therefore supports the conclusions of previous studies that found that parish apprentices were bound in local areas when opportunities were available.[13]

The apprenticeship certificates from the Worcestershire parishes of Northfield, Alvechurch and Bromsgrove indicate that pauper children from these areas were rarely apprenticed to Birmingham masters (Table 2.2). The parish of Northfield was located just six miles from Birmingham, but fewer than 10 per cent of their pauper apprentices were placed in the town, whereas around 25 per cent were bound to masters elsewhere in the West Midlands counties. A majority of children were apprenticed to local farmers in the home parish, but children were also bound to masters in Halesowen and Dudley in Worcestershire and Harborne, Walsall or Tipton in Staffordshire.[14] Overseers in Northfield appear to have established links with industrial parishes in south Staffordshire, following a pattern of placing children in either agriculture or a traditional local trade. It may also be the case, however, that overseers were unsuccessful in

---

10   WoCRO, DRB0019/83–89.

11   *Ibid.*

12   WoCRO, DRB0100/107–109; DRB0056/143–144.

13   Levene, 'Parish Apprenticeship', pp. 927–31; Honeyman, *Child Workers*, p. 78.

14   BAH, EP 14/157.

securing suitable placements for parish apprentices in Birmingham industries. Alvechurch apprenticed 194 pauper children between 1750 and 1835: 170 of these children remained in their home parish; 19 children were sent to other West Midlands parishes; and just five were bound to Birmingham masters. The Birmingham apprentices included 11-year-old Joseph Webb and his nine-year-old sister Sarah, who were bound to their step-father Edward Dukes, a locksmith, who received a payment of £4 15s 6d towards their clothing from the Alvechurch overseers. The apprenticeship certificates for Joseph and Sarah reveal that their mother, Mary Webb, was a widow 'now lawfully married to Edward Dukes'.[15] Similarly, while the overseers from the parish of Bromsgrove apprenticed a total of 535 pauper children over the same period, only five were placed in Birmingham. Around 80 per cent of the Bromsgrove pauper apprentices remained in the parish, typically being apprenticed in husbandry or housewifery, with a smaller number engaged in nailing and needle-making. Those children sent outside the parish were bound in similar industries in Belbroughton, Redditch, Halesowen or Dudley in Worcestershire and Rowley Regis or Sedgley in Staffordshire.[16] This suggests that overseers in Bromsgrove, in common with those in Northfield and Alvechurch, sought out and maintained links with tradesmen and women in nearby industrial parishes.

It has been identified that parish children from Worcestershire were frequently bound to masters in Staffordshire, but were pauper children from Staffordshire placed in Worcestershire? The three Staffordshire parishes of Harborne, Tamworth and Wednesbury apprenticed only 29 children in Birmingham over the entire period. From a total of 449 parish apprentices, 149 children remained in their home parish and 249 were placed in other parishes in Warwickshire, Worcestershire or Staffordshire. The evidence shows that children from Harborne, only three miles from Birmingham, were more likely to be dispatched to Wolverhampton or Wednesbury than to Birmingham (Table 2.3). Similarly, children apprenticed by the parish of Wednesbury were most likely to stay in their home parish or be placed in neighbouring south Staffordshire industrial villages such as Tipton, Willenhall, Darlaston or Bilston.[17] Pauper children from Wednesbury were rarely apprenticed to masters in Worcestershire, indicating there were greater opportunities for placements in Staffordshire industries. Nevertheless, girls from Wednesbury were sometimes apprenticed further afield: Sarah and Elizabeth Mumford were apprenticed as ribbon-weavers in Nuneaton, Warwickshire, in 1795; and in the same year six girls were bound to Peels, Yates & Co. cotton mill in Manchester. The youngest girl was Ann

---

15   WoCRO, 5498/9.

16   WoCRO, 9135/38–41.

17   SCRO, D4383/6/5.

Ackwood, aged nine, and the eldest Elizabeth Whitehouse, at 14; the other girls were Eleanor Spittle, aged 12, Martha Turner, aged 11, Sarah Wood, aged ten, and Elizabeth Greaves, aged ten. However, apprenticing girls to distant textile mills did not prove a popular choice for the overseers in Wednesbury, since only two further children were apprenticed to cotton mills and these were both sent to Joseph Peel's mill in Fazeley, Staffordshire.[18] Children from the Staffordshire parish of Tamworth were located some 16 miles from the town of Birmingham, but close to Peel's cotton mill at Fazeley. Five Tamworth girls were apprenticed to Peel's mill in 1797 and four girls were sent to Peel's calico mill in Lichfield in 1800. A number of other children were bound to ribbon-weavers and framework-knitters in Leicestershire and north Warwickshire, yet the majority of pauper apprentices from Tamworth were bound to industrial trades in the Staffordshire towns and villages of Walsall, Darlaston, Wednesfield and Wolverhampton.[19] The evidence from apprenticeship bindings from the Staffordshire and Worcestershire parishes thus shows that pauper children were most likely to be apprenticed in either their home parish or the traditional trades and industries of south Staffordshire and north Worcestershire. Similarly, London parishes had links with specific industries in local areas.[20]

Poor children from Warwickshire parishes were more frequently apprenticed to Birmingham masters than those from Staffordshire and Worcestershire, yet they were equally likely to be placed in other local parishes in the West Midlands. It is unclear whether parish overseers actively chose to place children in the industrial areas of south Staffordshire or were simply taking advantage of any available employment opportunities for pauper children. Historians have highlighted the importance of investigating apprenticeship employment patterns to identify where opportunities existed and which trades were willing to accept pauper apprentices.[21] Parish apprenticeship patterns are used to identify both rapidly expanding industries that needed a flexible workforce, such as the cotton industry, and contracting or impoverished industries less attractive to parents seeking private apprenticeships, such as cordwaining. Surprisingly, even the parishes of Harborne and Northfield, which were geographically close to Birmingham, bound very few children there. From a total of more than 2,000 apprenticeships examined in the sample parishes only 240 children were placed in Birmingham, a far smaller number than might have been expected.

It appears from these results that although a ready supply of child workers was available from the surrounding areas, and despite evidence that parish

---

18   *Ibid.*

19   SCRO, D3773/5/1059–1251.

20   Levene, 'Parish Apprenticeship', p. 939.

21   *Ibid.*, p. 918.

overseers had close links with masters in metal trades, there was little demand for parish apprentices in Birmingham. It may be the case that non-apprenticed children met the demand for child labour in Birmingham, or that pauper children from the Birmingham parishes of St Martin's and St Philip's took up any available opportunities. The pauper apprenticeship certificates for Birmingham during this period have not survived, but there are other records to show that pauper children from Birmingham were apprenticed to Lancashire cotton mills and to Staffordshire coal mines.[22] Nevertheless, the practice of dispatching Birmingham children to cotton mills had ceased by around 1800, according to evidence given by Birmingham magistrate Theodore Price to a parliamentary select committee in 1816. Price reported that Birmingham children had not been apprenticed to cotton mills following an unfavourable inspection visit report in 1800, adding that, since that time, 'in general cotton mills were spoken of unfavourably, as improper places for those children'.[23] Furthermore, the custom of Birmingham masters was to have 'out-door apprentices': that is, children who worked as assistants but lived at home with their families rather than living in the household of a master in the same way as parish apprentices did. One problem with this system, according to Theodore Price, was that outdoor apprentices were free at night to 'cause mischief' and become involved in the theft of metal because at the end of the working day they were no longer under the care and control of a master.[24]

Child labour and the changing demands of industry

What can parish apprenticeships tell us about continuity and change in occupations over time and did child labour under the old Poor Law reflect the expansion of industry in the town of Birmingham? As discussed above, overseers from the Warwickshire parishes found a greater number of places for pauper children in Birmingham, especially between the years 1790 to 1809, than did overseers from the other counties examined. From 1810 onwards there was a sharp drop in the overall numbers of children apprenticed by parishes, but a higher proportion of pauper apprentices were bound to Birmingham masters (see Appendix, table 3a).

The Warwickshire parish of Coleshill apprenticed its pauper children to a range of traditional crafts and metal trades in Birmingham.[25] For example, in 1770 they bound Thomas Dowler to a breeches-maker, James White to a blade-

---

22 BAH, 660982 Minutes of the Birmingham Overseers of the Poor, 1803–13.

23 BPP, 1816, 397, *Report of the Minutes of Evidence to the Select Committee on the State of Children Employed in the Manufactories of the United Kingdom*, p. 124.

24 *Ibid.*, p. 124.

25 WCRO, DRB0100/107–109.

maker and John Ward to a basket-maker. In 1776 John Ridden, aged 11, was apprenticed to a Birmingham locksmith, and William Clarkson, aged ten, to Sam Clemenson, a hinge-maker. Boys from Coleshill also became apprentice toy-makers, button-makers, steel-buckle-makers and cordwainers, reflecting the varied nature of Birmingham industry.[26] The relatively small number of girls from Coleshill who were apprenticed in Birmingham were usually bound in 'housewifery'. This term traditionally denoted agricultural service, whereby girls were expected to learn the domestic duties of a farmer's household. In an urban setting, a girl apprenticed in housewifery would have undertaken domestic duties within the household and may also have been expected to assist with routine work in the masters' business or workshop. The evidence from apprenticeship certificates suggests that very few girls were apprenticed in Birmingham's metal industries: in one example, Elizabeth Gray, aged seven, of Coleshill, was apprenticed as a button-burnisher in Birmingham in 1777.[27] Under the terms of her apprenticeship Elizabeth would have lived in the household of her master until the age of 21, during which time she would have been trained in the trade of a button-burnisher, rather than learning domestic skills. At the turn of the nineteenth century a majority of pauper children from Coleshill were apprenticed in three industries: the Staffordshire cotton mills, the Leicestershire framework-knitting industry and the Staffordshire lock-making industry.[28] From 1810 onwards, however, they were largely bound in the Birmingham trades of gunlock-filer, cabinet-maker, cabinet-locksmith, cordwainer and pearl-button-turner.[29]

Pauper children from Knowle and Tanworth in Arden were also apprenticed to a variety of occupations in Birmingham. In 1759 William Kimberley of Knowle was apprenticed to William Freeth, a Birmingham toy-maker, and in 1760 William Terry of Knowle was apprenticed to Charles Freeth, a Birmingham brass-founder, indicating the links between the overseers and Birmingham tradesmen.[30] The parish children of Tanworth in Arden were typically bound in agriculture, yet Birmingham apprenticeships increased from the 1790s onwards, to include trades such as button-making, buckle making, watch-chain-making, gun-finishing and awl-blade-making.[31] The Tanworth in Arden overseers had notable links with tradesmen in the Aston area of Birmingham: for example, they apprenticed William Handy to William Hodges, a compass-

---

26   *Ibid.*
27   *Ibid.*
28   *Ibid.*
29   *Ibid.*
30   WCRO, DRB0056/143–144.
31   WCRO, DRB0019/83–89.

maker in Aston in 1802; Henry Bissell to William Rollason, a whitesmith in Aston in 1803; Thomas Wadsworth to Joseph Rogers, a comb-maker in Aston; and William Edwards to John Ansell, an Aston cordwainer.[32] Boys from Tanworth in Arden were also bound by the parish in the Birmingham trades of rule-maker, steelyard- and beam-maker, bridle-bit- and stirrup-maker, gun-finisher, fish-hook-maker and wheelwright.[33]

The range of well-paid trades in Birmingham suggests that apprenticeships in the town were probably highly sought after, with parish officials competing with parents seeking private apprenticeships for their children. It is unsurprising, therefore, that relatively small numbers of pauper children were apprenticed to Birmingham masters (see Appendix, table 3b). For a tradesman such as a brass-founder or metal-button-maker, motivated by the need to be profitable in order to survive in a competitive environment, the choice of a 14-year-old outdoor apprentice who lived nearby with his own family over a ten- or 11-year-old parish apprentice who had to be housed, fed and clothed seems obvious. A preference for privately arranged apprenticeships is illustrated by advertisements in a 1791 edition of *Aris's Birmingham Gazette*. One advertiser offered 'A good Opportunity for Boys': three boys aged 12 to 14 years 'from honest industrious families' were offered the opportunity to become apprentices in the engraving business.[34] A second advertiser was seeking 'six boys aged 12 to 16 years' as apprentices in an established steel-toy business. Furthermore, it seems likely that Birmingham tradesmen who did take on a parish apprentice may have had connections with the child's family or with the parish. One example of a local link comes from the parish of Knowle: John Smith and Christopher Smith of Knowle were apprenticed by the parish in 1754 and 1756 to John Chinn, a toy-maker and button-maker in Birmingham.[35] The records show that John Chinn of Birmingham was originally from Knowle, having been a parish apprentice himself 28 years earlier in 1728, when he was bound to Joseph Hunt, a Birmingham button-maker. The significance of this example is in showing that John Chinn had not only completed his apprenticeship and followed the trade of a button-maker but also maintained a connection with his home parish of Knowle, so that in due course he was able to offer the same opportunity to other boys from a poor family.[36]

Apprenticeship certificates from the Worcestershire and Staffordshire parishes reveal that very few pauper children were placed in Birmingham

---

32   *Ibid.*

33   *Ibid.*

34   *Aris's Birmingham Gazette*, 13 June 1791.

35   WCRO, DRB0056/143–144.

36   *Ibid.*

trades: less than 3 per cent of the Worcestershire children and just 6.5 per cent of the Staffordshire children.[37] Moreover, the parish overseers did not appear to have access to apprenticeships in important local industries within their own counties. Although Worcestershire was a predominantly agricultural county, there were glove-making and porcelain industries in the county town of Worcester; yet none of the parish apprentices from the sample was apprenticed into these trades. Approximately 80 per cent of the 898 children from the three Worcestershire parishes were bound into agriculture, to be trained in husbandry and housewifery.[38] Among the remaining children, 26 from Alvechurch and 78 from Bromsgrove were placed in trades related to agriculture or in the traditional metal industries of north Worcestershire and south Staffordshire. For example, Joseph Shepherd from Alvechurch was apprenticed as a blacksmith in Alvechurch; Mary Warren from Alvechurch was apprenticed as a needle-maker in Redditch; Mary Layton and Francis Moreton from Bromsgrove were apprenticed as nailers; and Elizabeth Hunt, Martha Kings and Ann Taylor, also from Bromsgrove, were apprenticed as needle-makers.[39] By the early nineteenth century children from Worcestershire were also apprenticed in coal-mining and carpet-weaving: Joseph Tilt and James Reynolds became apprentice miners in Darlaston, Staffordshire, in 1811; Sarah and Susannah Lee were apprentice bombasine-weavers in Kidderminster; and John Lamsdale was an apprentice carpet-weaver in Kidderminster.[40]

Children from Worcestershire who were bound to Birmingham masters entered trades including gimlet-maker, bellows-maker, hairdresser and perruque-maker, locksmith, wood-turner and horn-button-maker.[41] Northfield parish apprenticed almost 70 per cent of its pauper children in agriculture and the remainder in crafts and trades or coal-mining.[42] The boys apprenticed in Birmingham trades included George Folley, an apprentice hardwood-turner; Edward Walker, an apprentice brush-maker; William Faulkner, an apprentice brass-founder; and Samuel Southall, an apprentice tailor. The last two parish boys from Northfield to be apprenticed in Birmingham were Joseph Evetts, aged ten, apprenticed in 1819 to a pearl-button-maker, and Benjamin Haycock, aged 15, apprenticed in 1820 to a pump-maker.[43]

---

37 WoCRO, 5498/9; 9135/38–41; BAH, EP 14/157; SCRO, D4383/6/5; D3773/5/1059–1251.

38 WoCRO, 5498/9; 9135/38–41; BAH, EP 14/157.

39 WoCRO, 5498/9; 9135/38–41.

40 *Ibid.*

41 WoCRO, 5498/9; 9135/38–41; BAH, EP 14/157.

42 BAH, EP 14/157.

43 *Ibid.*

The Staffordshire parish overseers were far more likely to bind pauper children in crafts and trades rather than agriculture, although none of the children on the registers was placed in the Staffordshire pottery industry. The parish of Tamworth apprenticed 128 pauper children in crafts and trades but only 21 in agriculture.[44] Boys were most likely to be placed in Staffordshire metal trades such as locksmith, gunlock-filer and steel-trap-maker, whereas girls were bound in housewifery or placed in silk-ribbon-weaving and cotton mills. A small number of Tamworth boys and girls were apprenticed in Birmingham trades: William Walters was bound to a wire-drawer, Thomas Doves to a hatter, William Arnold to a button-maker and John Fenton to a buckle-chape-maker[45]; Sarah Pigford was apprenticed as a leather-clog-maker and Anne Capewell as a steel-blade-grinder.[46] The parish of Harborne found few opportunities for its parish apprentices in nearby Birmingham, just 12 of its children being placed with Birmingham masters between 1750 and 1810.[47]

Children from Wednesbury in Staffordshire were the least likely to be found placements in Birmingham: only four children from a total of 224 parish apprentices over the period from 1750 to 1834 were apprenticed in the town. These four were Elizabeth Hall and Ann Whitall, who were apprenticed in housewifery to Birmingham tradesmen, William Robinson, who was apprenticed to a Birmingham gun-finisher, and John Stokes, who was apprenticed to a button-castor.[48] A majority of poor boys from Wednesbury were apprenticed by the parish to trades in south Staffordshire towns, notably in metal trades such as gun-finishing, gunlock-filing or brass-lock-making. A further 32 boys from Wednesbury were bound to coal-miners in the Staffordshire coalfields, many of them at the age of just seven or eight. Girls from Wednesbury were typically apprenticed in housewifery to tradesmen: examples include Mary Foster, who was bound in housewifery to a gunlock-filer, and Mary Holland, who was similarly bound to a box-lock-maker in Wednesbury. In addition to undertaking cleaning, cooking and sewing duties within the household, these girls were likely to have assisted in tasks around the workshop, such as cleaning and metal-polishing.[49]

The wide range of occupations children were bound into suggests that overseers found places for pauper children as and where they could be obtained. Parish apprenticeships were frequently in low-paid agricultural occupations,

---

44   SCRO, D3773/5/1059–1251.

45   A buckle-chape was a plate or fitting connecting a buckle to a belt or strap.

46   SCRO, D3773/5/1059–1251.

47   BAH, EP 61/7/8 Harborne Parish Apprenticeship Certificates.

48   SCRO, D4383/6/5.

49   *Ibid.*

such as husbandry and housewifery, or trades linked to local industries, such as nail-making and needle-making in north Worcestershire or lock-making and coal-mining in south Staffordshire. The relatively small number of parish children sent to Birmingham indicates that few opportunities were available for pauper apprenticeships in the town, despite the expansion of industry in the eighteenth and nineteenth centuries. A number of explanations might be offered for this: first, Birmingham's fame as the 'town of a thousand trades' meant that its industries mainly comprised numerous small manufactories and workshops, rather than the relatively few establishments employing large numbers of workers that characterised the textile towns. Second, the Birmingham men engaged in metal industries were usually skilled and well-paid tradesmen who would have little problem in employing local boys or girls as apprentices or assistants, often from within their own family. Third, the Birmingham industries that employed groups of young children, most notably the pin industry, also found sufficient child workers from the local population and so did not resort to bringing parish apprentices from other areas. Given the diversity of occupations and the small number of parish apprentices employed in each trade, it is difficult to draw any conclusions about changes in Birmingham occupations over time. Levene found that 76 per cent of London bindings were in manufacturing industries, including both traditional and developing sectors of the economy.[50] This is also reflected in the analysis of Birmingham bindings: 71 per cent of the parish apprenticeships in Birmingham were in metal or wood trades and a further 20 per cent in traditional service trades, such as cordwaining, shoe-making, tailoring, mantua-making and peruke-making.

Gender differences in child labour
The discussion so far has highlighted some of the gender differences in employment for parish boys and girls, an issue that Katrina Honeyman argues has been inadequately explored by historians.[51] Whereas Honeyman's study focuses largely on parish apprenticeship in textile industries, this analysis sheds light on parish apprenticeships in trades and crafts in the West Midlands. An important point to reiterate is that girls were mainly apprenticed in housewifery, a term that could apply in both agricultural and non-agricultural settings. When pauper girls were apprenticed in a trade, as opposed to housewifery, this was specifically stated on the apprenticeship certificate. From Alvechurch in Worcestershire Mary Mills was apprenticed as a maidservant in 1773, Harriet Francis as a needle-maker in 1807, and Sarah Wardle as an apprentice nailer

---

50   Levene, 'Parish Apprenticeship', pp. 927–31.
51   Honeyman, *Child Workers*, p. 151.

in 1807. Girls from Alvechurch and Bromsgrove were less likely than boys to be apprenticed away from their home parish and only two girls were placed in Birmingham. One of these was Sarah Webb, already mentioned above, who was apprenticed to her step-father, indicating the significance of family connections.[52] Girls from poor families in Northfield were usually apprenticed in housewifery to yeoman farmers in the parishes of Northfield, Kings Norton or Halesowen. In one case, nine-year-old Sarah Hollis from Northfield was apprenticed in the trade of nailing alongside her brother, William Hollis, who was eight.[53] None of the girls from Northfield was placed in Birmingham, although 15 boys from the parish were bound in Birmingham trades such as gunbarrel-grinding, cordwaining and brick-laying.[54]

In Staffordshire, the parish of Wednesbury apprenticed a total of 100 girls between 1750 and 1835, including 87 girls who were bound in housewifery, mostly to local tradesmen.[55] Agnes Brown, for example, was apprenticed in housewifery to a gunlock-filer in Wednesbury and Jane Bushell in housewifery to a Wednesbury shopkeeper. Ten girls from Wednesbury were apprenticed in the textile industry and, in a more unusual example, Mary Hale was apprenticed in 1803 'in the art of pipe making'.[56] In contrast to the girls' experiences, boys from Wednesbury parish were typically apprenticed in trades such as gunlock-filing or brass-lock-making, and a number were bound to Staffordshire coal-miners.[57] The parish of Tamworth found apprenticeships for 126 boys and 45 girls over this period. Boys were bound into metal trades such as buckle-making in Walsall, textile industries such as ribbon weaving in Nuneaton and linen weaving in Tamworth. Ten girls from Tamworth were sent to the Staffordshire cotton mills, 18 were bound in trades such as ribbon-weaving and 17 were apprenticed in housewifery.[58] The Staffordshire parish of Harborne was just three miles from Birmingham, yet only three girls from the parish were apprenticed in housewifery to Birmingham tradesmen: Elizabeth Pritchet was placed with a Birmingham gunbarrel-forger in 1753; Sarah Osbourn with a buckle-maker in 1781; and Mary Smith with a button-maker in 1785.[59] Boys from Harborne were bound in Birmingham trades including cordwaining, brass-founding and spectacle-frame-making. Harborne also

---

52   WoCRO, 5498/9; 9135/38–41.

53   BAH, EP 14/157.

54   *Ibid.*

55   SCRO, D4383/6/5.

56   *Ibid.*

57   *Ibid.*

58   SCRO, D3773/5/1059–1251.

59   BAH, EP 61/7/8.

apprenticed boys to a range of trades in nearby areas: for example, Thomas Darby was bound to a gardener in Rowley Regis and Samuel Thompson to a ramrod-maker in Halesowen.[60]

From the Warwickshire parish of Knowle, a total of 35 parish children were apprenticed to Birmingham masters. These were all boys apart from Sarah Bentley, who was bound to a relative, Martha Bentley, a milliner and mantua-maker.[61] Coleshill found apprenticeships for 80 of its poor children in Birmingham, including seven girls. Four of the girls were apprenticed in housewifery; one girl was a button-burnisher, one was a mantua-maker, and the last was a 'steale piercer'. The parish of Tanworth in Arden apprenticed 63 boys and six girls in Birmingham, including Phebe Hunt as a button-shanker; Mary Hodgkins as a watch-chain-maker; and Hannah Mills as a fish-hook-maker.[62] Overall, the three Warwickshire parishes apprenticed a total of 184 children to Birmingham masters, but only 14 of these were girls. The parishes of Coleshill and Knowle apprenticed far fewer girls than boys, perhaps because they did not formally bind children in agricultural roles. There were 168 boys and 48 girls apprenticed by the overseers of Coleshill over the period, whereas the Knowle overseers apprenticed 80 boys and five girls from the parish. In contrast, the parish of Tanworth in Arden apprenticed almost equal numbers of poor boys and girls in agriculture: 122 boys in husbandry and 119 girls in housewifery. However, they placed 97 boys in trades and crafts, compared with 37 girls.[63] These differing rates of parish apprenticeship suggest that there were relatively few opportunities available to girls from poor families in Warwickshire. Furthermore, it appears that overseers in these parishes were unwilling to bind girls in the 'rougher' trades of nail-making and needle-making.

Honeyman suggests that the parish apprenticeship system offered more opportunities for girls than the private system of apprenticeship, since parish officials were anxious to remove pauper children from the parish as early as possible.[64] Even so, parish girls were offered fewer training opportunities than boys, being largely confined to textiles and service trades. Furthermore, Honeyman found no evidence that parishes were more protective of girls than boys, as they were equally likely to be sent to distant textile mills.[65] This study of parish apprenticeship in Warwickshire, Worcestershire and Staffordshire parishes also found fewer opportunities were open to girls – the relatively

---

60   *Ibid.*

61   WCRO, DRB0056/143–144.

62   WCRO, DRB0019/83–89.

63   *Ibid.*

64   Honeyman, *Child Workers*, p. 152.

65   *Ibid.*

small number of girls apprenticed in occupations other than housewifery suggests that priority was given to the training and economic self-sufficiency of boys. Even when no suitable local placements were available, girls were not dispatched in large numbers to textile mills. Only 18 girls from Warwickshire were bound to cotton mills, despite the presence of mills at Warwick and Fazeley in Staffordshire. This indicates that factory employment may not have been considered a suitable option by some parish overseers. Interestingly, the cotton mill at Emscote near Warwick advertised for parish apprentices in local newspapers at Coventry, Warwick and Oxford, but did not advertise in the Birmingham newspapers.[66]

Levene's study of London parish apprenticeship registers found that 75.9 per cent of boys and 76.8 per cent of girls were employed in the manufacturing sector in traditional and factory settings.[67] From the three Warwickshire parishes 69.2 per cent of boys and 34.9 per cent of girls were apprenticed in manufacturing trades, suggesting that variation by gender in parish bindings was closely linked to local parish networks and the attitudes of parish overseers towards child labour. Furthermore, the relative absence of girls from parish apprenticeship registers may be explained by the practice of placing pauper children into service within the parish rather than into formal apprenticeship.[68] As Peter Jones points out, from the end of the eighteenth century onwards parishes frequently placed children in service, even agreeing to provide clothing for children already in service, in their anxiety to keep control of the spiralling poor rate.[69] It seems likely that girls from pauper families in rural parishes may have been absent from parish apprenticeship registers because they were placed in service with local farmers and landowners without any formal apprenticeship agreement.

Age of starting work

This section considers pauper children's age of starting work and asks whether there was an increase or decrease over time for children apprenticed in Birmingham. The average age of binding of parish children can also indicate parish overseers' attitudes towards child labour, as well as the attitudes of the masters who were willing to take on parish apprentices.[70] The practice of

---

66   Joan Lane, 'Apprenticeship in Warwickshire Cotton Mills, 1790–1830', *Textile History*, 10 (1979), pp. 161–74 at 162.

67   Levene, 'Parish Apprenticeship', p. 928.

68   Peter M. Jones, *Industrial Enlightenment: Science, Technology and Culture in Birmingham and the West Midlands, 1760–1820* (Manchester, 2009), pp. 38–9.

69   Jones, *Industrial Enlightenment*, p. 40.

70   Levene, 'Parish Apprenticeship', p. 919.

apprenticing very young children implies not only that a child worker was profitable for the master but that passing on economic responsibility for a child was an important imperative for the parish overseers. Levene's study of London parish apprentices found that the average age of binding was 12 years for boys and 12.5 years for girls, with a sustained lowering of ages in the 1790s and 1800s, when the average age fell below 12 years.[71] Honeyman found that children were bound to textile mills at various ages, with many ten years or younger, reinforcing the perception that mills employed younger children.[72] In contrast, the parish apprentices at the Warwick cotton mill were generally somewhat older when bound, ranging from 12 years to 17 years. Benjamin Smart's advertisement in the *Oxford Journal* of 1812 addressed to 'Overseers of the Poor' specified his requirement for 'active healthy girls about 14 years of age' to work in his Warwickshire cotton mill.[73]

The age of starting work for children from the sample parishes who were apprenticed in Birmingham was indicated on 193 of the certificates. A majority of these children were at least ten years old, and 45 per cent were 13 years or above. Nevertheless, 23 children (12 per cent) were apprenticed between the ages of seven and nine years into trades including cordwaining, gunbarrel-boring, domestic service or pin- and wire-working.[74] This indicates that Birmingham industries did not routinely welcome very young parish apprentices, showing a marked preference for older child workers who were more competent and could be properly trained. Children from Warwickshire were bound to Birmingham masters at between 11 and 13 years of age, although there were differences between the parishes. Tanworth in Arden often apprenticed children at a younger age: Daniel Smith was bound aged nine and Job Hemming aged eight to cordwainers, and Thomas Marchall aged eight to a Birmingham gun-finisher. On the other hand, John Crockett of Coleshill was bound at 14 years to a Birmingham tailor, John Boden at 14 years to a joiner and cabinet-maker, and Joseph Phillips to a gun- and pistol-stock-finisher at the age of 14.[75] These cases illustrate variations not only in the types of parish apprenticeship available, but also in the age of starting work. The pauper child's experience of early work and future employment prospects may therefore have depended on a number of factors, such as networking by parish overseers, the pressure from ratepayers and local attitudes towards child labour. The records of the parish of Knowle, discussed below, offer some

---

71   *Ibid.*, p. 924.

72   Honeyman, *Child Workers*, pp. 45–7.

73   Lane, 'Apprenticeship in Warwickshire Cotton Mills', p. 164.

74   WCRO, DRB0019/83–89.

75   WCRO, DRB0100/107–109; DRB0019/83–89.

additional insights into the economic and social conditions of poor families in a rural community.

Experiences of pauper children: case studies from Knowle, Warwickshire

What were the particular social and economic circumstances that resulted in children's removal from their families? The accounts and financial records for the Warwickshire parish of Knowle reveal that families of parish apprentices were recipients of regular assistance during times of hardship in the form of cash payments, fuel, clothing and shoes.[76] In one example, although Thomas Shakespear was apprenticed at the age of 11 in 1764 to a curry-comb-maker in Birmingham his family continued to receive support from the overseers in Knowle after his removal.[77] Cash payments of between 6d and 1s 0d were made to the family on 22 different occasions between April 1765 and April 1766, as well as 2s 4d for 'shoes for Shakespear's Girl', 8s 4d for coals and 12s 7d for '11 yards of cloth' (see Appendix, table 4).[78] In April 1770 the family received assistance of 8s 0d when they were suffering from smallpox and a further 7s 0d to pay for 'a Coffin for Shakespear's Child'. The family's state of destitution was revealed in 1774, when Elizabeth Shakespear received a total of £3 6s 6d in parish support while 'her husband was in prison'. In a second example, regular payments were made to the Bayliss family from Knowle; they received amounts of between 6d and 2s 0d on 15 occasions between 1765 and 1766, plus an additional sum of 3s 0d 'for a Pair of Shoes for Bayliss's son' and 7s 4d 'for clothes for Bayliss's son' (see Appendix, table 5).[79] John Bayliss was apprenticed by the overseers in 1766 to a Coventry weaver at the age of 13, and his brother Isaac was apprenticed the following year to a Birmingham toy-maker.[80] Sadly, the apprenticing of the two Bayliss boys did not bring an end to the family's distress, as an entry for December 1767 shows a payment of 2s 0d to the family 'For a coffin for Bayliss's Child'. The frequency of parish assistance to these families suggests they were in dire financial straits, forced to repeatedly turn to the Poor Law overseers for help to support their children.

Pauper letters to Poor Law overseers in England requesting relief were frequently centred on the parents' inability to find work and thus support their children.[81] Joanne Bailey points out that these requests tended to emphasise the temporary nature of difficulties and petitioners were anxious to be perceived as

76   WCRO, DRB0056/137 Overseers Accounts, Parish of Knowle, 1764–66.

77   WCRO, DRB0056/143–144.

78   WCRO, DRB0056/137, 1764–66.

79   *Ibid.*

80   WCRO, DRB0056/143–144.

81   Bailey, *Parenting in England*, p. 7.

hard-working and industrious. Paupers were well aware of the need to present themselves as deserving of relief and not as examples of the idle poor. A similar analysis of pauper letters to overseers in Berkshire and Hampshire by Peter D. Jones found that requests for clothing and issues around clothing were as important as problems relating to illness and ill-health. Such letters frequently emphasised their extreme economic distress through terms such as 'nakedness', indicating their lack of adequate clothing and placing a moral obligation on the parish to restore them to a state of 'decency'.[82] The numerous payments made to the Shakespear and Bayliss families by the Knowle overseers indicate that these families were in severe distress during the 1760s, forcing them into the position of making repeated pleas for parish assistance. In order to hold down the parish rates and encourage economic independence, parish overseers would undoubtedly have been anxious to secure apprenticeships for those children old enough to be bound.

Although mothers were expected to contribute financially in providing for their families, the low wages paid to women meant that this was very difficult without a male earner.[83] Women who were widowed with young children invariably needed to rely on the parish for support. 'Widow Bentley's' daughter, ten-year-old Sarah Bentley, was apprenticed in 1806 to Martha Bentley of Aston in Birmingham as a milliner and mantua-maker.[84] The Knowle overseers made two journeys to Birmingham at a cost of 6s 0d to arrange the formalities, paying a fee of £3 3s 0d to Martha Bentley and 8s 0d for the apprenticeship indentures to be signed and completed. Sarah's mother, perhaps with younger children to care for, remained in the parish and was still receiving a weekly payment of 4s 0d in 1811.[85] Another Knowle widow, 'Widow Gumley', was receiving a sum of 5s 0d weekly in 1811, but the amount was reduced to 2s 6d following the apprenticing of her two young sons. John Gumley, aged ten, was apprenticed to a brass-founder in Birmingham, and Matthew Gumley, aged 13, to a clock-maker in Aston.[86] As these cases illustrate, the absence or loss of a father through early death, desertion or imprisonment was clearly a common experience for many parish apprentices and particularly for those children who started work at a young age.

In view of the extreme difficulties these children experienced in early life, questions arise about what may have happened to parish apprentices in later life.

82   Peter D. Jones, '"I cannot keep my place without being deascent": Pauper Letters, Parish Clothing and Pragmatism in the South of England, 1750–1830', *Rural History*, 20/1 (2009), pp. 31–49 at 32–5.
83   Bailey, *Parenting in England*, p. 9.
84   WCRO, DRB0056/137, 1764–66.
85   *Ibid.*
86   WCRO, DRB0056/143–144.

How did children from Knowle who were parish apprentices in Birmingham fare as adults, and is it possible to trace any of them? Children apprenticed from 1810 onwards were those most likely to appear in the later census records. The apprenticeship records show that Knowle overseers apprenticed eight children in Birmingham between 1810 and 1833, and five of these have been successfully traced in the census records. The elder of the Gumley brothers mentioned above, Matthew Gumley, never married or had a family of his own and he died in 1840 at the age of 41. His younger brother, John Gumley, appears to have been more fortunate despite starting work in a brass foundry at the age of ten. The 1851 census shows that, at the age of 50, John Gumley was living in Birmingham and employed in the trade of brass-founder. He was married and had two sons living at home – John, aged 27, and Henry, aged 14 – both also employed as brass-founders.[87] William Bayliss was apprenticed in 1817 by the Knowle overseers to a relative, Isaac Bayliss, a cordwainer of Aston in Birmingham. The 1851 census shows that William Bayliss remained in Aston working at the trade of shoe-maker, and was married with six children.[88] John Gumley and William Bayliss illustrate that the opportunity to train for a trade had enabled these former parish apprentices to overcome the initial disadvantages of an impoverished childhood. However, the extent to which their living standards improved remains unclear. Whereas John Gumley was in the well-paid occupation of brass-founder, William Bayliss had a family of six children to support from his low-paid work as a shoe-maker.

In further examples from the parish of Knowle, two boys who had been apprenticed in Birmingham returned as adults to live in their home parish. Daniel Dyke was apprenticed by the parish in 1825 as a cordwainer in Birmingham and continued in this occupation as an adult.[89] By 1841 he had left Birmingham to return to live in the parish of Knowle, along with his wife Sophia and their children. Daniel continued to work as a cordwainer in Knowle in 1851, residing with his wife and six children. His two eldest sons – George, aged 15, and Samuel, aged 13 – were working as brick-yard labourers and a third son, 11-year-old Charles, was a farmer's labourer. It appears that Daniel Dyke's family were living on the edge of poverty, but managed to survive with contributions to the family income from the three eldest children. William Bant was bound by the parish of Knowle in 1833 to a plumber and glazier in Aston. At the end of his apprenticeship in 1840 William was married to Elizabeth and had returned to live in his home village of Knowle. His two children, William Henry and Eliza, were born in Knowle, but by 1851 the family had returned to

---

87 Census of England and Wales 1851.

88 Census of England and Wales, 1841 and 1851.

89 WCRO, DRB0056/143–144.

live in Aston, where William worked as a plumber and glazier. In 1861 William was still employed as a plumber and glazier in Aston and his wife was working as a laundress. His two children were also employed in the local area, his son as a nail-caster and his daughter as a spectacle-maker.[90] The examples from the parish of Knowle highlight that in some cases former parish apprentices were able to find regular employment and successfully raise their own families without relying on parish support. Nevertheless, it seems apparent that in order to survive many working families relied on the additional earnings of wives and older children.

Conclusion

Parish apprentices were a major source of child labour under the old Poor Law.[91] In a period of social and economic transition many parishes sought to reduce the demands on poor relief by off-loading parish apprentices to textile mills, coal mines and traditional craft industries. As a rapidly expanding industrial town, Birmingham may have been expected to attract parish apprentices from surrounding towns and villages in Warwickshire, Worcestershire and Staffordshire. However, very few children were apprenticed in Birmingham from neighbouring areas, even from parishes such as Harborne, which was only three miles from Birmingham. Where employment opportunities were available, parish apprentices were most likely to be bound in local areas and in occupations traditional to the locality. Many children were apprenticed in their home parish or a nearby parish, with little evidence of children being sent to distant locations. The ability of parish overseers to maintain links with local sectors of the economy was thus of crucial importance. Furthermore, Birmingham craftsmen and small manufacturers did not welcome pauper apprentices, possibly because they found a ready supply of child workers and older non-parish apprentices within the Birmingham population.

The attitudes of parish overseers towards pauper children and child labour reflected wider perceptions of the poor and gendered roles in society. It was important for boys to learn the habits of work and a future trade in order to become economically independent rather than dependent on the Poor Law. Girls were trained in domestic duties and the habits of work so that they could run a household and raise a family as well as contributing to family incomes. By apprenticing children from pauper families, parishes were able to reduce the poor rate and invest in human capital through the training of a future workforce. The examples in this chapter suggest that parish children who were apprenticed to masters in Birmingham were likely to remain there as

---

90   Census of England and Wales 1841, 1851, 1861.

91   Lane, *Apprenticeship in England*; Honeyman, *Child Workers*; Levene, 'Parish Apprenticeship'.

adults, obtaining employment not only for themselves but also for their wives and children. However, there was a lack of demand for parish apprentices in Birmingham, perhaps because child workers were available in sufficient numbers without the legal, economic and social responsibilities entailed in formal apprenticeship agreements. This raises new questions about the numbers of non-apprenticed children working in Birmingham industries, their occupations, and the attitudes of parents towards children's work. These are issues to be discussed in the chapters that follow.

3

Birmingham workhouse children[1]

Introduction

In the late eighteenth century the Guardians of the Poor in Birmingham adopted an innovative approach towards the problem of overcrowding in the workhouse and the rising cost of boarding out children by establishing a separate children's institution. The Birmingham Asylum for the Infant Poor opened in 1797, providing residential accommodation for pauper children complete with workshops in which children could be usefully employed.[2] The separation of workhouse children at some distance from adults became more widespread in England in the 1840s, when residential district or industrial schools were established, providing training for boys in agriculture, tailoring or shoe-making and for girls in sewing, knitting and domestic work.[3] These institutions followed the example of schools of industry, which promoted training in traditional crafts and skills as opposed to factory work.[4] However, the Guardians of the Poor in Birmingham initially avoided the educative approach taken by schools of industry or industrial schools, viewing pauper children instead as an economic resource that could be utilised in manufacturing. The minutes of meetings of the Birmingham Board of Guardians, which cover the years from the inception of the Asylum for the Infant Poor until its closure in 1852, offer insights into the attitudes of the guardians towards child labour and childhood during a period of important social and economic change.[5] Additional information is drawn from the census records to track a number of children who were resident in the asylum in 1851, following their progress into adulthood. Three main issues are addressed in this chapter: first, it examines the particular circumstances

---

1   A version of this chapter has been published as Mary Nejedly, 'Earning their Keep: Child Workers at the Birmingham Asylum for the Infant Poor', *Family and Community History*, 20/3 (2017), pp. 206–17. Reprinted by permission of the publisher, Taylor & Francis Ltd.

2   Nejedly, 'Earning their Keep'.

3   Patrick McCrory, 'Poor Law Education and the Urban Pauper Child: The Theory and Practice of the Urban District School, 1840–1896', in John Hurt (ed.), *Proceedings of the Annual Conference of the History of Education Society of Great Britain* (Leicester, 1980), pp. 83–100.

4   Malcolm Dick, 'English Conservatives and Schools for the Poor c1780–1833', PhD thesis (University of Leicester, 1979).

5   BAH, GP B/2/1–5 Minutes of the Birmingham Board of Guardians, 1783–1852.

in Birmingham that led up to the guardians' decision to establish an asylum for pauper children; second, it considers the extent to which children's work at the asylum differed from that undertaken in other institutions; and, third, it analyses changes in the attitudes of the guardians towards childhood and child labour over the period from 1797 to 1852.

An asylum for pauper children

The problem of how to deal with increasing numbers of pauper children, either resident in the workhouse or placed with foster families in the countryside, became an urgent issue for the Birmingham Guardians of the Poor at the end of the eighteenth century as the town's population expanded. At a meeting of the guardians in September 1795 Thomas Smallwood, a cabinet-maker from Bull Street, advised that he had established a small manufactory for children in the workhouse because 'there are in the workhouse thirty or forty children of the age of five years upwards unemployed and conceiving they cannot be too early initiated to habits of industry … they (could) be employed in the manufacturing of Laces'.[6] He reported that approximately 30 children in the workhouse and a further ten children 'at nurse' in nearby Castle Bromwich had been taught to weave lace in the course of just a few days. Smallwood suggested that, rather than placing 100 Birmingham children at nurse with foster families in nearby parishes, it would be more cost effective to place them under one roof in an 'infant manufactory'. This residential establishment would house the town's pauper children and 'habituate them to industry and preserve their morals'. Smallwood added that an infant manufactory might also be profitable, providing an income from the children's labour. At the same time it would solve the problem of unruly children placed in the countryside who 'for want of some employment range about the fields and are frequently found committing some depredations'.[7]

In line with Smallwood's proposals, the Guardians of the Poor made plans to build a 'new nursery' for the children in Summer Lane on the outskirts of Birmingham, some distance away from the workhouse on Lichfield Street. A committee was formed to oversee the running of the nursery and a matron, a schoolmistress and two female servants were appointed. By October 1797 more than 200 children had been admitted to the nursery and in the following year it was renamed the Asylum for the Infant Poor.[8] The new institution was presented as a refuge or place of safety for pauper children, removing them from the undesirable influence of adults in the workhouse and allowing them to enjoy the benefits of clean air on the edge of the town. This was despite the reality that

---

6   BAH, GP B/2/1/1 Minutes of the Birmingham Board of Guardians, 1783–1806, September 1795.

7   *Ibid.*, September 1795.

8   *Ibid.*, October 1797.

most children at the Asylum for the Infant Poor were destined to spend their days in the institution's workshops, labouring for long hours at pin- or lace-making.[9] The asylum committee reported savings on expenditure of more than £500 in the first year of operation, as well as reductions in overcrowding in the workhouse.[10] Furthermore, the institution had provided additional income from the children's labour and had proved successful as a method of controlling their behaviour.

An infant manufactory

The Birmingham Asylum for the Infant Poor was distinctive in putting workhouse children to work in manufacturing, rather than providing training in traditional skills. Children were expected to work for their keep in the asylum, earning their board and lodging from a very young age. Links were established in early 1796, a year before the infant asylum opened, with a local pin manufacturer and arrangements made for the employment of child workers. The guardians' meeting of February 1796 recorded: 'the Manufacturing Committee have agreed with Mr Samuel Ryland for the use of twenty three children to be employed in the Pin Manufactory at the rate of one shilling per head per week each from the 22nd Inst'.[11] It was also agreed that employed children would not be removed or apprenticed for at least one month, ensuring some continuity of child labour. At the same meeting the guardians decided to provide a Sunday school at the workhouse and appoint a tutor under the direction of the House Committee. Through these combined activities the Guardians of the Poor had set a timetable for pauper children in Birmingham to ensure they were fully occupied in manufacturing work during weekdays and with religious education on Sundays. They thus ensured there was no opportunity for pauper children to be unoccupied or unruly at any time while under the control of the poor law authorities.[12]

The number of children resident in the asylum fluctuated from month to month and from year to year. In September 1813 there were 264 children housed and 94 children employed, bringing an annual income from child labour of £288.[13] By September 1817 the number of resident children had increased to 397 with 150 employed, resulting in an annual income from child labour of £566. And in October of the following year three-quarters of the 388 resident children were employed 'in the Manufacture of Pins, Straw Platt and figuring British Lace', demonstrating the links that existed with local industries and small businesses.[14]

---

9   Nejedly, 'Earning their Keep', p. 209.

10   BAH, GP B/2/1/1, October 1797.

11   BAH, GP B/2/1/2 Minutes of the Birmingham Board of Guardians, 1807–26, February 1796.

12   Nejedly, 'Earning their Keep', p. 208.

13   BAH, GP B/2/1/2, September 1813.

14   BAH, GP B/2/1/2, October 1818.

Most of the children worked at pin-making, the industry famously cited by Adam Smith as an example of increased productivity associated with the division of labour. There were 135 boys and 90 girls making and carding pins for Phipson's Pin Manufactory, while a further 55 girls worked 'in the straw platt business for Mr & Mrs Sharpe' and 20 girls worked 'in the British lace business for Mrs Ford'.[15] Among the total of 388 children in the asylum at this time were 137 orphans and 135 with only one parent, highlighting that the loss of one or both parents was the primary reason for children's admittance to the asylum.[16]

The relationship between the Birmingham Asylum for the Infant Poor and local businesses, particularly pin manufacturing, contrasted with the philosophy underpinning the establishment of schools of industry in England during this period. Whereas the Birmingham asylum focused on preparing children for a lifetime of manual labour in workshops and manufactories, schools of industry were set up to teach children traditional craft occupations such as spinning, tailoring and weaving, together with domestic skills for girls. These schools for children of the poor emerged in the late eighteenth and early nineteenth centuries along with Sunday schools and charitable institutions for pauper, vagrant or criminal children.[17] A number of schools of industry were established by individual women philanthropists, notably Sarah Trimmer and Catherine Cappe, who were concerned about a perceived degeneration of morals, manners and family values among the labouring poor. These campaigners believed that the spread of industrialisation had brought about a breakdown in traditional family life largely related to the employment of women and young girls in manufactories and mills. A spinning school set up in York in 1783 by Catherine Cappe was specifically aimed at removing girls from 'the evils of employment' in a local hemp manufactory.[18] Cappe's view was that girls who were taught spinning would learn 'the habits of industry' and be prepared for respectable work in domestic service, rather than factory work, where women and young girls worked closely with men and boys. A number of schools of industry were set up around London, such as Sarah Trimmer's school in Brentford, and others were established at Bath, Cheltenham, Ipswich, Kendal and Exeter, as well as in the industrial towns of Bolton, Leeds, Wakefield and Wigan.[19]

Some schools of industry, such as the one at Kendal, were supported by voluntary subscriptions and overseen by committees of ladies who made regular visits. Other schools were run by Poor Law authorities, including the King Street School of Industry in London. Boys in rural schools learnt spinning, weaving

---

15   *Ibid.*

16   *Ibid.*

17   Dick, 'English Conservatives'.

18   *Ibid.*, pp. 194–5.

19   *Ibid.*, pp. 194–5.

and agricultural labour, whereas boys in towns were taught the crafts of tailoring and shoe-making.[20] Girls were typically taught spinning, sewing, knitting and domestic tasks. Training poor children in these traditional occupations and skills was regarded as an important way of avoiding the social disruption brought about by industrialisation.[21] However, the high cost of materials and equipment required by schools of industry contributed to their decline by the 1830s, and there is no evidence to show that these schools were able to become self-financing, as happened at the infant asylum in Birmingham. Early work was generally accepted as inevitable for the children of the poor but there were differences in attitudes towards the purpose of training and the type of work regarded as suitable for children. Supporters of the schools of industry believed that training in traditional skills suitably prepared children for a lifetime of labour while avoiding the degradation of industrial occupations, particularly for girls. On the other hand, the Birmingham Guardians of the Poor had no reservations about employing children in industry, as many of the guardians themselves were small-scale industrial manufacturers such as brass-founders or gunsmiths.[22] However, while they did not oppose child labour in industry the guardians were relatively open to emerging theories and ideologies about children and childhood. Changes in attitudes in the early nineteenth century towards educating pauper children are illustrated by increases in the amount of time children spent in the asylum schoolroom as opposed to the workshops.

Concerns about education and health in the infant asylum

The infant asylum committee decided in 1822 to engage a schoolmaster and mistress in response to concerns expressed by the Guardians of the Poor about the asylum children's lack of educational progress.[23] By September 1826 less than half of the 389 children in the asylum were employed in manufacturing occupations. The number of children engaged in pin-making had declined from 225 in 1818 to 73 by 1826, and the straw-plait trade had disappeared altogether from the list of occupations.[24] This reduction in pin-making activity may have been due to a lack of demand by the pin industry because of advances in mechanisation, or because there was an over-supply of available child labour. However, new manufacturing processes were introduced, such as bead-stringing, glass-cutting and the production of small wire items, again reflecting the asylum's connections with local Birmingham industries.

---

20 *Ibid.*, pp. 228–9.

21 *Ibid.*, p. 305.

22 Nejedly, 'Earning their Keep', p. 209.

23 BAH, GP B/2/1/2, October 1822.

24 BAH, GP B/2/1/3 Minutes of the Birmingham Board of Guardians, 1826–38, September 1826.

Additional concerns about the welfare of asylum children emerged in the 1830s when attention became focused on the impact of work on children's health. The guardians were called to a special meeting in August 1836 'to discuss the state and management of the Asylum for the Infant Poor'.[25] Visitors from the asylum committee had noticed the 'general unhealthy appearance' of the children, especially the youngest, and parents had complained that their children were ill-treated. An investigation found that children from the age of seven were being set to work for eight hours each day at pin-heading and lace-making, which was harmful to their health and did 'not qualify them for earning their subsistence after they quit the Asylum'.[26] The investigation report made three important recommendations: first, girls should be taught plain sewing and domestic work and boys should learn tailoring and shoe-making; second, children below nine should not work and those of nine and above for no longer than six hours daily; third, the amount of time spent in school each day should be increased.[27]

These measures were based largely on the 1833 Factories Act, which prohibited children below the age of nine from working in textile mills and specified that employed children between the ages of nine and 13 in textile mills must be provided with at least two hours of schooling each day. The emphasis on craft skills for boys and domestic service skills for girls mirrored the type of traditional training promoted by the schools of industry. By 1837 girls at the asylum were no longer employed in lace-making but had taken up needlework and domestic duties, and employers had been notified that pin-making was to be discontinued. The asylum committee was thus able to report at the end of 1837 that most of the improvements suggested by the investigating committee had been implemented.[28] Nevertheless, boys continued to be employed at pin-heading for another four years, suggesting that the guardians may have been reluctant to withdraw child workers from such lucrative work despite the recommendations to make changes for the benefit of children's health. This failure to act quickly highlights the tensions between the guardians' duty towards the welfare of children under their care and their duty to the Birmingham ratepayers to maintain low levels of expenditure.

Changes in attitudes towards child labour

Child labour at the infant asylum changed quite significantly over a period of five decades, reflecting some of the changes that took place in society's attitudes towards childhood and child labour. For much of the eighteenth century John Locke's theories on education and the poor law, such as his view that parishes

---

25 *Ibid.*, August 1836.

26 *Ibid.*, October 1836.

27 *Ibid.*, October 1836.

28 *Ibid.*, December 1837.

should provide 'working schools' for pauper children, had remained influential. This philosophy was shared by many influential members of society, including William Pitt, who in 1796 spoke in favour of employing children in manufacturing. Yet even by this date attitudes towards children and work had already begun to change in other sectors of society. Jean-Jacques Rousseau's treatise on education, *Émile*, which depicted children as innately good and innocent until corrupted by the outside world, appealed to early opponents of child labour such as Jonas Hanway and Samuel Taylor Coleridge.[29] Poets and artists belonging to the Romantic Movement, like Coleridge and William Blake, were inspired by the natural world and drew attention to the hardships endured by children working as chimney-sweeps or in cotton mills in the late eighteenth century. The idealisation of childhood and a belief that children needed to be protected from exploitation continued to spread during the early nineteenth century, influencing the debates around child factory workers. These debates, together with numerous political campaigns and a series of legislative measures passed between 1802 and 1833, aimed to improve the lives and working conditions of child workers.[30] It seems likely that the reforms introduced at the Birmingham Asylum for the Infant Poor by the guardians in the 1830s were part of a wider response to the ongoing discourses in society around childhood and child labour.

Industrial schools and district schools

The Guardians of the Poor in Birmingham made the decision in 1839 to close the city's residential establishment for pauper children and return them to the workhouse at the same time as other Poor Law Unions were on the point of opening residential industrial schools or combining to form district industrial schools. The Poor Law Amendment Act of 1834 required Boards of Guardians to provide education in their workhouses, but for many guardians education was a low priority in comparison with other demands. Two influential members of the Poor Law Board, Edward Carleton Tufnell and James Kay-Shuttleworth, favoured the provision of residential schools for pauper children that were separate from the workhouse. Tufnell believed that pauperism was hereditary, that pauper parents raised their children to be paupers and thus dependent on the poor rate. In order to break the cycle of dependency children needed to be separated from their families and from the workhouse environment.[31] One notable example of this policy was

29 Honeyman, *Child Workers*, p. 4; Cunningham, *Children and Childhood*, pp. 138–9.

30 Hopkins, *Childhood Transformed*, pp. 74–7; Kathryn Gleadle, 'We *Will* Have It: Children and Protest in the Ten Hours Movement', in Nigel Goose and Katrina Honeyman (eds), *Childhood and Child Labour in Industrial England: Diversity and Agency, 1750–1914* (Farnham, 2013), pp. 215–30 at 215–19.

31 R.J. Phillips, 'E.C. Tufnell: Inspector of Poor Law Schools, 1847–1874', *Journal of the History of Education Society*, 5/3 (1976), pp. 227–40.

THE INDUSTRIOUS CHILD WORKER

the Bridgnorth Union's Farm School at Quatt in Shropshire, set up in 1845 in a house owned by William Whitmore, who was a Guardian of the Poor. This rural school catered for around 80 children and provided training in agriculture for boys and domestic service for girls. Whitmore claimed in his memoir that the school provided numerous long-term benefits for the children as well as ratepayers, as well as making a profit of approximately £67 per year, although he emphasised that producing a profit was less significant than providing appropriate education and training for the children: 'The question of profit, though of importance, is trifling when compared with the benefits derived, by the children immediately and the ratepayers ultimately, from the improved system of education.'[32] This farm school offered a model system for training pauper children in long-established agricultural skills that became widely known as 'the Quatt System'.[33]

The district industrial schools advocated by Kay-Shuttleworth and Tufnell were more suited to urban areas than rural districts. Manchester and Liverpool were the first Poor Law authorities to build large residential schools accommodating up to 1,000 pauper children.[34] Liverpool's Kirkdale Industrial Schools, built in 1845, provided skills in tailoring, shoe-making and carpentry for boys, as well as preparation for life at sea. Girls at the school were taught household skills, cooking, knitting and needlework to prepare for employment in domestic service. Manchester's Swinton Industrial Schools opened in 1846, as did the Leeds Moral and Industrial Training Schools. Three large district schools opened in London in 1849, and in the West Midlands the Walsall and West Bromwich unions joined together to set up the Wigmore Schools in 1869. Within a relatively short time, however, overcrowding in these district schools (also known as 'barrack schools' because of the emphasis on regimentation) led to health problems and the rapid spread of contagious diseases among the children. Moreover, the constant movement of children in and out of the schools disrupted the education and training provided, undermining potential levels of achievement.[35] Such movement was possible because, unlike the 'certified' Industrial Schools and Reformatory Schools established after 1857, the children at Poor Law industrial and district schools were not committed to the school by a magistrate, but were free to leave according to their family situation.[36]

---

32 William W. Whitmore, *A Memoir relating to the Industrial School at Quatt, addressed to the Ratepayers of the South East Shropshire District School*, LSE Selected Pamphlets (London, 1894), p. 4.

33 BPP, 1855, XXVIII, *Eighth Annual Report of the Poor Law Board*, p. 59.

34 McCrory, 'Poor Law Education', pp. 83–99.

35 McCrory, 'Poor Law Education', pp. 83–99.

36 Gillian Gear, 'Industrial Schools in England, 1857–1933', PhD thesis (University of London Institute of Education, 1999), p. 11.

A blueprint for industrial schools

The Birmingham Asylum for the Infant Poor provided what might be regarded as a blueprint or model for the district schools and industrial schools established during the mid-1840s in industrial Manchester and Liverpool, despite the fact that by this time the Birmingham institution had already been earmarked for closure. In December 1841 the infant asylum accommodated 240 children, including 63 boys who were employed at tailoring, shoe-making and knitting, earning a total of £38 8s 8d per week for the asylum from these traditional crafts. Shoe-making proved to be the most profitable occupation, bringing in £22 9s 2d per week. Girls of nine and above were engaged in unpaid domestic work within the asylum, possibly including the care of younger children, which saved on staff wages.[37] Children's labour in the infant asylum had by this time changed in a number of ways: first, approximately 50 per cent of the children were no longer expected to work because they were below nine years of age; second, among children over the age of nine gender differences in employment were more pronounced than previously, as girls were restricted to domestic work; third, employment for boys was no longer connected to local metal-working industries but had been replaced with traditional crafts of tailoring and shoe-making. Overall, children were being trained for future work in trades and roles that were deemed 'respectable', rather than working at repetitive manufacturing processes. Despite the length of time taken to implement these changes, the asylum had been transformed by 1841 into an institution similar in many respects to the industrial and district schools that followed. This pattern of schooling combined with traditional training continued throughout the 1840s (Table 3.1).

Table 3.1 Children resident in the Birmingham Asylum for the Infant Poor, 1845–47.

	1845	1846	1847
Average number of children	356	325	293
Average weekly maintenance per head	1s/0d	1s/9d	n/r
Boys employed at tailoring	30	36	27
Boys employed at shoemaking	32	27	23
Girls employed at knitting	26	24	11
Girls employed in sewing	40	35	50
Girls employed in domestic work	31	31	31
Children below 9 years	197	172	151

Source: BAH, GP B/2/1/5, Minutes of the Birmingham Board of Guardians, 1845–49.

---

37   BAH, GP B/2/1/4 Minutes of the Birmingham Board of Guardians, 1838–45, December 1841.

Making a profit from child labour

From its earliest beginnings the Birmingham Asylum for the Infant Poor was designed as an institution that would reduce expenditure on pauper children by making savings on the cost of their maintenance and possibly by profiting from the children's labour.[38] One of the main stated objectives of the asylum committee was 'to train up the Children to habits of industry'.[39] Finding employment for large numbers of children required additional workshops to be added to the asylum buildings, but the evidence shows these costs were 'defrayed by the produce of the Children's Labour'.[40] For example, the income for 1818 from children's labour was £900, whereas expenditure on wages for employees in the asylum amounted to an annual total of £139 19s 0d. This sum covered the cost of wages for the governor and governess of the asylum, two cooks, five chambermaids, one sick room assistant, three school room assistants, a gardener and three visiting staff.[41] As this example demonstrates, earnings from children's employment far exceeded expenditure on the wages of staff employed to care for them. Even when other running costs are taken into account, it seems evident that children's labour at the infant asylum provided a substantial source of income for the Birmingham Guardians of the Poor in the early nineteenth century. One of the chief problems they faced was the continual movement of children in and out of the institution, since the guardians had no control over the length of time they remained. During the three months from November 1818 to January 1819, for example, eight children were admitted to the asylum and 30 children left, chiefly at the request of their parents.[42] A significant factor in enabling parents to remove their children was the children's potential earnings ability. Once children had acquired some proficiency in pin-making or lace-making during their stay at the infant asylum they were able to contribute to the family income, offering a route for families to leave the workhouse system.

Throughout 1819 an average of 390 children were accommodated at the asylum, which resulted in over-crowding. This issue was highlighted by the visiting medical officers, who reported the need for larger premises. When the asylum committee presented their case for expansion to the Board of Guardians they made it clear that, despite the difficulties of constantly fluctuating numbers, the institution had become self-financing from the profits earned by the children's labour:

---

38 Nejedly, 'Earning their Keep', p. 212.
39 BAH, GP B/2/1/1, September 1795.
40 BAH, GP B/2/1/2, January 1819.
41 *Ibid.*, January 1819.
42 *Ibid.*, January 1819.

It is equally well known that the expense of building these premises as well as the sum required for the purchase of the Estate on which they are situated amounting to upwards of £4500 has been defrayed solely by the product of the children's labor, in addition to which the committee has had the satisfaction of paying over to Mr James Welch the Sum of £225 arising from the same source and to be appropriated to general purposes.[43]

The guardians made no objections to the financial claims put forward by the infant asylum committee, with the result that work on the additional buildings had already begun by the time of the next quarterly meeting of the Board of Guardians. This evidence is significant in highlighting that profits from the children's work not only supported the asylum's running costs but also repaid the original cost of the land and buildings. Moreover, surplus income from child labour was apparently helping to fund general poor relief in Birmingham, perhaps supporting the children's own parents in the workhouse.

The additional buildings were completed by January 1820, providing new dormitories, a new infirmary and 'a day room for instruction in reading'.[44] The extra provision brought the number of children accommodated up to 442 by the summer of 1820, yet the asylum committee was able to report that children engaged in the pin, straw-plait and lace trades were all fully employed and 'at the usual prices'.[45] As outlined above, however, this situation changed during the 1830s, when employment was restricted to older boys only and girls to domestic duties, bringing a loss of income from child labour. In January 1839 there were 321 children in the asylum incurring average costs of 2s per week each. Among the boys who were employed, 80 were engaged in pin-heading, eight in tailoring and four in mending shoes. Maintenance costs for 321 children amounted to approximately £32 per week, whereas the income from children's earnings was in the region of £23 per week – a substantial shortfall compared with the profitability of children's labour in earlier years.[46] Despite the loss of income and increased expenditure, a report by the asylum visitors concluded that the advantages to the children in terms of physical health and morality 'far outweigh all the money and attention which have been bestowed upon them and are a noble example of the Humanity, Liberality and Wisdom of the Guardians

---

43   *Ibid.*, June 1819.

44   *Ibid.*, January 1820.

45   *Ibid.*, Board of Guardians Minutes, 1807 to 1826, July 1820.

46   BAH, GP B/2/1/4, January 1839.

of Birmingham'.[47] Thus the asylum visitors, although appearing to be genuinely concerned with improvements to the children's health and well-being, completely failed to recognise the important economic contributions made by the children themselves to the asylum finances.

A decision made by the guardians in 1839 to build a new workhouse and close the infant asylum was justified on the basis of savings in expenditure and providing closer supervision of the poor. Financial issues were the main priority and, even though it seems clear that the existing asylum premises had become inadequate for the number of children to be housed, there was no suggestion that children might benefit from living alongside their families. The workhouse site in Lichfield Street was valued at £11,000, the asylum site at £5,000, and a sum of £4,194 was on deposit with the Bank of England. This provided a total of £20,194 to cover the £15,000 estimated building costs for a large new workhouse complex to be built on land at Winson Green, on the outskirts of Birmingham.[48] It has already been noted that profits from the children's labour had repaid the original costs of the asylum land and buildings. It seems to be the case, then, that the asylum children had also contributed up to a third of the cost of building the new Birmingham workhouse.

Pin-making finally ceased at the infant asylum in 1840, yet earnings from child labour continued to be significant when compared with those of other children's institutions. The Kirkdale Industrial Schools in Liverpool accommodated more than 1,000 children and provided training for boys in shoe-making and tailoring, yet earnings from this work were far lower than those achieved at the Birmingham asylum. Whereas 63 boys at the Birmingham asylum earned more than £38 per week from tailoring and shoe-making in 1841, the boys at the Kirkdale Industrial School earned just over £120 in six months in 1850.[49] The equivalent earnings over six months at Birmingham would have amounted to approximately £988, a huge difference. It is possible, of course, that earnings were recorded differently, perhaps because the Kirkdale child workers were employed mainly in making clothing and shoes for children in the school. Nevertheless, it appears that child workers in the Birmingham asylum continued to make substantial contributions to the costs of running the institution, even from traditional craft occupations. The ability of the Birmingham Guardians of the Poor to make a profit from child labour, of any description, seems to have been quite exceptional.[50]

---

47   Ibid., January 1839.

48   Ibid., June 1839.

49   Anne Brogden, 'Clothing Provision by Liverpool's Other Poor Law Institution: Kirkdale Industrial Schools', Costume, 37/1 (2003), pp. 71–4.

50   Nejedly, 'Earning their Keep', p. 213.

Children's health and closure of the asylum

At the end of the 1830s reports concerning child health and the number of deaths of children at the asylum became more prominent. In September 1838 11 cases of illness were recorded in the sick room, which included 'two cases of atrophy or wasting disease; three cases of inflamed eyes; three cases of fever; one case of canker of the mouth; one case of scald head; one case of Hooping cough'.[51] These illnesses subsequently resulted in three deaths: Catherine Stanley died from tuberculosis 'and the disease called wasting'; William Higgs was admitted with fever and died from congestion of the lungs; and Ann Egginton, an infant in the nursery, was 'affected with canker in the mouth ... she gradually grew worse and died from exhaustion'.[52] These illnesses do not have any direct connection with child labour, other than the three cases of inflamed eyes, which may have been related to conditions of work. However, they are an indication of the poor physical condition of children admitted to the infant asylum and the risks of infection among large numbers of children confined in close quarters. The asylum visitors' report of 1839 highlighted improvements in the children's general physical condition, especially among the boys, who appeared to be 'healthy, intelligent and cheerful', concluding that improvements were due to the reduction of working hours from eight to four hours per day. Children had also benefited from additional schooling and 'frequent access to the extensive new play ground, being formerly confined to the yard paved with stones'.[53] These comments suggest that the Birmingham guardians were prioritising the health and education of pauper children above any potential financial burden on local ratepayers. Nevertheless, shortly after receiving this favourable report on the children's health, the guardians decided to build a new workhouse for adults and children at Winson Green. The infant asylum site in Summer Lane was situated 'in a low valley exposed to prevalent winds which resulted in a cold and damp environment' and was thus damaging to health.[54] The decision by the guardians to close the infant asylum on health grounds contradicts the positive view of children's health included in the visitor's report of just a few months earlier. It seems possible, therefore, that the recent loss of income from child labour may have been a significant factor in the decision to close the infant asylum in addition to concerns about children's health.

From 1841 until its closure in 1852 the asylum accommodated an average of 300 children at any time, reaching more than 400 children in 1849. A

---

51   BAH, GP B/2/1/4, October 1838.

52   *Ibid.*, October 1838.

53   *Ibid.*, January 1839.

54   *Ibid.*, June 1839.

schoolmaster and mistress provided boys and girls with daily instruction in reading, writing, arithmetic and the principles of the Christian religion, and by the late 1840s asylum children spent longer periods in the classroom and fewer hours at work.[55] Children continued to work in traditional occupations, but reports to the guardians became notably focused on health and education rather than on income from child labour. For example, smallpox was prevalent in the borough in 1845, yet there were no cases of smallpox at the asylum owing to its policy of vaccinating all children before admittance.[56] The guardians demonstrated forward thinking in this aspect of public health several years in advance of the 1853 Vaccination Act, which introduced compulsory smallpox vaccinations for children. Despite this, however, renewed concerns were raised in 1849 by Dr Thomas Green, the medical officer, when a total of 422 children were being accommodated.[57] This had resulted in considerable overcrowding, especially in the lower nursery, which contained 66 children despite being certified for a maximum of 38. Dr Green reported that the children presented with 'dull eyes, a vacant countenance and listless attitude' due to 'impure air in badly ventilated rooms'.[58] More significantly, six deaths of asylum children from scrofula during the previous three months were ascribed to the poor environmental conditions.

Dr Green's concerns about the environment were confirmed by members of the maintenance committee, who reported that the buildings were inefficiently drained and ventilated, resulting in a 'foul and fetid atmosphere'.[59] Shortly afterwards architects were invited to submit plans for a new workhouse housing up to 1,550 residents including 600 children. Separate schoolrooms and classrooms were to be provided on the workhouse site.[60] It is not clear whether overcrowding and pressing health problems at the infant asylum in 1849 triggered the request for workhouse plans. However, the Birmingham guardians appear to have become pro-active with regard to public health, taking any potential threats very seriously, and so it may have been these issues that finally prompted the relocation of children to premises on the new workhouse site.

55   BAH, GP B/2/1/5 Minutes of the Birmingham Board of Guardians, 1845–49, January 1839.

56   *Ibid.*, August 1845.

57   *Ibid.*, April 1849.

58   *Ibid.*, April 1849.

59   *Ibid.*

60   *Ibid.*

Leaving the infant asylum

The constant movement of adults in and out of the workhouse led to a corresponding steady transfer of pauper children in and out of the infant asylum. The records for October 1822 show that 54 children had been admitted in the previous 12 months, whereas 112 children had been withdrawn by parents or relatives and 32 children were apprenticed.[61] The removal of a large number of older children from the asylum led to a reduced income from child labour, although some expenditure on maintenance costs was also reduced. A similar pattern of fluctuating income and expenditure was noted a few years later, in December 1826, when 96 children were removed from the asylum over a three-month period, mostly by their parents. The asylum committee were informed that very few children in the asylum were old enough to be apprenticed, noting that the 'demand for apprentices for several years has been greater than the supply … an indication of a preference for children educated in the institution.'[62]

This evidence suggests that during the 1820s families with younger children experienced the greatest financial pressures, forcing them to turn to the workhouse for support. Families with slightly older children were able to leave the workhouse because their incomes could be bolstered by children's earnings from pin- or lace-making. It also appears that families may have removed their children from the infant asylum as soon as possible in order to avoid them being apprenticed under the Poor Law, resulting in a shortage of parish apprentices. It seems likely, therefore, that children who had reached the age of nine or ten were viewed by their families as economic assets because of their earning potential as child workers in Birmingham industries. Pauperised families thus developed complex survival strategies including the use of the workhouse system for temporary support during times of greatest financial hardship.

Parish apprentices from Birmingham

Children who were orphaned or whose families were unable to care for them because of the death or illness of a parent were those most likely to be apprenticed in cotton mills or coal mines by the Birmingham guardians. An overseer's inspection report on Birmingham parish apprentices at Lancashire cotton mills in 1796 provides a detailed description of the long working hours and harsh conditions endured by these children.[63] The children apprenticed to Ratcliffe Bridge Mill were expected to work from 5am to 8pm each day,

---

61   BAH, GP B/2/1/2, October 1822.

62   BAH, GP B/2/1/3, December 1826.

63   BAH, GP B/2/1/1, June 1796.

leaving no time for schooling. They wore poor clothing and worked in bare feet as shoes were not provided for them. The conditions at the mill were so harsh that when the overseers arrived from Birmingham for the inspection 'the boys begged they might not stay'.[64] Parish children sent to Hind Mill and Somerset Mill in the Lancashire town of Bury fared little better, working from 6am to 7pm each day. These children wore poor clothing and were beaten with sticks as punishment so that 'many of the children cryed to come home'.[65] Following these reports of shocking ill-treatment and the desperate condition of cotton-mill apprentices, the Birmingham guardians decided to cease apprenticing pauper children to the Lancashire mills. Nevertheless, they continued to apprentice children to textile mills in Staffordshire and the East Midlands and to coal mines in South Staffordshire.[66] Conditions in the Lancashire cotton mills seem to have been particularly severe, which may explain the guardians' decision to send children to mills, mines and workshops in neighbouring Midlands counties, where they could be visited on a regular basis.

In a second example, an overseer's inspection visit in August 1805 to cotton mills in Staffordshire, Leicestershire and Nottinghamshire highlights the quite substantial numbers of Birmingham pauper children who were apprenticed. This visit involved an investigation of the living and working conditions of 60 children at Alrewas, 50 children at Tutbury, 29 children at Cuckney, 26 children at Bulwell, 30 children at Ashby, eight children at Measham and 30 children at Appleby. The overseer inspected 203 children during this visit, out of the total number of 233 apprentices from Birmingham, noting the healthy appearance of the children and giving a favourable report on their accommodation. Apart from one complaint made by a child about severe treatment from a mill overlooker, the views of the apprentices were not recorded in these official records and might have provided a different perspective from that of the overseer. At the same time, the inspection report provides an insight into the views of the Birmingham overseers, suggesting that 'preference should at all time be given to placing the Children of Paupers in these healthy situations and Clean Trades to the impure air and dirty Manufactories of Birmingham'.[67] Furthermore, the report recommended that it might be 'highly beneficial to the Parish of Birmingham to establish similar employment for Poor Children in a Manufactory of its own'.[68]

---

64   BAH, GP B/2/1/1, June 1796.

65   *Ibid.*

66   BAH, 660982.

67   *Ibid.*, August 1805.

68   *Ibid.*

The Birmingham Guardians of the Poor did not adopt the suggestion to establish a textile mill in Birmingham so that parish children could be apprenticed in 'clean' manufacturing work rather than an unhealthy metal trade. It seems unlikely that such an idea would appeal to them in view of their tight control of public finances and the capital investment required for a textile mill. The guardians clearly believed that parish children should be provided with the basic necessities of food, shelter and clothing, but they also felt it was their duty to place pauper children in full-time employment at the earliest possible opportunity. By removing these children from the parish, any future financial burden was shifted away from the Birmingham ratepayers. Although children in the infant asylum were able to produce a profit from their labour, the guardians frequently preferred to apprentice children who were without family support away from Birmingham rather than accept long-term responsibility for their welfare.

Life after the infant asylum

In view of the number of Birmingham children who spent at least part of their childhood at the infant asylum, an important issue to be considered is how these children fared as adults. The census returns are an important source of information about individual children living at the asylum, as they provide names and approximate ages of the residents. The 1851 census indicates that children were most likely to be living in the asylum between the ages of five to ten years, with boys outnumbering girls in nearly all age groups (Table 3.2). Four boys and three girls from the 1851 census have been traced through later census and parish records, showing that some of them experienced considerable difficulties as adults. Hezekiah Bibb, for example, who was just four years old in 1851, was later imprisoned at Warwick Quarter Sessions in 1866 for stealing a bag of soot as a 19-year-old.[69] After serving a sentence of two months with hard labour Hezekiah settled in the town of Tamworth in Staffordshire and found employment as a chimney-sweep. However, he was in trouble with the law again in July 1874 when, along with two colliers, he was charged with making an unprovoked attack on three Irishmen. On this occasion he was sentenced to six weeks' imprisonment with hard labour for the 'very brutal assault'.[70] Shortly after his release in September 1874 Hezekiah was charged with being drunk and disorderly on licensed premises after refusing to leave the Rose and Crown Inn in Tamworth. He was fined £1 with costs of 14s 9d or one month's imprisonment in default of payment.[71] Just two months

---

69   *Coventry Standard*, 7 July 1866.

70   *Tamworth Herald*, 18 July 1874.

71   *Tamworth Herald*, 19 September 1874.

later he was remanded in custody at Tamworth Borough Sessions on a charge of stealing a large quantity of calico from a draper's shop in Church Street.[72] His career as a petty criminal appears to have come to an end in December 1882, when he was charged with trespassing on land at Wigginton 'in pursuit of game' and fined 20s with 5s 3d in costs.[73] Finally, the *Tamworth Herald* reported his death on 26 January 1896 at the age of 52.[74] His sister Jane Bibb had died several years earlier, in 1866, at the age of 23.

Table 3.2 Children in the Birmingham Asylum for the Infant Poor in 1851.

Age	Boys	Girls	Total
2 to 4 years	17	9	26
5 to 7 years	39	30	69
8 to 10 years	67	43	110
11 to 13 years	30	25	55
14 + years	5	9	14
Totals	158	116	274

Source: Census of England and Wales, 1851.

Another former resident, Alfred Ashbrook, was recorded in 1861 at the age of 17 in full-time employment as a metal-cutter and living as a boarder with a family in Birmingham. Alfred married three years later, but his wife died soon after giving birth, leaving him widowed at the age of 23 with a baby son. A decade later, in 1871, Alfred had remarried and found employment as a surgical-instrument-maker in Birmingham, where he lived with his second wife and young son.[75] Former child resident Moses Jesson has been traced in the 1881 and 1891 census returns. In 1881 Moses was a 42-year-old basket-maker living with his wife and five children in Birmingham, but ten years later he was recorded as a boarder in the household of another family at Court 15, Essex Street, in Birmingham.[76] One possible explanation for the change in circumstances is that Moses may have been a widower with adult children by this time, perhaps living in the household of his married daughter.

Sisters Selina and Harriet Selvey were aged 13 and ten respectively at the time of their stay in the asylum in 1851. Ten years later, 23-year-old Selina was boarding with a family in Caroline Street, Birmingham, although without any

---

72   *Tamworth Herald*, 12 December 1874.

73   *Tamworth Herald*, 30 December 1882.

74   *Tamworth Herald*, 8 February 1896.

75   Census of England and Wales, 1851–71.

76   Census of England and Wales, 1881–91.

apparent occupation. She appeared in official records again in 1868, having died at the age of 28. Harriet was recorded in the 1891 census as the proprietor of a sweet shop in Boulton Road, Handsworth, while her father William Selvey, a 79-year-old retired jeweller, was a patient in the Birmingham workhouse infirmary. In a final example, in 1881 former asylum resident Joseph Hollick was employed as a boot-maker and lived with his wife and five children in Wolverhampton. He continued to live and work in Wolverhampton with his family, dying in 1916 at the age of 75.[77]

These life stories of former infant asylum children provide evidence that some individuals were able to overcome the early setbacks of their childhood. Alfred Ashbrook, Moses Jesson and Joseph Hollick were successful in establishing stable occupations, marrying and raising families of their own. Harriet Selvey pursued an independent lifestyle as the proprietor of a sweet shop in the Birmingham suburb of Handsworth, a noteworthy achievement for a working-class woman. Some children were less fortunate than others in later life, however, perhaps becoming involved in criminal activities, like Hezekiah Bibb, or the victim of an early death. The variety of outcomes encountered by this sample of children raises further questions about the impact of childhood experiences in an institution on an individual's subsequent life-chances. For example, how were children's lives affected by the age at which they entered the infant asylum, the length of stay, or the educational provision?

Conclusion

Children were transferred from the infant asylum to children's accommodation blocks at the new workhouse in 1852, bringing to an end the practice of housing pauper children on a separate site from their parents. Asylum children had made significant profits for the asylum, repaying more than the original costs of the land and buildings – a considerable economic contribution that has not previously been recognised. Following the final withdrawal of manufacturing processes in 1840, the asylum children divided their time between schoolwork and occupations such as tailoring, shoe-making or domestic work, but even when children were engaged in these more traditional activities the guardians continued to extract a profit from child labour, highlighting the distinctiveness of the infant asylum as a Poor Law institution. This investigation of policies at the infant asylum over five decades has offered new insights into changing attitudes towards childhood and child labour in response to the wider political, social and cultural context of the period and argued that changes in attitudes towards childhood and child labour during the early decades of the nineteenth century forced the Birmingham guardians to alter their policies towards

---

77   Census of England and Wales, 1881–91.

children's work and education in the infant asylum. Furthermore, it uncovers some of the strategies adopted by pauper families in their interactions with the Poor Law, and the extent to which children from these families were expected to contribute to their own upkeep. The demand for child workers in Birmingham's workshops and manufacturing industries is explored and discussed in the next chapter.

4

The industrious child worker

Introduction

The previous chapters have shown there was little demand for parish apprentices in Birmingham industries during the eighteenth and nineteenth centuries. This was in contrast to the high level of demand in the textiles districts of England, where parish apprentices have been identified as an important part of the early industrial labour force.[1] The reluctance of Birmingham tradesmen and industrialists to employ pauper apprentices, however, did not mean there was a corresponding absence of child workers in its manufacturing enterprises. This chapter aims to demonstrate that significant numbers of non-apprenticed children were employed in Birmingham workshops and factories and that child workers were an essential part of Birmingham's economic expansion. Jan de Vries has argued that an 'industrious revolution' occurred before and during the Industrial Revolution, involving an intensification of work by adult males and widespread participation of women and children in the labour market, driven by a desire among all social classes to acquire new consumer goods.[2] This included increased consumption of fuel for lighting and heating, clothing, and household goods such as crockery. Child workers, who were typically under-fed and poorly clothed, became part of this industrious revolution because of their families' need for additional financial support. This pattern of working, with whole families included in the paid labour force, declined only during the second half of the nineteenth century, when the sole male bread-winner family began to predominate.[3] In the light of this interpretation, a second aim of this chapter is to illuminate how far the employment of child workers contributed towards an 'industrious revolution' in Birmingham. It suggests that child workers laboured to support the basic needs of their own families, while at the same time working to meet the consumer demands of others for the manufactured goods they produced. A third aim is to question the timeline for the demise of child labour in England. Humphries and Kirby have identified the early decades of the nineteenth

---

1   Honeyman, *Child Workers*; Lane, *Apprenticeship in England*; Levene, 'Parish Apprenticeship'.

2   Jan de Vries, *The Industrious Revolution: Consumer Behavior and the Household Economy, 1650 to the Present* (New York, 2008), p. 121.

3   de Vries, *Industrious Revolution*, p. 121.

century as the peak participation period for child labour, with a decline from mid-century onwards.[4] This chapter explores the question of whether the employment of child workers in Birmingham similarly declined in the mid-nineteenth century.

The sources for research into non-apprenticed child workers are particularly problematic in two ways. Firstly, business records from this period are notoriously scarce and those records that have survived are unlikely to record details of child workers because wages were paid either to the parent or to the workman who was directly employing the child.[5] In a few cases, surviving Birmingham business records have been identified that include details of weekly wages. For example, the Soho Foundry paid wages of £313 7s 6d for the week of 27 October 1826. These included payments to carpenters, smiths, fitters, labourers, brick-layers, foundry men and pattern-makers, but there is no list of individual workers or indication of payments to child assistants.[6] Similarly, wages records for the coin manufacturing firm of Ralph Heaton & Sons of Birmingham list all weekly payments from 1840 to 1861.[7] During the week of 4 January 1840 the company employed 24 workers whose wages ranged from 2s 6d, paid to Elizabeth Hinks, to £3 4s 0d, paid to Thomas Adams. The sum received by Elizabeth Hinks suggests that she was probably a child worker, but the wages records do not confirm her age, occupation or the hours worked. By April 1861 the company employed 189 workers who received weekly payments of between 2s 6d and £7 0s 2d, but, again, there is no further information on ages and occupations.

A second issue is that, except for a few large-scale enterprises, Birmingham industry until at least the mid-nineteenth century was characterised by numerous small-scale firms and masters who each employed a handful of workers.[8] In order to obtain an overall picture of child labour a substantial number of business records would be needed. Evidence of child labour in eighteenth-century industry is particularly problematic, existing largely in the personal diaries of visitors who noted the presence of child workers in Birmingham manufactories. Inspections of manufacturing industries undertaken in the nineteenth century by the Factories Inquiry Commission and the Children's Employment Commissions, however, not only provide statistical information but offer a range of direct testimonies from employers,

---

4   Humphries, *Childhood and Child Labour*; Kirby, *Child Labour*.

5   Kirby, *Child Labour*, p. 16.

6   BAH, MS 3147/8 Boulton and Watt Collection, Staff and Employment Records, 1784–1888.

7   BAH, MS 1010/8–9 Ralph Heaton & Son, Wages Books, 1840–73.

8   Hopkins, *Birmingham*; Clive Behagg, 'Myths of Cohesion: Capital and Compromise in the Historiography of Nineteenth-Century Birmingham', *Social History*, 11 (1986), pp. 375–84.

supervisors, adult workers and child workers themselves.[9] Evidence from these reports, therefore, forms the basis of research in this chapter.

A number of influences impacted on the level of industriousness among child workers in Birmingham. One important factor was the widespread belief that early work was preferable to 'idleness' for children from poorer families who could not afford school fees, because this brought in extra income, prepared them for future employment and removed them from the streets. A second factor was the relative lack of employment opportunities, other than casual and temporary work, for adult male workers who were inexperienced and unskilled in manufacturing work. This led to a reliance on children's earnings, particularly among families newly arrived in Birmingham from agricultural districts. The introduction of the Poor Law Amendment Act in 1834 was an additional factor that pushed families to rely on children's earnings, as it became more difficult to obtain outdoor relief during times of unemployment or ill health. However, gradual changes in attitudes towards childhood, which became perceived as a life-stage in which children from all social classes should be educated and protected from the harshness of the adult world, led slowly over the course of the nineteenth century to a decline in child labour among the youngest children in Birmingham. The main questions considered here are: what was the extent and nature of child labour in Birmingham industries? Were child workers regarded as essential in manufacturing processes? Was there an intensification of child labour amounting to an 'industrious revolution' and when did child labour decline? And, finally, what were the attitudes towards child labour and how did these change over time?

Birmingham industry and child labour
The tradition of metal-working in Birmingham has a long history. John Leland famously described Birmingham in 1538 as a market town with one parish church and 'many smithes in the towne that use to make knives and all manner of cuttynge tools'.[10] The important Birmingham trade of gun making was established in the seventeenth century and by the early eighteenth century a variety of metal goods was being produced in the town, contributing towards

---

9   BPP, 1833, 450, XX.I, *Factories Enquiry Commission, First Report*; BPP, 1843, 430, XIII, *Children's Employment Commission, Second Report*; BPP, 1863, 3170, *Children's Employment Commission 1862, First Report*; BPP, 1864, 3414, *Children's Employment Commission 1862, Second and Third Reports*.

10 John Leland, *The Itinerary of John Leland In or About the Years 1535–1543* (London, 1907), pp. 96–7.

its reputation as the 'city of a thousand trades'.[11] Industrial expansion during the eighteenth century involved the establishment of a number of large-scale manufacturing firms alongside countless small-scale industries and workshops that evolved from the Birmingham tradition of self-employed workers and small masters.[12] The large-scale manufacturers included Matthew Boulton's Soho Manufactory, which employed 800 to 1,000 workers by 1770, and John Taylor's button-making factory, which employed 500 workers. Another notable manufacturer was John Baskerville, who established important printing, japanning and papier-mâché industries in eighteenth-century Birmingham.[13] The reputation of Birmingham as a centre for the manufacture of metal 'toys' such as buttons, buckles, watch-chains, snuff boxes, pins and silver-plated tableware attracted a succession of visitors to the town to see new methods of production and new consumer goods.[14] The Soho Manufactory showrooms displayed desirable luxury goods that proved a particular magnet for overseas visitors, attracting French, Spanish, German and Norwegian buyers as well as prominent Russian visitors.[15] Matthew Boulton established an important and long-term relationship with the Russian Embassy, welcoming the ambassador to Soho in 1770 for the first of many visits to purchase articles on behalf of the Empress Catherine, a leading patron of the decorative arts.[16]

Despite the establishment of some large-scale manufacturing enterprises, Birmingham industry remained heavily reliant on hand-operated machinery such as the stamp and the press, which were especially important in the metal toy and jewellery trades. Two leading Birmingham manufacturers, John Taylor and Samuel Garbett, stated in evidence to a House of Commons committee in 1759 that at least 20,000 people were employed in the toy trade in Birmingham

---

11 'Economic and Social History: Industry and Trade, 1500–1880', in Victoria County History, *A History of the County of Warwick, the City of Birmingham, Vol. 7*, ed. W.B. Stephens (London, 1964), pp. 81–139 <http://www.british-history.ac.uk/vch/warks/vol7/81–139>, accessed 12 September 2017; Malcolm Dick, 'The City of a Thousand Trades, 1700–1945', in Carl Chinn and Malcolm Dick (eds), *Birmingham: The Workshop of the World* (Liverpool, 2016), pp. 125–57; Peter Jones, 'Birmingham and the West Midlands in the Eighteenth and Early Nineteenth Centuries', in Malcolm Dick (ed.), *Matthew Boulton: A Revolutionary Player* (Studley, 2009), pp. 3–29.

12 Hopkins, *Birmingham*; Jones, *Industrial Enlightenment*, pp. 172–3; Behagg, 'Myths of Cohesion', p. 379; Berg, *The Age of Manufactures*, pp. 264–9; Harry Smith, 'William Hutton and the Myths of Birmingham', *Midland History*, 40/1 (2015), pp. 53–73.

13 'Economic and Social History: Industry and Trade, 1500–1880', in Victoria County History, *The City of Birmingham*.

14 Jones, 'Birmingham and the West Midlands', pp. 13–29; Berg, *Age of Manufactures*, p. 267.

15 Jones, *Industrial Enlightenment*, pp. 172–3.

16 Olga Baird, 'His Excellency Count Woronzow the Russian Ambassador and the Hardware Man: The History of a Friendship', in Malcolm Dick (ed.), *Matthew Boulton: A Revolutionary Player* (Studley, 2009), pp. 92–106.

and nearby towns.[17] The toy trade included coin and button manufacturing that utilised the hand-operated press, stamp and lathe, and pin-making, which involved the use of the draw-bench to draw out wire to a uniform thickness. Eric Hopkins has argued that these four machines were vital for production in the toy trade, adding that 'children were used to keep the Birmingham machines working' in the same way that children were employed to keep spinning and weaving machinery working in the textile regions.[18] Hopkins' view of the central role of child labour in Birmingham industry is substantiated by first-hand accounts written by visitors to the town's manufacturing industries in the mid-eighteenth century.

Child workers and the division of labour

The dean of Gloucester, Josiah Tucker, was an early visitor to the Birmingham manufactories, recording details of his visit in the *Collected Works of Josiah Tucker*, published in 1758.[19] He described the Birmingham workmen's custom of employing one or more child workers as assistants, a method of production that increased output by taking advantage of the division of labour. He cited an example of processes he witnessed at a Birmingham button manufactory to illustrate its economic advantages:

> When a man stamps a metal Button by means of an Engine, a Child stands by him to place the Button in readiness to receive the Stamp and to remove it when received, and then to place another. By these means, the Operator can stamp at least twice the Number, which he could otherwise have done, had he been Obliged to have stopped each Time to have Shifted the Buttons.[20]

In the course of his visit Dean Tucker learnt that an adult button-maker could earn 14d to 18d per day, but paid a child assistant just 1d to 2d per day, making it far more profitable for the workman to employ at least one assistant. Furthermore, such a method of production 'trains up Children to an Habit of Industry, almost as soon as they can speak. And hence it is, that the bijoux d'Angleterre, or Birmingham Toys, are rendered so exceedingly cheap as to astonish all Europe.'[21] Dean Tucker's description of production methods in the button industry thus provides important first-hand evidence that child

17   Hopkins, *Birmingham*, pp. 6–9.

18   *Ibid.*, pp. 7–9.

19   Josiah Tucker, *Collected Works of Josiah Tucker, Economics and Social Policy Volume III: Instructions for Travellers* (London, 1758; reprinted 1993), p. 34.

20   Tucker, *Instructions for Travellers*, p. 34.

21   *Ibid.*, p. 35.

workers were employed in Birmingham manufacturing as early as 1758. It also illustrates the popular mid-eighteenth-century point of view that children could be usefully set to work from a very young age.

Further contemporary accounts of child labour come from a visit to Birmingham in 1766 by Lord and Lady Shelburne. These visitors toured the premises and showrooms of many of Birmingham's leading manufacturers, including Samuel Garbett, Matthew Boulton, John Baskerville and John Taylor. Lady Shelburne recorded that their tour of the Baskervilles' garden and hothouse was followed by a visit to the japanning premises led by Mrs Baskerville, 'which business she has chiefly the management of'.[22] Lord Shelburne described their visit to the button factories, noting the significance of child workers: 'a button passes through fifty hands, and each hand perhaps passes a thousand in a day; likewise, by this means, the work becomes so simple that, five times in six, children of six or eight years old do it as well as men, and earn from ten pence to eight shillings a week.'[23] Carlo Castone, an Italian visitor, described in 1787 the volume of buttons produced: 'women, men and children do a huge amount of work and produce several kinds of buttons, which grow into thousands and thousands into a heap.'[24] He observed that some low-skilled tasks were undertaken by women and children rather than male workers: 'Work is simply done without effort and quickly. Badly paid women and children are involved in the production and not men.'[25]

The combined evidence from these first-hand accounts illustrates the extent to which child workers were employed in Birmingham industries in the mid-eighteenth century and identify child labour as an essential part of production methods. However, because child workers in Birmingham were employed by individual workmen rather than by firms, they are more difficult to locate than the groups of children who were apprenticed in textile mills or coal mines. This method of direct employment by workmen or workshop overseers, who were themselves self-employed, also resulted in the exclusion of Birmingham child workers from protective employment legislation for much of the nineteenth century. The Factory Acts introduced from the early nineteenth century onwards aimed to regulate the hours of work and conditions of employment for child workers, but applied only to the textile industries. The Health and Morals of Apprentices Act of 1802 prohibited the apprenticeship of children below nine years of age in the cotton industry and limited work to 12 hours per

---

22   Edmund Fitzmaurice, *Life of William, Earl of Shelburne* (London, 1912), pp. 274–7.

23   Fitzmaurice, *Life of Shelburne*, pp. 274–7.

24   Malcolm Dick, 'Discourses for the New Industrial World: Industrialisation and the Education of the Public in Late Eighteenth-century Britain', *History of Education*, 37/4 (2008), pp. 567–84 at 572.

25   *Ibid.*

day for apprenticed children aged from nine to 16 years. A further Act in 1819 extended these regulations to non-apprenticed children in the cotton industry. This was later followed by the Factory Act of 1833, which brought children in other textile industries under the same regulations, apart from those working in silk mills. However, the regulations did not extend to children in manufacturing apart from textiles, despite the fact that Birmingham industries had been visited by the Factories Inquiry Commission.[26] Factory inspectors Horner and Woolriche reported to the Inquiry Commission that much of the manufacturing in Birmingham was undertaken on the basis of piece-work and completed by home-based workers: 'there is no establishment in Birmingham where children are collected in large numbers to work together, as is the case in cotton, woollen and flax mills.'[27] Thus, a great deal of manufacturing production was organised through intermediary agents known in Birmingham as 'undertakers', who provided raw materials to small domestic workshops and set the rates of payment per piece. This system encouraged families to put even the youngest children to work to maximise family incomes. In consequence, the factory inspectors found that, although 'many thousand children [were] employed in the manufactures of the town', they were scattered around in small workshops and frequently worked at home with their parents.[28]

'The unhappy pin-headers': a case study of the pin industry
The inspectors for the 1833 Factories Inquiry Commission reported that no firms in Birmingham employed large numbers of child labourers, yet they had visited Phipson's pin manufactory, where more than 100 children worked, as well as the button factory of Thomas Ledsam & Sons, which employed 87 child workers.[29] According to William Bishop, who was employed as a pin-pointer there, children provided the majority of the workforce at Phipson's.[30] In evidence to the Inquiry he said that more than 100 children were employed out of a workforce of 150 to 160. The regular working hours for adults and children were 7am to 7pm on Mondays to Fridays and 7am to 5pm on Saturdays, excluding two hours for meals, which added up to a working week of 58 hours. Bishop stated that approximately 40 of the children were below the age of nine and a few were younger than seven, but children did not find the work exhausting and there were no complaints of ill health. A second workman, wire-drawer William Miles (34), also thought that children's health was not

---

26   BPP, 1833, 450, XX.I, 145:1–10.
27   *Ibid.*, 145:2.
28   *Ibid.*, 145:2.
29   *Ibid.*, 145:2.
30   *Ibid.*, 145:7.

affected by the work or the long hours. He had worked in the pin trade for 27 years and his own health was good, although wages were too low. Despite these positive comments from adult workers employed in the pin-making industry, it seems likely that they were anxious to retain their own positions within the firm and would have avoided making any criticism of the working conditions.

The pin factory proprietor Richard Phipson confirmed that around 130 children worked at his premises on a piece-work basis, engaged in either pin-heading or sticking pins onto paper. The children were employed by five overlookers, who were responsible for giving out the work and determining the rates of pay.[31] The hours of work and age of child workers was confirmed by the statements of children interviewed by the inspectors. Elizabeth Crofts, aged 14, had worked at Phipson's since the age of nine, working for nine and a half hours each day and earning wages of 5s 0d per week. Elizabeth had never attended a day school, but had been to Sunday school for a short time: 'I was not long there to learn.'[32] A second girl, Sarah Foster, aged 12, had earnings of 2s 9d weekly and lived with her widowed mother and four siblings. When questioned by the inspector about tiredness both girls maintained they were not tired in the evenings, despite the long hours at work.[33]

Inspectors also visited button manufacturing premises owned by Thomas Ledsam and John Turner. Children employed in these factories worked for nine or ten hours daily, usually from 7am to 7pm with two hours for meal breaks. John Sexty, the manager of Ledsam & Sons, explained that apprentices were not employed in the button industry because they were troublesome to employers: 'I should be glad if we never had another, as they are not under the same control as those children who can be turned away when we like.'[34] This statement is significant because it reveals that some small employers and workmen in Birmingham preferred to control child workers through the threat of dismissal and loss of income rather than taking on the responsibility of an apprentice. Whereas formal apprenticeship agreements were written and legally binding, these less formal employment arrangements were verbal and temporary, and have thus remained largely undocumented in the archives. The consequent lack of evidence means that the full extent of child labour, particularly in manufacturing industry, has not been fully explored by historians.

Manufacturers preferred not to employ children below the age of nine, but because many families could not afford school fees it was believed the children

---

31   *Ibid.*, 145:8.

32   *Ibid.*, 145:8.

33   *Ibid.*, 145:8.

34   *Ibid.*, 145:9.

'would be much better in the factory, working, as they often do, with their father, than running about in idleness, acquiring bad habits'.[35] Child labour in Birmingham was thus seen at least partly as a form of social control for children who were not attending school. Furthermore, it was believed that many parents, especially widows, depended on the earnings of their children and that limiting the age of starting work would be problematic for those families. Children working in Birmingham industries in the 1830s were not perceived as in need of protective legislation because they were not found in large groups like those in cotton or woollen mills. Even in the pin industry, children were employed either as home workers in domestic workshops or by overseers in relatively small groups of 20 children. In addition, children in Birmingham typically worked for a total of nine or ten hours each day, which was the central demand of the Ten Hours Movement in the textiles districts. Furthermore, Birmingham industries utilised hand tools and presses, rather than the large machinery regarded as hazardous to children's health in textile mills. For these reasons, the legislation on child labour included in the 1833 Factory Act did not apply to children working in Birmingham industries.

The Factories Inquiry of 1833 reported favourably on conditions for child workers in Birmingham, noting the 'kind friendly feeling so generally subsisting between the master and his work-people'.[36] Within a decade, however, the attitudes of officials towards child labour had changed appreciably, as evidenced by investigations for the Children's Employment Commission of 1843 and perhaps a reflection of the growing middle-class commitment to schooling for all children regardless of their social status. Sub-Commissioner Grainger reported that large numbers of very young children were employed in the Birmingham pin industry and were 'in every respect ill-used'.[37] These children worked in cold, dark premises that were overcrowded and dilapidated for 12 hours every day at sedentary tasks that left no opportunity for healthy exercise or relaxation. The sub-commissioner described them as 'pale and sickly looking' children who were dressed in rags, without shoes or stockings. They were continually watched by overlookers who punished them for the slightest loss of attention to their monotonous work. In some of Birmingham's pin workshops the children faced such cruelty and ill-treatment that Sub-Commissioner Grainger concluded: 'In the whole of my inquiries I have met no class more urgently requiring legislative protection than the unhappy pin-headers.'[38]

---

35 *Ibid.*, p. 109.

36 *Ibid.*, p. 108.

37 BPP, 1843, 430, XIII, p. 79.

38 *Ibid.*, p. 80.

The intensification of children's work in the pin industry

Phipson's Pin Manufactory, located at Broad Street in Birmingham, was visited on several occasions in November and December 1840 by Sub-Commissioner Grainger.[39] He reported that between 90 and 100 children were employed in small workshops at the premises, where they were expected to remain at work until 8pm, even though most of the adult workers finished work at 7pm. According to Samuel Phipson, children from the age of eight upwards were employed, but the sub-commissioner found several younger children at work on the premises. In one case, a woman who lived two miles from the factory 'had carried her child, who was too young to walk so far, and set him down at the factory door'.[40] Phipson stated that children working in the pin factory often came from among the poorest and most desperate families in Birmingham. He believed that the parents fell into poverty 'through lack of work or dissipation' and then sent their children to work in the pin trade because no previous experience was needed. The factory manager employed by Phipson confirmed that pin-heading was undertaken exclusively by women and children because it was the most laborious and worst-paid part of the pin-making process. The more skilled processes of pin-making, such as wire-drawing, pin-pointing and head-cutting, were undertaken by workmen assisted by children who were sometimes their own sons. The final process of sticking the pins into sheets of paper was mostly completed by girls.[41]

Children working as pin-headers at Phipson's were employed by two workshop masters, John Field and Hampton Jay, who were each responsible for around 40 children. The terms of employment were agreed verbally between a child's parents and the workshop master, often involving an advance payment of a few shillings to the parents that was to be repaid from the child's wages. Hampton Jay reiterated that these children were from the poorest families in Birmingham, including migrants from Ireland and those from the lowest class of 'beggars and other vagrants'.[42] In general, the children were inadequately clothed and poorly cared for by their parents. Mary Bowling, aged 13, had worked as a pin-header for six years from the age of seven; she worked alongside her younger sister, who had started work at just five years old. Mary and her sister earned joint wages of 5s per week, which were paid directly to their father, but they received nothing for themselves. In this family the mother had died and the father apparently worked from time to time at unloading coal carts but was not regularly employed, so the family were dependent on the

---

39 BPP, 1843, 431, XIV, p. 119.

40 *Ibid.*, p. 119.

41 *Ibid.*, pp. 119–21.

42 *Ibid.*, p. 121.

children's income from pin-making. Mary's health was not good and she said other children in the pin workshop also complained of feeling unwell because they were ill-treated by the overlookers: 'they are bad in the head … the cane is often used. The children are struck on the head, back or anywhere … some of the children made ill by being beat.'[43] Another child worker, 11-year-old Charles Hughes, had worked at Phipson's for two years earning 2s 6d per week, which he gave to his mother, receiving 3d to keep for himself. Charles' father worked as a stone-breaker for the parish, earning 4s a week, but he had previously worked at making silver pencil cases, for which the wages were 13s to 14s a week. Because of their father's lack of well-paid work Charles and his brother had been sent to work at pin-heading.[44] The child workers at Phipson's pin manufactory were clearly from families living in dire poverty and were sent to work at an early age because their parents were unable or unwilling to fully support their families as a result of ill-health, the absence of one parent or a lack of regular and well-paid work. One factor affecting the ability of parents to support their children during times of hardship was the Poor Law Amendment Act of 1834. Peter Kirby has argued that the introduction of more stringent policies towards outdoor relief for able-bodied adults had the effect of increasing dependence on children's earnings.[45] It seems highly likely that this was the case in Birmingham, as families who had fallen on hard times or who had recently arrived from Ireland or elsewhere faced a stark choice between sending their children out to work or to the workhouse.

At Palmer and Holt's pin manufactory 46 children were employed in old and very dilapidated premises by workshop master George Latham. One of the employees was 21-year-old Sarah Clarke, who had started work at pin-making at the age of ten. Sarah believed that many of the children were sent to work all day without breakfast or midday dinner because they were neglected by their families: 'the parents of the "headers" care very little about them, except to get their wages to spend in drink.'[46] Palmer and Holt had a contract with the Birmingham Asylum for the Infant Poor for the manufacture of pins. In December 1840 the asylum housed 82 boys who were working as pin-headers, but they were restricted to working for a maximum of four hours per day, a regulation that did not apply to children employed elsewhere. The asylum governor suggested that after learning the trade of pin-heading in the asylum, boys were sometimes removed by their parents with the intention of sending

---

43 *Ibid.*, p. 122.

44 *Ibid.*, p. 123.

45 Kirby, *Child Labour*, p. 95.

46 BPP, 1843, 431, XIV, p. 124.

them out to work.[47] Thus, parents were allegedly using the infant asylum as a period of temporary welfare relief where their children could acquire basic skills in pin-making.

There was a widespread perception in Birmingham at this time that child workers from the most destitute families were supporting their families financially. This was highlighted in the sub-commissioner's report of visits to children working from home at pin-heading, where he found a number of families who were dependent on their children's earnings because the parents were unemployed:

> It seems to be the universal opinion of all persons, high and low, with whom I have spoken on the subject, that the pin-headers and their families to which they belong, are the most wretched part of the population of the town; that no decent mechanic would allow his children to go to this work.[48]

The evidence from the pin industry shows that children comprised a large section of the workforce in 1840s Birmingham. It also suggests that child workers were often the principal breadwinners for their families, as there was sometimes a greater demand for child workers than for adults. The inability of parents to obtain well-paid employment, combined with the effects of the Poor Law Amendment Act, appears to have left some families with no choice other than to rely on their children's earnings. Interviews that were conducted with the children themselves reveal evidence of ill-health among child workers in Birmingham and incidents of ill-treatment by overlookers. Following his investigations, Sub-Commissioner Grainger asserted that child workers in the Birmingham pin industry were in need of protective legislation along with other industrial child workers. Despite this recommendation, government attention was firmly focused on children employed in coal mines and textile mills.

In 1842 the Mines and Collieries Act prevented underground working by women and children below the age of ten. This legislation was enacted in part as a result of the public outcry in response to the commission's report, which revealed that women and children worked partially clothed when underground.[49] The Factory Act passed in 1844 actually lowered the permitted age of employment from nine to eight years, but there was a proviso that children between the ages of eight and 12 should attend school for three hours each day, reducing their hours of work. However, the 1844 factory

---

47   *Ibid.*, p. 126.
48   *Ibid.*, p. 126.
49   Kirby, *Child Labour*, p. 100.

legislation applied only to children employed in the textiles industry and did not extend to child workers in other types of industries. Where Birmingham was concerned this omission can be explained partly by the organisation of production in small factories and workshops, which made detailed inspection and enforcement of employment legislation difficult. A second reason was that far fewer children were employed in Birmingham industries than in coal-mining or textiles.[50] Figures from the 1851 census for England and Wales show that the cotton industry employed 54,651 children between the ages of ten to 14 and the coal industry employed 23,038 boys aged ten to 14. Before the 1842 Mines Act young children below the age of ten were widely employed in coal mines across the West Midlands, as were child workers in a broad range of manufacturing industries. Some of these are illustrated in the case studies that follow.

'In the power of the butties': coal-mining children in the West Midlands

The Royal Commission on Children's Employment in Mines and Manufactories (1842) investigated a number of coalfields in the West Midlands, including the south Staffordshire coalfields to the north and west of Birmingham, the Shropshire coalfield district of Coalbrookdale between Wolverhampton and Shrewsbury, and the Warwickshire coalfield in the north-east of the county.[51] The sub-commissioner, Dr James Mitchell, reported that in south Staffordshire children began working in the mines between the ages of seven and nine years. In the Coalbrookdale district of Shropshire children began as young as six, and in one case the sub-commissioner met a miner who regularly took his four-year-old child down into the pit. Children began work at a similar age in the Warwickshire coalfields according to evidence from a Bedworth surgeon, John Sommers, who confirmed that boys were sent down to the pits at the age of six or seven. Dr Mitchell found no evidence of underground working by girls in any of the West Midlands coalfields, although many young women were employed as bankswomen on the coal banks and the canals, where they loaded coal onto canal boats. This work was 'laborious though not beyond their strength.'[52]

The method of working in the Staffordshire, Shropshire and Warwickshire coalfields was based on a system of contracting out underground work to 'butties' or 'charter masters', who were paid at a certain rate, or charter, for each ton of coal extracted. The butty hired the men and boys required to dig out the coal and transport it to the foot of the mine shaft, where it was then

---

50   *Ibid.*, pp. 53–5.

51   BPP, 1842, 380, *Children's Employment Commission, 1842, First Report*, Appendix.

52   *Ibid.*, Appendix.

raised up by labourers employed directly by the proprietor. Butties were paid a charter of 2s 6d to 3s 6d per ton, rising to 4s per ton in some pits, and were responsible for providing tools, carts and horses in the mines in addition to paying the wages of their workers.[53] Boys working underground were a combination of apprenticed and non-apprenticed children. Parish apprentices were rarely found in the Shropshire and Warwickshire coalfields, but they were very common in the south Staffordshire coalfields, where they were 'wholly in the power of the butties'.[54] Boys were sent to these districts from Union workhouses in Wolverhampton, Walsall, Dudley and Stourbridge at the ages of eight or nine for a trial period. At the age of nine they were formally bound as apprentices until the age of 21, receiving board and lodgings but no wages in exchange for their labour. William Grove, a mine agent at the Bilston Colliery in Staffordshire, said there were 200 to 300 parish apprentices at the mine and that they were often badly treated by the butties, being forced to work where other boys refused to go. Another agent, William Hartell Bayliss, said that boys had lost limbs or been killed in accidents at the mine. In fact, the reputation of the south Staffordshire minefields was so well known that some parishes would not apprentice their pauper children there.

Dr Mitchell visited coal mines at Holly Hall and Kingswinford near Dudley. The children in these mines started work at the age of seven or eight years and worked from 6am to 6pm each day with one hour for a dinner break. William Orton, then aged 17, had started work at the age of seven on the pit bank, carrying coal to the blacksmith's workshop. He had first worked underground in the pit at the age of ten, initially earning 10d per day for carrying slack, and then 1s. Charles Bleaden also earned 1s per day for carrying slack as a ten-year-old, explaining: 'it's hard work for boys, but easier for boys than men, it is so thin to go under'. John Greaves had worked in the pit from the age of seven at opening doors, earning 6d to 8d a day. At ten years old he began clearing away the slack for the miners, who would use a leather strap to keep the boys at work. He earned 1s 6d to 2s a day for this work, later earning 3s a day for cutting coal. Greaves thought the pits were a dangerous place to work because of falling coal, and knew of men who had been killed by falls. Boys who were apprenticed to the butties received the worst treatment: they were made to work where other boys would not go, and were sometimes forced to work all day and all night.[55]

---

53   *Ibid.*
54   *Ibid.*
55   *Ibid.*

'Forced to work through the night':
children in the Wolverhampton metal industries

The town of Wolverhampton in Staffordshire was home to a population of 36,382 in the early 1840s. There were numerous small metal-workers in the town, including 260 locksmiths, 60 to 70 key-makers and 20 to 30 in each of screw-maker, latch-maker, bolt-maker, snuffer-maker, tobacco-box-maker, spectacle-frame-maker and spectacle-case-maker. These trades were conducted in workshops behind houses, apart from a few large manufacturers, and each workman employed one, two or three children as assistants. Children and young people were also employed in the trades of japanning, tin-plating, nail-making and manufacturing of goods in iron and steel.[56] Sub-Commissioner Horne reported that children were generally employed by the adult workman they assisted, with the terms settled between the parents and the master. It was common for the masters to advance money to the parents, to be repaid by the children's labour from earnings of 1s 6d to 2s 6d weekly. Children in Wolverhampton typically began work at eight years of age and worked the same hours as adults, from 7am to 7pm or 8pm with two hours for meal breaks. The sub-commissioner found the children were generally in poor physical condition, short in stature, with poor diets and inadequate clothing. At work they were treated badly, especially by the small locksmiths, with punishments including beatings, going without meals and being forced to work beyond the normal hours, even through the night. In many cases the parents were held responsible for the ill-treatment of their children, with widespread drunkenness among fathers and a lack of domestic skills in mothers. According to the report findings, very few parents would support measures to restrict the age at which children might be employed because they were dependent on their children's earnings.[57]

'Haggard, dirty and worn out':
child workers in the Kidderminster carpet industry

The Worcestershire town of Kidderminster was highly dependent on its carpet industry, which employed 80 per cent of the population either directly or indirectly.[58] On Thursdays and Saturdays factory masters gave out yarn on bobbins to the carpet-weavers, who were expected to produce 36 yards of woven carpet in six days, for which they received between 8d and 1s 8d per yard. Each weaver employed a child or young person as an assistant to draw the wires, earning from 2s 6d to 5s 6d weekly. Sub-Commissioner Samuel Scriven

---

56   BPP, 1843, 432, XV, *Children's Employment Commission,1842, Second Report*, Appendix II.

57   *Ibid.*, Appendix II.

58   BPP, 1843, 431, XIV, Appendix I.

interviewed a number of child workers in the carpet industry: Thomas Carter, then aged 12, had worked as a draw boy for three years and earned 4s per week. He had attended day school before starting work, but now appeared to be supporting his family, as his father had not worked for 11 years. Thomas spent his wages on food for his mother, father and four siblings. Jane Warrington, then 13, had worked as a drawer for more than four years. She was from a large family of eight children, with three of them at work and earning a total of 11s 8d per week. Jane's father was a carpet-weaver but had not worked for 12 months, although he was in good health. The whole family were supported by the three working children, living mainly on bread and dripping. The family received no parish relief because the father would not ask for support.

'The sadly abused nailers': children in the nail-making trade

Nail-making was a common industry in the West Midlands from Wolverhampton in Staffordshire to Bromsgrove in Worcestershire, a distance of some 20 miles which included the districts of Sedgley, Dudley, Cradley Heath, Halesowen, Netherton and Old Swinford. The manufacture of hand-made nails typically involved whole families and took place in forges or nailshops attached to the small houses occupied by the workers. In the parish of Old Swinford children were 'put to the nail-block as soon as they can earn a few pence', according to the Reverend S. Cragg.[59] The curate's attempts to persuade the parents to send their children to school, rather than to work, were met with the response that they could not afford to lose their children's labour. Although there were many day schools and Sunday schools in the parish, children left at a very early age and acquired little education. In the districts of Netherton, Rowley Regis and Cradley Heath Sub-Commissioner Horne found that children from nailing families were put to work at the age of five, six or seven, as soon as they could blow the bellows or use a hammer. Girls as young as five were expected to care for infants so that mothers could work, and then started working in the forge themselves at the age of eight or nine.

The child workers in Netherton and Rowley Regis, near Stourbridge, were described by the sub-commissioner as 'poorly fed, dressed in rags and constantly overworked'.[60] However, James Bolton, aged ten, of Cradley Heath, who worked at nail-making with his father, mother and sisters from 6am to 5pm, did not find the work very hard and attended night school at 6pm, where he was learning to read and write. Anna Powell, aged 11, from Cradley Heath, worked at nailing with her mother from 7am to 8.30pm, with three hours for breaks. Anna was healthy, clean and well-clothed in appearance and was able

59   BPP, 1843, 432, XV, Appendix II.
60   *Ibid.*

to read and do needlework, although she could not write. Sub-Commissioner Horne also visited the district of Sedgley and its surrounding villages, where he found the majority of nail-making families' houses were 'wretched and sty-like' and the forges 'like a dilapidated coal-hole or little black den'.[61] Children started work at the age of seven or eight, working from 6am to 7pm or 8pm. By the age of ten or 12 years boys and girls were expected to produce 1,000 nails per day, despite being provided with insufficient food and miserable clothing. Many of the children in this district were 'left to run wild' by their parents and even those who attended school were removed at the age of six or seven. Mary Humphries, aged 11, worked at nailing from 6.30 am to 8.45pm, earning 1s per week, which she gave to her mother. Mary attended Sunday school and could read some words, but she was 'a poor emaciated object, very little for her age, filthy dirty, and in dirty rags'.[62]

'The glass trade apprentices': boys in the Stourbridge glass industry

In contrast to the children who worked in nail-making, boys employed in the glass trades of Stourbridge in Worcestershire did not start work until the age of 12 and were paid 3s to 4s weekly, rising to 9s to 10s per week for older youths. Sub-Commissioner Horne reported that there were several large glassworks in the district, which were found to be clean, well-ventilated and in good repair.[63] In the glass-making branch of the trade workers were exposed to intense heat from the furnaces in the glass-houses, but provision was made for them to wash and change their clothes at the end of a six-hour shift. The glass-cutting and polishing works of Thomas Webb at Amblecote were extremely clean, with railings around machinery, providing a model of good practice for all similar works in this branch of the trade. The glass-cutters were respectable men who took on boys as outdoor apprentices through a contract with the parents. No girls were employed at the works.

The demand for child workers: diversity in child labour

One of the factors behind the failure to regulate child labour in Birmingham industries was, as discussed above, the diverse range of employment in small-scale firms. Children in 1840s Birmingham were employed in numerous occupations, including making buttons from metal, bone, horn, glass or mother-of-pearl shells; brass-casting; japanning; lacquering; glass-making and polishing; glass-blowing; gun-making; spoon-polishing; and nail-making.[64]

---

61 *Ibid.*

62 *Ibid.*

63 *Ibid.*

64 BPP, 1843, 431, XIV, pp. 126–40.

This range of occupations gives some indication of the high level of demand for child labour in Birmingham's manufacturing industries. When interviewed by the Children's Employment Commission, button factory clerk Daniel Baker confirmed that many young children from the age of six were employed in the button trade. Boys who were employed to assist the adult stamp operators in the button trade were paid directly by the workmen rather than by the workshop master or the proprietor.[65] Normal working hours were from 8am to 7pm with half an hour for breakfast and one hour for dinner breaks, but if the men worked late to meet demand the boys were also required to stay. Adult workers often employed their own sons as assistants but in the horn-button trade each man required three assistants. William Elliott's button factory was one of the largest in Birmingham, employing up to 500 workers when demand for buttons was high.[66] When Sub-Commissioner Grainger visited in 1841 he found that 50 boys and girls below the age of 13 were employed at the factory. During an interview William Elliott said he expected his employees to follow a policy of strict moral conduct within and outside the workplace. In principle, he disagreed with the employment of children below the age of nine, but he also thought that children excluded from manufacturing work would be neglected by their parents and left to roam the streets. His views thus coincided with a contemporary belief that children from the lower classes who were not occupied at school should be at work where they could be supervised and controlled by adults.

Despite Elliott's stated views on the employment of very young children, some of those at his button factory in 1841 were below the age of nine. Seven-year-old Betsey Toe worked at 'putting in' the blank buttons ready for the adult to stamp with the press, for which she earned 1s 6d per week.[67] Another girl, five-year-old Amelia Delaney, had been working at 'putting in' for 12 months, indicating that she had started work in the button factory when she was just four years old.[68] The firm of Elliott's was featured in an article on Birmingham industry in an 1844 edition of the *Penny Magazine*, but its description of button-making failed to mention the involvement of child workers. According to this article, female workers were employed in large numbers, but stamping presses were operated solely by male workers: 'The man places the button on the lower die, raises a heavy weight to the lower part of which the upper die is attached, and allows it to fall with great force'.[69] In contrast, an article in

---

65   *Ibid.*, p. 128.

66   *Ibid.*, pp. 135–6.

67   *Ibid.*, p. 136.

68   *Ibid.*, p. 136.

69   'A Day at the Birmingham Factories', *The Penny Magazine*, 30 November 1844.

Household Words in April 1852, which also referred to Elliott's button factory, stated that nearly all of the 400 workers were women and children, with very few men employed: 'We see hundreds of women, scores of children, and a few men'.[70] The *Penny Magazine* article was one of a series of supplements aimed at promoting the merits of Birmingham, hence the failure to mention child workers. It did, however, refer to button production as being under a 'factory-system', employing hundreds of workers in one building.[71] The accompanying illustration of Elliott's factory showed a large, clean and well-lit workshop in which a number of women and older girls were engaged in button-making. The workers were comfortably seated and respectably clothed, providing the appearance of an organised and well-paid workforce.

The impression conveyed by the *Penny Magazine* article was that the Birmingham button industry provided clean, light work for young females in congenial surroundings, which was in contrast to many of the findings of the Children's Employment Commission report published in the previous year. Sub-Commissioner Grainger interviewed six children at Smith and Kemp's Button Manufactory: Betsey Woodroff, aged nine; Emma Reeves, aged 12; Mary Ann Tibbits, aged 12; William Chaplin, aged 13; and Thomas Baldwin, aged nine. Emma had started work in the button factory at the age of five as a 'putter in' and subsequently worked at lacquering alongside Mary Ann. The lacquering required them to work over a very hot stove, which Mary Ann reported gave her headaches. Because of the greater skills involved, Emma and Mary Ann were paid at a higher rate of 3s 3d to 3s 6d per week. Following a visit to Hasluck's button factory in Summer Lane, the sub-commissioner reported that the workshops were small and crowded, with one room occupied by nine women working the presses. They were assisted by nine girls employed to put in the blank buttons, including an eight-year-old girl and two girls aged nine.[72] Samuel Page, a button-maker at Haslucks, said he sometimes worked from 6am until 12 midnight when trade was busy, keeping the boy assistant with him as his work was essential to the process. Page added that, because of poor trade and low wages, 'the children have to help very much in supporting their parents. There is more demand for the labour of children and young people than for that of adults; half as much again'.[73] As this statement demonstrates, child workers were seen as essential to manufacturing in the Birmingham button trade because adult button-makers relied on the labour of child assistants. Page's evidence

---

70 'What there is in a button', *Household Words*, 17 April 1852, p. 108.

71 *The Penny Magazine*, 30 November 1844.

72 BPP, 1843, 431, XIV, pp. 137–8.

73 *Ibid.*, pp. 134–5.

to the Children's Employment Commission further reinforces the belief that children provided vital financial support for poor families because the demand for child workers was often greater than for adults.

The intensification of children's work in various industries

The demand for child labour was not restricted to the pin-making and button-making industries in the 1840s. As highlighted by the Children's Employment Commission, children were employed in countless Birmingham industries, where they were expected to work for long hours from an early age. Thomas Andrews, aged 14, had been employed in the blacksmith's shop of a brass foundry for three years, earning 7s per week; Thomas Harper, aged 12, had worked as a brass-filer for three years, earning 3s per week; Benjamin Bradley, aged seven, worked at japanning; Eliza Leadbeater, aged 14, had worked at lacquering for three years.[74] At Ledsam and Sons, a brass nail factory on Great Charles Street in Birmingham, each adult caster employed three or four boys aged from seven or eight years as assistants. The fact that these assistants were often the sons of the workmen indicates that adults in these well-paid trades were willing to put their own young children to work. In one example, nine-year-old Benjamin Beach worked as an assistant to his father, who was a brass-caster. Benjamin was expected to start work at 6am each morning, bringing his breakfast with him, even though his father did not arrive for work until between 7am and 9am. After finishing work for the day Benjamin walked the one mile home and said he was 'very tired at night; is glad to go to bed'.[75] Whatever the limitations of the sources, these examples provide further evidence that children were routinely expected to work long hours in harsh conditions, even those more fortunate children from relatively prosperous families who were employed by their own relatives. The high demand for child workers in Birmingham industries was due to the organisation of production for manufactured goods, which depended on the labour of very low-paid assistants. These children could, therefore, be considered part of an 'industrious revolution'.[76]

Young child workers such as Benjamin Beach forfeited their leisure, either voluntarily or involuntarily, so that families could improve their standards of living. An increased demand for consumer goods of all kinds by the general population was the driving force behind an intensification of work in Birmingham, including among child workers. However, there were differences in the economic circumstances of individual child workers' families. On the one hand, Benjamin Beach's father was a skilled brass-caster with the ability

---

74   *Ibid.*, pp. 142–3.

75   *Ibid.*, p. 145.

76   de Vries, *Industrious Revolution*, pp. 71–2.

to earn a good income for his family without the need to rely on his son's earnings. On the other hand, girls such as Emma Reeves and Amelia Delaney, who had worked in button factories from the age of five, were from some of the poorest families in Birmingham. It is important to note, therefore, that although the intensification in child labour was driven in some instances by a desire to acquire more wealth and consumer goods, it was also important in providing families with the basic requirements of food, housing, fuel and clothing. Furthermore, industriousness among child workers extended well beyond the early decades of the nineteenth century.

Gender differences in employment

The evidence on child workers obtained by the Children's Employment Commission is supported by locally conducted surveys undertaken by the Birmingham New Meeting Sunday Schools in 1841 and by the Birmingham Educational Association in 1857. A survey of 273 children attending the New Meeting Sunday Schools in July 1841 recorded details of occupations, age of starting work, hours of work, time allowed for meals and weekly wages.[77] Among the 168 boys in the survey, 73 per cent were employed as assistants in manufacturing industries such as brass-founding, gun-finishing and other metal industries. These included John Parkes, aged 13, who was a spoon-maker working from 6am to 9pm daily and whose wages were paid entirely to his father; Thomas Oldbury, aged 11, a pearl-button-maker working from 7am to 4pm and paid 2s 6d per week; James Wilson, aged 12, a gun-finisher working from 8am to 5pm and earning 2s 6d per week; and William Bell, aged nine, working as a brass-founder from 6am to 7pm and earning 1s 6d per week. Some of the older boys with several years' work experience were able to earn considerably more. Charles Kirby, a 17-year-old gun-finisher with seven years' experience, was paid 6s 9d weekly; Joseph Reginton, aged 17, who had begun work at ten years old, earned 12s per week as a snuffer-maker; and William Yates, aged 18, who had started work at the age of seven, was earning 10s per week as a metal-roller.[78] A further 6 per cent of boys were employed in trades such as printing, engraving or brick-laying, and two boys were working as errand boys. Peter Rooke, a nine-year-old errand boy, was paid 2s per week for working from 8am to 7pm daily; George Bayliss, aged 11, earned 2s per week in the printing trade; and Thomas Branwick, aged nine, earned 2s per week as a japanner. The remaining 21 per cent of boys in the survey were recorded as either at school or 'at home'.[79]

---

77 BPP, 1843, 431, XIV, pp. 200–03.

78 *Ibid.*

79 *Ibid.*

Among the 105 girls attending the New Meeting Sunday Schools, 46 per cent were employed in manufacturing industries and 42 per cent were at home or at school. The remaining 12 per cent included nine girls in service, two girls working as 'nurses' (minding infants) and two errand girls.[80] The girls employed in manufacturing included Sarah Turner, aged 12, who worked at coffin furniture manufacture and earned 4s per week; Laura Payne, aged ten, who was a button-maker earning 3s per week; and 12-year-old Ellen Elks, who earned 3s 6d weekly making umbrella wires. Older girls such as Mary Anne Bissell, a 15-year-old button-maker, could earn 6s per week in manufacturing industry. This was far more than the wages of girls who were in service, such as Sarah Purden, aged 14, and Elen Hughes, aged 13, who each earned just 6d per week in wages in addition to board and accommodation. The two girls who described themselves as nurses, Eliza Parker and Mary Ann Williams, were both nine years old and earned 1s 6d per week. Minding infants for a relative or neighbour was a common occupation for girls at around the age of nine, and perhaps also accounted for some of the girls in the survey who were 'at home' taking care of siblings. This was confirmed by the headmistress of St Mary's Girls Day School in Birmingham, who reported that 'girls leave at 8 or 9, as soon as they can nurse a baby or earn something at work.'[81] The Sunday Schools survey lists fewer girls than boys in paid employment, but it is likely that some girls were working within their own families as unpaid childminders or domestic helpers. Overall, 79 per cent of boys and 58 per cent of girls in the 1841 survey were occupied in paid employment.

Further details of changes in child employment patterns over time come from an extensive survey of child labour conducted by the Birmingham Educational Association in 1857. This survey covered 14 districts of Birmingham, obtaining information on the employment status and education of 753 boys and 620 girls between the ages of seven and 13 years.[82] Among the boys, 39 per cent were employed, 41 per cent were at school and 20 per cent were 'idle' or at home. Few of the younger boys were at work in the 1857 survey, but more than 70 per cent of boys aged 11 to 13 were working. A majority of boys worked in manufacturing, including brass-founding, button-making, glass-working, umbrella-making and spoon-making. Boys engaged in non-manufacturing occupations included errand boys, shoe-makers and blacksmiths.[83] Among the girls in the 1857 survey, 26 per cent were employed, 42 per cent were at school and 31 per cent were 'idle' or at home. Again, few

---

80 *Ibid.*

81 *Ibid.*

82 BPP, 1864, 3414, *Third Report*, Appendix B, pp. 154–61.

83 *Ibid.*, pp. 160–61.

of the younger girls were at work, but this increased to more than 50 per cent of girls aged 11 to 13. A majority of girls worked in manufacturing, including 34 who worked in button-making, whereas 25 girls were in service and eight girls worked in warehouses. For children between the ages of ten to 11 years there were significant gender differences: 44 per cent of boys in this age group were at work, compared with 27 per cent of girls; 41 per cent of boys aged ten to 11 were at school, compared with 33 per cent of girls. However, 39 per cent of girls aged ten to 11 were 'idle' or at home, suggesting that girls in this age group were those most likely to be engaged in unpaid child-minding and domestic work.[84] By the age of ten years, therefore, gender differences had become pronounced. Boys were more likely to be in paid employment or attending school than girls of the same age.

The age of starting work

Historians have identified children apprenticed by their parish under the old Poor Law as being some of the youngest child workers, especially those sent to work in textile mills and coal mines. Honeyman found that in the early nineteenth century children were frequently apprenticed to cotton mills at the age of ten or younger, whereas a study of London parish apprentices found the average age of binding was 12 years for boys and 12.5 years for girls.[85] However, evidence from the 1841 Birmingham survey indicates that non-apprenticed child workers in the manufacturing industries typically started work at eight or nine years.[86] Boys who started work at nine years of age included Henry Taylor, a gun-finisher; John Oldbury, a bullet-mould-maker; James Taylor, a brass-founder; and Josiah Probert, a gilt-toy-maker. Some boys began work at an even earlier age. Samuel Jones, for example, was five when he started work as a stamper, while John Atfield, a button-maker, William Field, a die sinker, and Thomas Jones, a tea-pot-maker, were all aged six.[87] Girls started work mainly at eight years of age: Eliza Timmins was a gilt-toy-maker, Martha Eddowes a button-burnisher, Sarah Cartwright a piercer and Anna Hammond a button carder at this age. Anne Davis started work at just four years of age as a 'tye stitcher'. As these examples indicate, employment was available in Birmingham for boys and girls at a young age and in a wide range of trades and occupations. An additional factor was that women's participation in the labour force was often dependent on the ready availability of childcare, which was routinely provided by young girls of eight or nine.

---

84   *Ibid.*, pp. 154–61.

85   Honeyman, *Child Workers*, pp. 45–7; Levene, 'Parish Apprenticeship', p. 924.

86   BPP, 1843, 431, XIV, pp. 200–03.

87   *Ibid.*

According to the Birmingham Educational Association's survey, the average age of starting work had increased slightly for boys, from nine years in 1841 to nine and a half years in 1857. For girls the average age had increased from eight years in 1841 to ten years in 1857.[88] By the time of the survey the youngest children were more likely to be at school than at work: 62 per cent of boys and 53 per cent of girls aged seven to eight years were in education, indicating that some progress had been made during the intervening period. Nevertheless, 82 per cent of boys and 60 per cent of girls were in paid employment by the age of 13, indicating a continued high demand for child workers and the willingness of parents to send their children out to work, perhaps through economic necessity. Interestingly, where occupations have been recorded for mothers of children in the survey approximately one-third were framed as 'domestic duties'. The most frequently cited paid occupations for mothers were laundress, shopkeeper, needlewoman, charwoman and shoe-binder. Only a small number of mothers were employed in manufacturing, suggesting that concerns about married women with children preferring factory work to domestic duties may have been exaggerated.[89] Furthermore, an overall rise in the age of starting work by 1857 is evident, suggesting that there was a stronger and more widespread commitment to full-time education for children up to the age of nine or ten, a significant shift in attitudes when compared with earlier decades. Even so, employment remained at high levels for boys and girls aged 11 to 13.

Child labour and the changing demands of industry

The increased proportion of younger children at school rather than work reflected not only the changing attitudes towards childhood but also some of the technological changes taking place in industries such as pin-making. When child labour in Birmingham was investigated by the Children's Employment Commission of 1862 the child workers who had previously been employed at pin-heading had already been replaced by machinery capable of producing 220 pins per minute. These new machines were installed at the Birmingham firm of Edelsten & Williams, where a single employee controlled four machines producing 3,000,000 pins per week.[90] The development of new technology for the pin-making trade and the introduction of machine-made cut nails, rather than hand-made nails, reduced the demand for child workers in these industries to just a few children by the 1860s. But, although demand in these traditional manufacturing trades had declined, large numbers of children were still employed. The population of Birmingham increased from 183,000 in 1841

---

88   BPP, 1864, 3414, *Third Report*, Appendix B, p. 160.

89   *Ibid.*, p. 161.

90   *Ibid.*, p. 108.

to 310,000 in 1861, providing industrial employment for 18,460 children and young people under the age of 20, including approximately 2,000 children under the age of ten years by 1861.[91] It seems reasonable, therefore, to estimate that around 6,000 children below the age of 14 were employed in Birmingham industries engaged in the manufacture of brass, guns, jewellery, electro-plate, metal bedsteads, buttons, hooks and eyes, steel pens, tools, nails, screws and numerous other items.

The tradition in Birmingham of children working directly for workmen or women rather than for firms continued into the 1860s. This practice was described by Assistant Children's Commissioner White as 'very much to the prejudice of the children and young persons so employed' because they were under the control of individual workers.[92] It was therefore less easy to identify those children who were working excessive hours or suffering from other forms of ill-treatment at work. Although the stated hours of work in Birmingham industries were not considered to be excessive, the actual hours worked by children varied considerably. Most workmen worked fewer hours in the early part of the week, making up their time with long hours towards the end of the week and often working through the night on Fridays in order to complete work by Saturday afternoon, when they would be paid. This naturally had an impact on working children's health and leisure time. It also limited their access to education, as illustrated by the experiences of three boys in a brass foundry who were interviewed by Assistant Commissioner White.[93] Frederick Clarke, aged 11, George Rose, aged 14, and Joseph Bowell, aged 12, had all attended day school for five or six years before starting work and they continued to attend Sunday school and night school unless they had to work late. This shows a commitment to continue in education by these boys whenever possible, even after joining the workforce. It seems likely, however, that working children and their families experienced a tension between their commitment to education and the need for children to make a financial contribution to the family.

Some factory owners expressed the view that parents in Birmingham were not interested in education for their children, since they were anxious only to exploit the earnings potential of their offspring. Mr Watson, the proprietor of a brass foundry, stated that he employed only men and older youths because brass-casting was 'a very unhealthy occupation' and not a suitable place for children. 'They are so penned up in factories during the day that they do not care to go to evening schools, but go into streets ... many persons here

---

91   *Ibid.*, p. x.
92   *Ibid.*, p. xii.
93   *Ibid.*, p. 64.

raise children merely for the sake of sending them to work.[94] Watson also disagreed with the employment of women and girls in factories, suggesting that Birmingham girls preferred manufacturing work to being in service because it provided higher earnings and independence. Mothers also chose to work in factories to the extent that 'The destitute state of children here can nearly always be traced to the fact of females being so much employed.'[95] Watson's opposition to the employment of women and children in industry may have represented a typical middle-class Victorian perspective on family life, but important Birmingham industries such as the button trade depended on the cheap labour provided by women and children.

'The forlorn little button girls': a case study of the 1860s button industry
It has been suggested that child labour in England reached a peak in the early decades of the nineteenth century and then declined.[96] The reality, however, may have been very different for some child workers. At this time the button factory owned by William Aston employed 800 workers, including 100 girls aged seven to 13 who were paid directly by workshop overseers.[97] The workshops in this factory consisted of rows of female press operators who sat on one side of the workbench facing rows of young girls who placed the blank pieces under the presses. Assistant Commissioner White reported: 'Many of the girls are ragged and apparently ill-fed, and 13 young boys employed in a mere dark outhouse or hovel in cracking vegetable ivory nuts appeared especially rough and neglected.'[98] The normal hours of work were from 8am to 7pm with breaks for meals, but if a press operator worked late the child assistant was also forced to remain, as the work could not continue without them.

The girls in the press shops at Aston's factory started work at 'putting in' when they were seven or eight years old, and within a few years might be working the presses themselves. The younger girls interviewed by the assistant commissioner were Bridget Conway, aged seven, Harriett Rickett, aged seven, Emma Robinson, aged eight, Emma Anson, aged seven, Sarah Ebb, aged nine, Susan Stokes, aged nine, Betsey Walls, aged ten, and Mary Conroy, aged 12.[99] These child assistants earned around 1s 3d per week, whereas the older girls who operated the presses were paid 2s 6d or 3s per week. Many of the press

---

94   *Ibid.*, p. 66.

95   *Ibid.*, p. 66.

96   Maxine Berg and Pat Hudson, 'Rehabilitating the Industrial Revolution', *Economic History Review*, 2/45 (1992), pp. 24–50 at 35.

97   BPP, 1864, 3414, *Third Report*, Appendix B, p. 91.

98   *Ibid.*

99   *Ibid.*

operators, such as Elizabeth Hope, Esther Crowder, Ann Crompton, Sarah Hooper and Mary Ann Collins, were between 13 and 15 years of age. Sarah Hooper, who earned 3s per week, said, 'I am not strong in health. We doesn't have sufficient to eat as we ought. Mother is a cripple with children and father is dead.'[100] The employment of 100 girls below the age of 14 at William Aston's button factory, including a number of very young girls, highlights both the strength of demand for child labour in the 1860s Birmingham button industry and the family poverty that ensured a plentiful supply of child workers.

Mr J.P. Turner, a proprietor of Hammond, Turner & Sons, confirmed to the 1862 Children's Employment Commission that the button industry employed more women and girls than any other trade in Birmingham, but he thought that married women should not be working in factories because 'it makes them neglect their homes and families'.[101] However, Mr J.S. Wright of Smith & Wright's button factory took a different view. He believed that fathers were mostly responsible for sending their children out to work because they were 'unable to resist the temptations which public-houses … hold out to our industrious and skilful artisans'.[102] Wright emphasised the importance of child workers to the button trade because they could perform many operations more swiftly and effectively than adults. In addition to the children who assisted with the presses, a large number of girls worked from home at sewing buttons or hooks and eyes onto cards. Cheap child labour was particularly important to the button and other metal trades because of competition from manufactured goods produced abroad, especially in Germany,[103] but this demand, together with the willingness of parents to send their children out to work, combined to produce industrious but frequently unhealthy children. In his report, Assistant Commissioner White identified that, among Birmingham child workers, 'the most delicate and forlorn looking are to be found amongst the little button girls'.[104]

'Boys worked beyond their strength': child workers in iron and metal trades

Assistant Commissioner F.D. Longe visited blast furnaces, rolling mills, forges and metal-works in south Staffordshire and Worcestershire in 1863. He estimated that 200 boys below the age of 13 years were employed at blast furnaces; around 1,000 boys below 13 were employed in iron rolling mills and forges; and very large numbers of children were employed in the numerous

---

100 BPP, 1864, 3414, *Third Report*, Appendix B, p. 93.

101 *Ibid.*, p. 95.

102 *Ibid.*

103 *Ibid.*

104 BPP, 1864, 3414, *Third Report*, Appendix B, p. 60.

metal trades of Wolverhampton and district.[105] Boys working at the blast furnaces were employed by adult workmen as 'box-fillers' to fill up boxes and barrows with coal, coke, ironstone and limestone and wheel them to the worker at the furnace mouth. They worked alongside the men in two shifts from 6am to 6pm or 6pm to 6am, for which they received 6s per week. In the iron mills and forges boys from the age of nine upwards worked at heating iron rods and carrying them to the adult workers. Older youths were employed to pass the red-hot bars through the rollers while younger boys removed thin rods or wire using tongs and carried them away. The majority of boys employed to run with the hot iron were between ten and 14 years of age, and averaged 11 miles or more during each shift, but they 'rarely get through many turns without burns'.[106] The boys and youths in rolling mills were employed directly by the adult workman or master roller, earning between 5s to 10s per week depending on their age and experience. The highest paid workmen or master rollers could earn between £4 and £5 per week, and often employed their own sons as assistants. However, the medical officer, Dr Greenhow, said that boys started work too early and were worked beyond their strength.

The numerous metal trades of the Wolverhampton district employed so many children and young people that Assistant Commissioner Longe was unable to estimate the numbers. Boys worked in iron foundries and brass foundries throughout the district as assistants to the casters. Each caster employed two or three boys paid 6d to 1s per day. In the chain-works of Wolverhampton, Tipton, Bilston and Walsall, the youngest boys and girls were employed to blow bellows at 1s 6d to 3s 6d per week, and boys of ten to 14 years worked with a hammer as 'strikers', earning 4s to 6s weekly. One chain-maker in Wednesfield employed his ten-year-old and 11-year-old daughters as strikers and an eight-year-old daughter as a bellows blower. The family earned a total of £2 2s per week for their labours.[107] Small workshops in Wolverhampton, Willenhall, Darlaston, Walsall and Bloxwich were home to locksmiths, keysmiths, gunlock-makers, awl-blade-makers, hinge-, bolt-, file- and bellows-makers. The locksmiths and keysmiths were the poorest of the metal-workers, earning 12s to 18s per week, and were most likely to take on parish apprentices who received board and lodgings but no wages.

'The rough and untaught nailers': children in nail-making
The town of Halesowen, on the road between Birmingham and Stourbridge, had a population of 6,000 to 7,000 and nearly all the small houses of the town

---

105 BPP, 1864, 3414, *Third Report*, Appendix A.

106 *Ibid.*

107 BPP, 1864, 3414, *Third Report*, Appendix B, p. 135.

were built with an adjoining forge or workshop for the manufacture of wrought nails. The majority of nailers in Halesowen were women and children, as many of the men were employed in nearby coal mines and iron-works.[108] Children began work at nailing at the age of seven or eight years and tended to be thin and unhealthy due to the long hours in dark, very hot workshops. According to the Reverend Henry Fisher of Halesowen, the nailing families were generally 'rough and untaught', with most adults unable to read or write. Halesowen had a good National School and Sunday schools, but children were unlikely to attend owing to their long working hours. On the other hand, Monday afternoon classes in reading and writing for girls and young women were well attended. Ann Wood was left a widow with seven children when her nailer husband died of consumption. She worked at nailing with her two daughters, aged 16 and 17, from 7am to 11pm each day. Two of her sons had also begun nailing with the family at the age of ten, but now worked at a nearby spade factory, earning 6s per week.[109]

'The rough and unmannerly brickyard girls': children in brick-making

Along with the Stourbridge glass industry, brick-making was another important industry in the district. Among its products were the white fire-clay bricks used in furnaces. At the firm of R. North's Brickworks, in Brockmoor, women and girls were employed by the male brick-makers who operated the brick kilns. The work of the girls was to carry lumps of clay from the clay pits to the women who moulded the bricks. Each girl usually carried enough clay for six bricks at 10lbs per brick, earning 8d to 1s per day. Assistant Commissioner White reported that 'The girls look healthy, although very rough and unmannerly.'[110] Sarah Ann Harper, aged 13, had been working for a woman brick-moulder for two years, earning 2s 6d per week, which was paid to her elder sister. She had never attended day school and did not go to Sunday school either, because she could not go without shoes. Another brick-yard girl, 16-year-old Jemima Batham, said that she could read a little but did not know her letters and did not go to Sunday school. At the fire brick company of E. Baker & Co., in Brierley Hill, Ann Powell, aged 12, had been carrying bricks for two years and was paid 6d per day. Ann had been at day school and seemed intelligent and hard working.[111] Annie Holt, aged 12, worked from 6am to 5pm at rolling and carrying clay, earning 5s per week. She attended the Ragged School on Sundays but could not do sums.

---

108 *Ibid.*, p. 135.
109 *Ibid.*, p. 138.
110 *Ibid.*, p. 139.
111 *Ibid.*, pp. 138–9.

Demand for child workers in 1860s Birmingham

In addition to the button trade and brass foundries, children in Birmingham worked in a wide variety of metal industries, such as screw manufacture, wire-working, stamping and piercing, thimble-making, gold-chain-making, jewellery, gun-making, tin-plate, japanning and steel-pen-making.[112] Beckett Brothers manufactured small tin-plate items such as lucifer match boxes, toys, mugs and plates. The owner of this firm said they could manage without child workers if all employers agreed, but 'many parents come to live in the town for the sake of their children's earnings. It pays a man to do so, even if he only makes half as much himself as he did elsewhere.'[113] Whereas a male agricultural labourer could earn only 7s or 8s a week, a man plus his working children could earn £2 to £3 per week in Birmingham. This information had become widespread, encouraging more families to come to Birmingham to obtain work for their children and leading to the presence of a large number of unskilled male workers. Beckett's views represented a contemporary perception that many families migrated to Birmingham from rural districts to take advantage of child employment opportunities. The combination of low agricultural wages together with the availability of work for whole families in manufacturing provided a powerful economic incentive for migration. Intense competition between small firms may also have acted as a factor in prolonging child labour, while the availability of child labour may have actually discouraged the introduction of new machinery requiring capital investment, furthering the reliance on traditional production methods and working practices.

The experience of child workers in 1860s Birmingham

By the early 1860s the chief industry in Birmingham was the brass trade, followed closely by gun-making and the jewellery trade. Rather than being dependent on these three industries, however, the town was noted for its huge variety of trades in which numerous small masters employed a few skilled workmen.[114] Boys were predominantly employed in the brass trade, where they could earn between 3s 6d and 7s per week.[115] Girls in the button industry earned from 1s to 1s 6d per week.[116] The Birmingham button industry in 1865 provided employment for approximately 6,000 workers, including 4,000 women and children.[117] At Iliffe and Player's button factory in Newhall

---

112 *Ibid.*, p. 82.

113 *Ibid.*, p. 84.

114 Samuel Timmins, *Birmingham and the Midland Hardware District* (London, 1866), pp. 222–3.

115 *Ibid.*, p. 285.

116 *Ibid.*, p. 444.

117 *Ibid.*, p. 443.

Street, children were employed as 'putters in' of linen buttons and older girls at presswork. Sarah Anne Greely, aged nine, had worked there for 'two or three years and at another button place for two years before'. Elizabeth Porter, aged six, was 'here for three months, and was at another button place before, where I worked from 8 to 7. The woman pays me 1s 1d a week.' Caroline Perks, aged 13, a japanner, had started work at eight years old as a 'putter in'.[118] These children provide evidence that girls were beginning work in the button industry at five to eight years of age in the 1860s, despite the campaigns against child labour, and contradict the findings of the 1857 survey by the Birmingham Educational Association, which found that girls were not beginning work until around ten years of age. It appears that for some children there had been little change since the early decades of the nineteenth century in terms of the age of starting work and weekly earnings.

Child workers were also involved in new methods of production. Kirby's Hook & Eye factory employed boys as machine minders in control of new machinery. According to the statements given by John Hinks, aged 12, he was employed to 'Mind machine'. He '[w]as never at day-school. Do not know any letters.' Albert Pipkin, aged ten, said that he 'Mind[ed] seven machines, have minded 11. Here 11 months. Wasn't at day school long.' Henry Bradley, aged ten, said that he 'Mind[ed] an eyelet machine. If it gets wrong I stop it and get the scrap off the punch. Clean it on Saturday at 1, after it stops. Get 2s per week. Was at nails before. Can read, not so very well.'[119] It thus appears that children were placed in charge of factory machinery with little supervision by adult workers, regardless of the safety implications. The advantages for employers were twofold: child workers were not only adaptable and quick to learn new methods but, more importantly, very cheap to employ.

The differences between adult and child workers in terms of wages costs are clear in examples from one of the leading Birmingham industries. The jewellery and gilt-toy trade employed approximately 7,500 workers in Birmingham by 1865, with artisans earning average wages of 30s to 50s per week and enamellers £3 to £5 per week. Few women were employed directly in the trade, other than approximately 500 women and girls employed in making gold and silver chains.[120] The firm of B. Goode in St Paul's Square was a leading manufacturer of gold chain. Each of the women workers making chains employed one or two girl assistants, who were paid 1s per week.[121] Many of the workers were young people who had been employed in the trade for several years. For example,

---

118   BPP, 1864, 3414, *Third Report*, Appendix B, p. 99.

119   *Ibid.*, p. 107.

120   Timmins, *Birmingham*, p. 453.

121   BPP, 1864, 3414, *Third Report*, Appendix B, p. 118.

Sarah Anne Bone, aged 15, said that she '[m]a[d]e chains with pliers and links at a gas pipe, sometimes using the blow pipe. Have done so for three years and a half. Have a sore throat. Have it most in summer.' Jane Adderly, aged 14, had worked at the firm for three years and also complained of a sore throat. She '[p]ress[ed] links at a hand press. The hours are from 8am till 7pm, or if we are busy, till 9pm. Went to work at buttons at about 6 years old.'[122] John Kimberley, aged 17, worked as a wire-drawer at Goode's. After attending day school for a year, he had left at the age of nine to start work, then attended Sunday school and night school for a time. John said that he was unable to continue at school because the family could not afford suitable clothing: 'Left because I had no clothes. Father gets such low wages, 10s or 12s or 14s a week, and there are nine of us. I get 9s a week, one of my brothers 19s, another 15s and another 5s.'[123] Even though the father and four boys in the Kimberley family were working, they were a large family unable to afford clothing suitable for John to attend school at night or on Sundays. It seems possible, however, that younger children in the family may have been able to go to school instead of starting work at a young age with the financial support of older siblings. That two of the older Kimberley brothers were earning higher weekly wages than their father highlights the preference of Birmingham industries for juvenile workers.

The steel pen industry was one of the newer manufacturing industries in Birmingham, dating from the 1820s. The industry employed 360 men and 2,050 women in 1861, plus a large number of workers employed indirectly in the manufacture of paper boxes and accessories for the pen trade.[124] Twelve firms were involved in the Birmingham pen trade, including Joseph Gillott's factory on Victoria Street. Here, some 500 workers were employed in 'very large works, conveniently arranged, and the work rooms clean, fresh and cheerful'.[125] The stated company rule was not to employ any children below 13 years of age, but two children aged 12, Eliza Jackson and George Swain, were found operating machinery at the factory when the premises were visited by the Children's Employment Commission. At Josiah Mason's steel pen factory Henry Warner, aged 13, was employed at steel rolling, earning 4s 6d a week. Samuel Enfield, aged ten, said that he had been there 'nearly four years. Lacquer pens, turning them in a barrel by a handle. Worked at umbrellas before and went there when going seven.' Charles Walters, aged ten, was also in his second job: 'Harden pens. Fill pens, and about every half hour for five minutes pull them out of the muffle with an iron, and help the man. Get 4s a week. Was at gun work before,

---

122 *Ibid.*, p. 119.

123 *Ibid.*

124 Timmins, *Birmingham*, p. 633.

125 BPP, 1864, 3414, *Third Report*, Appendix B, p. 89.

and minded a machine.'[126] John Caraghan, aged nine, had worked at Hinks and Wells' Steel Pen Works and Rolling Mills for about a year: 'Used to be at the rollers, and have scoured them four or five times, but now my work is to carry steel coils from one mill to another; carry several coils at a time.' Albert Flint, aged ten, had worked at the firm for six months: 'Was at guns before for a short time, at a big place. My work was to carry guns to another place. Before that played about in the streets. Mother said I ought to go to school, and would have paid for me, 2d a week, but I didn't want. My brother and sister go.'[127]

These examples from the steel pen industry suggest that in general the newer Birmingham industries employed fewer children than the more traditional workshop industries. Only two children under 13 were found employed at Joseph Gillott's factory, for example, from a workforce of more than 500. They appear also to have earned relatively high wages of 4s to 4s 6d per week, though perhaps for more demanding or hazardous work. Five years after the publication of the 1862 report, the 1867 Factory Act and 1867 Workshops Regulation Act finally extended the existing legislation on child labour to all factories and workshops. Children could no longer be legally employed below the age of eight years and children from eight to 13 years could work only half-time. In 1878 the minimum age of employment was increased to ten years.

Conclusion

This chapter has discussed the extent and nature of child labour in Birmingham and the West Midlands, exploring children's employment, particularly in manufacturing industries, from the mid-eighteenth century to the later decades of the nineteenth century. Parish apprentices were unlikely to be found in Birmingham industries, and in general child workers were not directly employed by the owners of firms. Instead, the organisation of production in Birmingham's manufacturing industries encouraged the employment of thousands of young children by individual workmen and women. In some trades, notably pin-making, children were employed in groups of 20 by overseers or supervisors, permitting owners of firms to claim that they neither approved of nor employed child labour. Nevertheless, child workers made a significant contribution to the development of manufacturing industry in Birmingham and to its competitiveness in international markets. Child labour also boosted family incomes, providing a vital safety net for families who may have been close to destitution because of unemployment or ill-health. Demand for child labour in Birmingham was so strong that many people believed families migrated to the town purely to obtain work for their children, and

126 *Ibid.*, p. 87.
127 *Ibid.*, p. 88.

there was often greater availability of work for children and adolescents than for adults. A gradual decline in child labour in Birmingham was seen in the 1860s, especially among younger children, as attitudes towards education and child labour changed over time. Even in the 1860s, however, the majority of children began work at the age of ten or 11. In the second half of the nineteenth century the tendency of older employed children to remain in the family home may have significantly reduced the need for younger children in a family to find employment. Fundamentally, however, children from working-class backgrounds had little choice about starting work, being largely dependent on the decisions made by their parents and the economic circumstances of their families. The importance of children's earnings to family incomes is discussed in further detail in the next chapter.

5

Child labour and the family economy

Introduction

Children were widely employed in Birmingham and West Midlands industries, thus supporting Eric Hopkins' contention that it was traditional for children from working-class families in the region to go out to work as soon as they were old enough and physically strong enough to do so.[1] This chapter considers the relationship between child labour and the family economy in the nineteenth century with a particular focus on Birmingham. Family labour was widespread in industries such as textiles, metal-working and coal-mining: under this system a principal worker was employed on a piece-rate basis with responsibility for employing his assistant workers, usually members of his own family. Coal-miners in the early nineteenth century, for example, frequently employed their wives and children as a family labour unit and did not support measures to exclude women and children from underground working.[2] Despite a growing opposition to child labour in England in the early nineteenth century, such views were not necessarily shared by labouring families, who regarded all family members as economic contributors.

Family poverty was an obvious reason for child employment at an early age, with children from unskilled households and single-parent families the most likely to be at work.[3] In view of Birmingham's reputation for well-paid employment opportunities, how far was family poverty an important factor in child labour? Why, and to what extent, did parents in Birmingham seek employment for their children, and what economic contribution did children make to family incomes?

Male incomes, family incomes and expenditure in Birmingham

The population of Birmingham expanded rapidly from 23,688 in 1750 to 73,670 in 1801, and more than doubled to 182,922 by 1841.[4] Birmingham had a reputation for highly paid employment, but the availability of work was subject to fluctuations in trade conditions, with severe depressions from 1793 onwards

---

1   Hopkins, *Birmingham*, p. 158.

2   Jane Mark-Lawson and Anne Witz, 'From Family Labour to Family Wage? The Case of Women's Labour in Nineteenth-Century Coalmining', *Social History*, 13/2 (1988), pp. 151–74.

3   Kirby, *Child Labour*, p. 28.

4   Hopkins, *Birmingham*, p. 119.

during the French wars.[5] Restrictions on trade with Europe and America introduced in 1807 and 1809 resulted in such severe hardship that petitions against the Orders in Council were made by Birmingham manufacturers in 1812.[6] Thomas Attwood, a banker and high bailiff of Birmingham, gave evidence to the House of Commons: 'Great numbers of workmen have been dismissed in the last twelve months', and men who had previously earned 20s per week 'cannot now obtain more than 10s or 12s, and hundreds of them are to be had at 12s a week'.[7] According to the evidence of export merchant Thomas Potts, every branch of trade in Birmingham was depressed at this time, with at least 20,000 to 25,000 men unemployed for half the week. Whereas a button-burnisher or plater had previously earned 40s to 50s per week, and lesser skilled workmen 25s to 30s per week, the same men could now earn only half these amounts.[8] Button manufacturer Henry Dunbar had significantly reduced his workforce, placing the remaining workers on short-time earnings of 10s to 15s per week instead of 40s to 50s per week.[9] Regardless of fluctuations in trade and the availability of work, the Birmingham Statistical Society in 1837 estimated that the town's population had increased to approximately 180,000, including 45,000 children and young people between the ages of five and 15 years.[10] Throughout the nineteenth century Birmingham was a magnet for young families in search of employment opportunities despite further economic depressions in the mid-1820s and early 1840s. How, then, did wages in Birmingham industries compare with average earnings in other regions and industries? Evidence is available from a survey of average wages in Birmingham complied by a provident society and included in the Chadwick Report of 1842 (Table 5.1).

Table 5.1 Average weekly wages – Birmingham, 1842.

	Weekly amount	Nos
Male wages (over 21)	24s 2d	134
Female wages (over 21)	7s 10d	68
Juvenile males (age 14–20)	5s 10d	211
Juvenile females (age 14–20)	5s 2d	62
Boys (up to 14)	3s 1d	278
Girls (up to 14)	2s 5d	34

Source: BPP, 1842, 007, xxvii, *Sanitary Inquiry England, Local Reports*, pp. 209–10.

---

5   *Ibid.*, pp. 70–73.

6   BPP, 1812, III, *Minutes of Evidence for Petitions against the Orders in Council*.

7   *Ibid.*, p. 2.

8   *Ibid.*, p. 28.

9   *Ibid.*, p. 105.

10   BAH, MS 1683/1 Birmingham Statistical Society Report, 1837.

The provident society survey detailed 623 male and 164 female workers employed in 110 different occupations. As the Chadwick Report points out, these savers were relatively affluent manual workers: 'the circumstance of their depositing a portion of their earnings in this society shows the members of it to be a more provident and better class of workpeople.'[11] According to the findings of the report, 'a very numerous class of workpeople' earned considerably more than average wages.[12] Some workmen earned 30s to 50s a week and young women could earn 10s to 14s in Birmingham factories and workshops. Moreover, Chadwick stated that members of the same family rarely worked in the same trade, so that if one trade was depressed, another might be expanding.[13] Nevertheless, some provident society members were young boys and girls of seven or eight years of age, suggesting that, although their families could afford to put money aside for future events, these children were regarded by their parents as economic contributors to the family, the loss of whose earnings would be significant for the family budget.

In contrast to Chadwick's findings, members of the Heaton family of Birmingham worked together in the trade of 'coin, metal, wire and tube making' at the firm of Ralph Heaton & Sons.[14] Four family members were employed in 1842, headed by Ralph Heaton, who was paid 80s per week. Ralph Heaton Junior and Elizabeth Heaton each earned 5s per week and Harry Heaton earned 1s per week, suggesting that the two eldest children were around 13 or 14 years old and the youngest around eight years old. Wages for the first quarter of 1842 show that although one or two employees received the same amount each week – such as Richard Sutherland, who earned 25s weekly – nearly all other employees earned varying amounts each week, indicating they were paid on piece-work rates. The lowest-paid workers were women or girls: Jane Brown earned 2s 2d per week; Elizabeth Hinks between 2s and 4s weekly; Charlotte Brisband 4s to 7s; and Harriet Morton 5s to 8s weekly. The lowest-paid male workers were Luke Brisband, earning an average of 7s weekly, and Thomas Butler, averaging 14s per week, whereas six workers earned an average of 24s or more per week. The highest-paid employee was Thomas Adams who earned 85s 7d in the first week of January 1842 and was paid an average of 47s per week over the year; he was clearly one of the elite workmen identified by the Chadwick Report. These business records show that Ralph Heaton was employing members of his own family in 1842, a decision that may have

---

11 BPP, 1842, 007, XXVII, Sanitary Inquiry England, Local Reports, 210 (henceforth Chadwick's Report, 1842)

12 Chadwick's Report, 1842, p. 210.

13 *Ibid.*

14 BAH, MS 1010/8, 1840–61.

contributed to the successful expansion of the firm, which by 1862 employed more than 200 workers.[15]

The evidence on average wages for Birmingham workers relates largely to those employed in the town's metal industries. Additional evidence of typical weekly earnings during this period is provided by the Statistics of Wages in the Building Trades compiled and published by the Royal Statistical Society. This reveals that in 1843 average weekly wages for carpenters in Birmingham were 25s per week, compared with 26s in Manchester, 24s in Liverpool and 23s in Oldham and Derby.[16] Average earnings for skilled workers in Birmingham were roughly similar to those in other industrial towns. On the other hand, a comparison of Birmingham rates of pay with earnings in various occupations as compiled by Sarah Horrell and Jane Humphries, indicates that manual workers in Birmingham industries were highly paid, earning at least twice the weekly pay of agricultural workers.[17]

Table 5.2 Comparison of national average weekly wages with average wages in Birmingham, 1841–45.

	Male wages	Family wages
Textile factory	19s	30s
Trades	15s	15s 9d
Mining	16s 6d	23s 9d
Agriculture (high)	12s	13s 5d
Agriculture (low)	8s 6d	12s 3d
Birmingham	24s 2d	37s 6d (estimated)

Source: Horrell and Humphries, 'Old Questions', pp. 855–9; *Chadwick's Report*, 1842.

Weekly earnings for agricultural workers averaged from 8s 6d to 12s for the years 1841–45 (Table 5.2), whereas the Royal Statistical Society calculated average annual incomes for agricultural workers of £30 11s 0d per annum or 11s 9d per week in 1833.[18] Considerable income differentials such as these made Birmingham an attractive destination for migrating families in the nineteenth century, particularly those from rural areas of Warwickshire and the neighbouring counties of Worcestershire, Staffordshire and Leicestershire.

---

15 *Ibid.*

16 A.L. Bowley, 'The Statistics of Wages in the United Kingdom. (Part V.) Wages in the Building Trades in English Towns', *Journal of the Royal Statistical Society*, 63/2 (1900), pp. 302–08.

17 Horrell and Humphries, 'Old Questions', pp. 855–9.

18 A.L. Bowley, 'The Statistics of Wages in the United Kingdom During the Last Hundred Years. (Part IV.) Agricultural Wages', *Journal of the Royal Statistical Society*, 62/3 (1899), pp. 555–70.

Whether these newcomers, along with migrants fleeing from the famine in Ireland, were able to rapidly acquire the industrial trade skills required for well-paid work in Birmingham seems unlikely. A lack of appropriate skills and experience may therefore provide an additional explanation for the value attached to the earnings of children and young people. Nicola Verdon's analysis of the Poor Law Commission's 1830s survey found that children's earnings were often more important than women's in rural districts, though the most significant contributions to family incomes were made in non-agricultural occupations.[19] In Cornwall, for example, children were employed in copper or tin mines and the china clay industry. In Wiltshire children worked in domestic silk-weaving, and in rural areas of Staffordshire and Worcestershire nail-making provided opportunities for child employment. Verdon concluded that the greatest impact in offsetting low male earnings was seen in rural counties with non-agricultural work for children.[20] The 1841 Royal Commission on Hand-Loom Weavers found that single-handed silk-ribbon-weavers in villages near Coventry in Warwickshire earned just 5s per week,[21] and families in Nuneaton, Bulkington and Foleshill were living in 'extreme distress' where there were small children and the wife was unable to work. The joint earnings of a ribbon-weaver and his wife amounted to the wages of an agricultural labourer and only began to increase when the children were old enough to work. Given the high demand for child workers in Birmingham, it seems reasonable to suggest that a similar reliance on children's earnings may have existed among recently arrived families, particularly in the early decades of the nineteenth century when population expansion was rapid.

Newly arrived families, along with families of unskilled or unemployed workers and those headed by lone parents, were those most likely to rely on children to contribute to the family's living expenses. Chadwick's 1842 report found that most working families in Birmingham were housed in courts of back-to-back housing, paying rents of 2s 6d to 3s 6d per week.[22] They were likely to use two hundredweight of coal per week at a cost of 14d for heating and cooking. Although there is no breakdown of expenditure on food for a family, a cooked dinner of meat and potatoes for a workman was available from cook-shops for 4d and stewing meat was sold at 9d a pound. However, women and children were unlikely to receive a share of the good meat as 'the more careful housewife buys what are called bits of meat at 5d a pound – these she stews with potatoes and onions, and forms a wholesome and nutritious

---

19   Verdon, 'The Rural Labour Market', p. 319.

20   *Ibid.*, p. 320.

21   BPP, 1841, *Royal Commission on Hand-Loom Weavers*, Vol. II, p. 302.

22   Chadwick's Report, 1842, p. 195.

meal for herself and her children.'[23] Assuming there was some continuity of employment, the evidence from Chadwick's investigation suggests that the basic requirements of food, shelter, and heating were well within the means of workmen on average wages of 24s per week, especially if the incomes of working wives and children were added. For instance, the combined cost of a family's rent and heating of around 4s 2d per week could be covered by the wages of a boy aged 13 or 14 years.[24]

Birmingham's population expanded to 232,000 in 1851, an increase that seems to have been linked to high average wages and the availability of work for children and young people, which drew in migrants. The typical wages for skilled workers in Birmingham were between 30s and 40s per week by 1866 (Table 5.3), with elite workmen earning as much as £4 or £5 for some weeks. The typical wages for unskilled workers and labourers were considerably lower, at 15s to 20s per week. However, the proportion of the workforce who were skilled workers earning the higher amounts is unknown. The wages record of Ralph Heaton & Sons (Figure 5.1) shows that approximately 98 workers, almost half the workforce, were earning 10s a week or less, with a further 63 employees earning more than 10s but less than 30s weekly.[25] Only 33 employees received the 'average' wages of 30s per week or more. This data indicates that the majority of workers at this firm were women and young people, although the ages of workers are not specified in the wages records. At the same time, some of the skilled workmen appear to have earned considerably more than

Table 5.3 Average weekly wages in Birmingham metal trades, 1866.

Industry	Skilled male workers	Highest earnings	Unskilled/ Labourers	Boys	Women	Girls
Button trade	25s	40s to 80s			7s to 9s	1s to 1s 6d
Jewellery trade	30s to 50s	60s to 100s	10s to 11s	4s		
Hemp and wire rope	30s to 40s				6s to 10s	
Wire drawing	35s	50s to 65s				
Hinges	30s				5s to 10s	
Cut nails	25s to 50s		15s to 20s	10s to 15s	10s to 15s	
Steel pen trade	30s to 80s	90s to 100s	18s to 20s	4s 6d to 16s	15s to 20s	2s 6d to 12s
Brass tubes	30s		15s to 18s	4s 6d to 10s	10s to 12s	4s to 8s
Hydraulic machinery	30s to 40s	55s	30s to 40s			

Source: Timmins, Birmingham, pp. 285, 362, 432, 444, 453, 616, 636, 647.

23   Ibid., p. 212.
24   Ibid., p. 209.
25   BAH, MS 1010/8, 1840–61.

Figure 5.1 Weekly wages at R. Heaton & Sons, 1 March 1861.

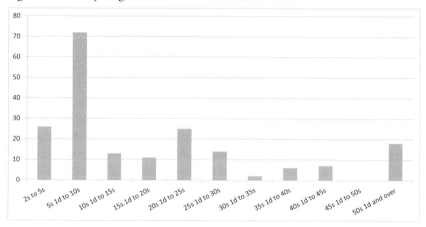

Source: BAH, MS1010/8, Ralph Heaton & Sons, Wages Book, 1840–61.

the average wage for skilled workers. Two of the highest paid employees were J. Willder, who earned £29 2s 4d in the week ending 1 March 1861, and William Hems, who was paid £28 5s 11d for the same week.[26] These amounts do not appear to have been isolated payments, as Hems earned a total of £284 11s 5d in the first quarter of 1861, averaging almost £22 per week. These amounts suggest that Wilder and Hems employed their own teams of workers and possibly supplied their own raw materials, the costs of which would have been covered by the high weekly payments. Similarly high-earning workmen in the same week included T. Simmonds, who was paid £19 0s 2d, Joseph Moore, paid £14 5s 4d, John Evans, paid £7 18s 5d, and Thomas Fisher, paid £7 3s 0d. Skilled workmen in Birmingham were therefore able to command high wages and, in a few cases, quite exceptional weekly earnings. However – if Ralph Heaton & Sons was a typical employer – skilled workers also comprised a relatively small proportion of the workforce. The majority of workers were earning less than 20s per week, illustrating the importance of women and children in the workforce and their value to the family economy.

In the case of one particular workman the firm of Ralph Heaton & Sons not only provided him with employment for many years, it also employed several members of his family. Moses Howlett was listed in the wages' records for March 1842, earning wages of between 22s 6d and 24s per week. Twenty years later Howlett continued to be employed by the firm, earning 66s for the week ending 1 March 1861.[27] The increased pay since 1841 placed him in the category

---

26   *Ibid.*

27   BAH, MS 1010/9, 1861–73.

of 'high-earning' skilled workers by 1862, according to the information drawn from contemporary sources.[28] Listed in the wages records alongside Moses Howlett were his three children: John Howlett was paid 12s 2d, Moses Howlett Jnr was paid 8s 2d and Elizabeth Howlett was paid 8s 9d, making a weekly total for the family of £4 15s 1d. The 1861 census recorded Moses Howlett as a 47-year-old tool-maker, living with his family in Brearley Street near the Birmingham jewellery quarter.[29] His sons John, aged 16, and Moses, aged 15, were also toolmakers, and his 19-year-old daughter Betsy was a warehouse woman. Additional family members living in the Howlett household were daughter Mary Ann, aged 21, who was employed as a harness stitcher, and two younger sons, William, aged 13, and George, aged 12, both gold-chain-makers. The fortunes of the Howlett family, headed by a well-paid workman with six older children at work, indicate that Birmingham's reputation for good employment opportunities was certainly true for some families. William Hems, mentioned above, who was paid an average of £22 per week at R. Heaton & Sons appears in the 1861 census records as a 38-year-old copper-roller living with his wife and four young children.[30] Mrs Hems had no occupation listed and the children were recorded as 'scholars'. It appears to be the case that there was no financial necessity for William Hems' wife and children to work, since the head of the household was able to provide comfortably for his family.

Children at work, at school or 'at home'

The Birmingham Statistical Society for the Improvement of Education conducted a survey in 1835 on the state of education in Birmingham.[31] It reported that, from a total of 45,000 children between the ages of five and 15 years in Birmingham, only 11,645, or around 25 per cent, were attending day or evening schools. This indicates that more than 30,000 children within the age group were either at home or at work on weekdays, although the survey gave no indication of the numbers in employment. A second survey conducted in 1841 by the New Meeting Sunday Schools of 273 children attending Sunday schools found that 44 per cent of children aged between five and nine years were at school and 22 per cent were at work. On the other hand, among children aged ten to 13 years only 11 per cent were at school and 78 per cent were at work.[32] A third and more extensive survey, conducted by the Birmingham Education Society in 1867, involved 15,847 families with a total of 45,056 children aged

---

28   Timmins, *Birmingham*, pp. 453, 636.

29   Census of England and Wales, 1861.

30   *Ibid.*

31   BAH, MS 1683/1.

32   BPP, 1843, 431, XIV, pp. 200–03.

between three and 15 years of age.[33] This survey concluded that less than 1 per cent of Birmingham children aged five to nine were employed, a figure lower than the national figure of 2 per cent for this age group as calculated by Hugh Cunningham using the 1851 census data.[34] It is also significantly lower than the 1851 census data for the county of Warwickshire, which recorded that 3.4 per cent of boys and 1.4 per cent of girls in this age group were employed. Among children aged ten to 13 years in Birmingham, 36.9 per cent of boys and 23.6 per cent of girls were in employment, compared with national figures of 37 per cent of boys and 20 per cent of girls in this age group as shown by the 1851 census. For the county of Warwickshire, the comparable figures are 44.8 per cent of boys and 24.8 per cent of girls.[35]

Overall, 4,026 children under the age of 14 in the Birmingham survey were employed in 1867, or 12 per cent of the 33,321 children in the age group between five and 13 years. This suggests there was a substantial reduction in child workers compared with the numbers employed in 1841 and 1851, but the survey results also show that only 50.1 per cent of five- to nine-year-olds were 'at school now' (at the time of the survey), and that 10,065 children in this age group were neither at school nor at work. Among children aged ten to 13 years, 3,818, or 30.3 per cent of the age group, were 'at school now', with a further 4,926 children who were neither at school nor at work. Approximately 15,000 children between the ages of five and 13 were therefore unoccupied in either school work or employment. The Birmingham Education Society was formed in 1867 as a campaigning organisation with the ultimate aim of achieving universal free education in Birmingham, and it is possible that the 1867 survey may have been designed with an in-built bias, for example, by assuming that parents failed to send their children to school because they could not afford the school fees. An alternative explanation might be that some families were reliant on children's earnings and that a loss of these was more significant than the cost of school fees.

Children's earnings and family budgets

The Birmingham Education Society visited 15,847 families in 1867, of whom 10,227 had incomes that averaged 20s 9d per week.[36] This amount was well below the average wage for skilled workers in Birmingham at the time, but reflected the wages typically paid to unskilled workers and labourers. The remaining families in the survey consisted of 1,222 families who had no

33   BAH, LB.48 Birmingham Education Society First Annual Report, 1868.
34   Cunningham, 'The employment and unemployment of children', pp. 115–50.
35   *Ibid.*
36   BAH, LB.48.

work, 1,587 families headed by widows or deserted women and 2,811 families for whom information on wages was not given.[37] The Society also obtained more detailed information for about 300 of the poorest families visited (see Appendix, table 7a). These families had an average of six members who lived on a weekly income of 9s 3d per family, a considerably lower income than the average wages of 30s per week paid to a skilled worker.[38] The Society provided a further breakdown of the economic circumstances of 80 families headed by widows or women deserted by their husbands. These single-parent families lived on extremely low incomes, averaging just 8s 3d per week for a family of six people. It is also particularly noteworthy that within this group only four children from a total of 414 were attending school.

Members of the Education Society paid an annual subscription of £1 1s 0d so that the Society could support poorer families by paying all or part of their children's school fees. The Society's first report, in 1868, recorded that school fees of 2½d per week had been paid for 3,097 children, with an average school attendance of 8¼ half-days per week.[39] However, they found that 25 per cent of the free school orders had not been taken up. After making allowances for children who were ill or who had gone to work, the Society reported that 'a large number of children and parents remain indifferent to the advantages offered them.'[40] They suggested that poor families consisted of two classes with differing attitudes towards education: one class of families was prevented from sending their children to school owing to poverty and were making good use of the free school orders provided by the Society, sending their children to school regularly. The second had no interest in education and failed to send their children to school even when the fees were paid. The Society concluded that children from the second class of families could be drawn into education only by compulsion. Interestingly, they focused on children who did not take up the opportunity of a free school place, rather than on children absent from school due to work. Although the Society's aim was to increase the numbers of children in education, in this report it did not appear to be critical of working children who were contributing to the family finances. Later reports by the Society's successor, the National Education League, however, did comment on parents' reliance on their children's earnings. A National Education League leaflet published in 1871 insisted that compulsory and free education was necessary because parents were not only too poor to pay for school fees but were 'aggrieved by any interference with

37   *Ibid.*, p. 19.
38   *Ibid.*, p. 9.
39   BAH, LB.48, p. 10.
40   *Ibid.*

their right to the earnings of their children.[41]

The importance of clothing

The Birmingham Education Society's 1867 report identified a third group of children whose parents could not afford school fees, but who could not be offered free school places by the society 'through want of clothes'.[42] The society's investigators reported that this group, which comprised a total of 931 children, lived with their families in such extreme poverty they were 'almost naked', meaning that no school would be able to accept them. The report noted that in many cases 'families of children are found with nothing that can be called a garment on them', highlighting the significant numbers of children who were from families so poor as to be beyond the help of the charity. The importance of clothing or, more accurately, the absence of suitable clothing has been identified by a number of writers as a barrier to accessing education and employment. Writing about his childhood in 1890s Salford, Jack Lanigan recalled that his widowed mother took in washing to pay the rent and that, although Jack and his brother went to school, they were unable to attend Sunday school because they did not possess adequate clothing and shoes. In Jack's neighbourhood 'You were considered posh if you could attend Sunday school.'[43] Similarly, historians researching pauper letters in parish records of the early nineteenth century have found a predominance of requests for clothing and shoes to relieve extreme poverty.[44]

For the Birmingham children whose families were too poor to clothe them there would also have been no opportunity to assist their families through paid work, unless the work could be undertaken at home. At the same time, the earnings declared by children in the 1867 survey seem particularly low, ranging from 1s 0¾d to a maximum of 3s 1¼d per week for children aged eight to 13 years, which was below average wages for boys and girls.[45] One explanation for this may be that respondents were under-reporting their earnings. Alternatively, many of the children may have been undertaking low-paid work at home, alongside other family members. What seems clear, however, is that incomes reported in this survey were far lower than average incomes for families of skilled workers in Birmingham. This suggests that a

---

41   BAH, MS 4248 National Education League Leaflet, 1871.

42   BAH, LB.48, p. 17.

43   Burnett, *Destiny Obscure*, p. 88.

44   Jones, '"I cannot keep my place without being deascent"'; Peter Jones, 'Clothing the Poor in Early-Nineteenth-Century England', *Textile History*, 37/1 (2006), pp. 17–37; Joanne Bailey, '"Think wot a mother must feel": Parenting in English Pauper Letters, c1760–1834', *Family and Community History*, 13/1 (2010), pp. 5–19.

45   BAH, LB.48.

substantial proportion of Birmingham families were headed by unskilled male workers whose earnings needed to be supplemented by the earnings of their wives and children.

Case studies: George Jacob Holyoake and Will Thorne

Differences in average earnings and the extent to which Birmingham parents may have relied upon children's earnings are further illuminated by an examination of the autobiographies of George Jacob Holyoake and Will Thorne. Holyoake, born in Birmingham in 1817, was from a hard-working family whose children were expected to work from an early age.[46] Holyoake's mother, Catherine, was a horn-button-maker with her own workshop attached to the house. She had run this business before marriage, employing several workers, receiving orders, purchasing raw materials and supervising the manufacture of the buttons. After marrying, she continued to run her business from the family home in Inge Street, alongside raising a family of 11 children. As Holyoake writes, 'There were no "Rights of Women" thought of in her day, but she was an entirely self-acting, managing mistress.'[47] He adds that it was 'a peculiarity of Birmingham' that numerous small trades existed in households, providing families with independence and prosperity when trade was good. From a young age George had been trained to work in his mother's business, using the lathe and press: 'I learned to wind the copper wire on a flat steel turned by a lathe, to stamp the coil into shank form under a press, and to cut the shanks with shears which often strained my little hands.'[48] He also helped with processes which involved using a hammer, vice and file before the buttons were dried and polished in a long bag: 'They were then strung into grosses, and delivered to the merchants who ordered them.'[49]

Following this early career as a button-maker, Holyoake worked for a 'tinman' making lanterns. He undertook this work in the evenings after school, indicating that his family could afford to send him to school, although perhaps his employment paid for the school fees. The work involved using a soldering iron to solder handles onto metal lanterns, for which he could earn up to 3s 6d per week, although he often burned his hands on the soldering iron.[50] Holyoake was therefore able to make a very useful contribution to the family income, even as a part-time worker after school. Nevertheless, it appears that he wanted to leave school as soon as possible in order to work full-time:

---

46 George Jacob Holyoake, *Sixty Years of an Agitator's Life* (London, 1900).

47 Holyoake, *Sixty Years*, p. 10.

48 *Ibid.*, p. 19.

49 *Ibid.*

50 *Ibid.*

'Afterwards, I persuaded my father to take me with him to the Eagle Foundry, from a desire to be at work. I must have been very young then, as I remember asking my father to let me hold his hand … .'[51] By the age of 12 or 13 Holyoake was working full-time at the foundry, learning the trade of whitesmith. Writing his autobiography some 60 years later, he recalled his good fortune in acquiring a life-long skill: 'The capacity to work as a whitesmith or engineer has always been a source of pride to me. Anything I could do in my mechanic days I could do ever after. It gave me a sense of independence.'[52] This belief supported him during his adult years when he became a lecturer and a leader in the co-operative movement.

George Holyoake's account of his childhood throws light on a number of points about attitudes towards child labour in Birmingham during the early decades of the nineteenth century. First, it seems clear that, although the family was financially stable, with the head of the household employed at the Eagle Foundry for more than 40 years, Holyoake worked as a very young child alongside his mother and siblings in a home-based workshop. This example fits with the view that children in Birmingham were traditionally expected to work as soon as possible and contribute to the family income, especially in family businesses. Second, Holyoake writes about working in the evenings after school, thus implying that attending school and then going to work was quite normal for a boy in his neighbourhood. This indicates that the Holyoake family recognised that children needed to acquire basic educational skills, but they also believed in the value of hard work and self-help, especially for children from a large family. Third, his autobiography suggests that he was not only happy to work after school, but also that he chose to work full-time in the foundry alongside his father. This desire for self-sufficiency as a skilled workman became a matter of pride that remained with him throughout his lifetime. Finally, there is nothing in Holyoake's account to suggest he resented his parents' expectation that he should work as a child. In fact, he was willing and eager to learn and proud to be able to make a financial contribution to his family.

Will Thorne was born in Hockley, Birmingham, in 1857, approximately 40 years after George Holyoake. He achieved success in adult life as general secretary of the National Union of Gas Workers and General Labourers in 1889, and was elected as a member of parliament in 1906. His lack of education during childhood was remedied by evening classes at an institute of adult education in East London, where he met George Bernard Shaw and other leading socialists. On becoming secretary of the gas workers' union, Thorne was fortunate in being able to rely on Eleanor Marx, the daughter of Karl Marx,

---

51   *Ibid.*

52   *Ibid.*

for assistance with report writing and drafting union rules.[53] His early life, however, was dominated by hard work and severe hardship following the death of his father when he was only seven years old.[54] Thorne began work at just six years of age at Rob's Rope Walk in Duddeston Mill Road, Birmingham. His job was to assist a rope- and twine-spinner by turning a wheel, for which he was paid 2s 6d a week for a 12-hour working day. On Saturdays, after finishing at the rope walk at 1pm, he worked in his uncle's barber's shop until 11pm, and returned on Sundays for a further six hours, earning an additional 1s per week. Thorne describes how, after the death of his father in 1864, life became even more difficult. His mother and sister worked at sewing hooks and eyes onto cards for a tiny reward, but the family had to turn to the Poor Law for relief, receiving 4s and four loaves of bread per week for a family of five.[55] He went to work for an uncle at a brick and tile works (adding a three-mile walk to the beginning and end of his 12-hour working day), for which he earned 7s a week.

After being dismissed for falling asleep during night-time work, Thorne found work at another brickyard at 8s per week, but was forced by his mother to give this up when he started to develop a hump-back. As Thorne describes his life at this time, 'Here was I, a boy of nine years of age, that should have been in school, getting up in the cold of early morning, leaving home at about 4.30, walking four miles to work, and then after a twelve-hour day, walking back again … '[56] Following this experience he worked as a plumber's mate and general handyman. After this came a stint with a firm that collected cow and pig hair from butchers' shops before, at the age of 14, he was employed at a Birmingham metal-rolling and ammunition works. The work here – removing metal bars from furnaces into pickling tubs containing a solution of acid that burnt the skin and clothes – was hot, noisy and dangerous.[57] Like Holyoake, Thorne made no criticism of his mother, but he pointed out the lack of legislation to protect children, the ignorance about health and safety in the workplace and the general exploitation of workers by employers. His early experience of 'long years of drudging work' created a life-long desire to improve working conditions through the trade union movement. In contrast to Holyoake's experience, Thorne was from a single-parent family and forced to work in order to support his family, rather than making a contribution. The declaration in his autobiography that 'I can never forget the horror of my childhood days and the misery and suffering I have seen' highlights the differing

53   Rachel Holmes, *Eleanor Marx: A Life* (London, 2014), pp. 322–3.

54   Thorne, *My Life's Battles*, p. 15.

55   *Ibid.*, p. 16.

56   *Ibid.*, p. 19.

57   *Ibid.*, p. 21.

work experiences of children, depending on the individual circumstances of their family.[58]

Conclusion

This chapter has examined the relationship between child labour and the family economy in nineteenth-century Birmingham. It was traditional in Birmingham and the West Midlands for children to begin work at a relatively early age in order to supplement family incomes and become self-sufficient. As Hopkins has emphasised, individual success was expected to be achieved through self-help, hard work and initiative, with less value placed on advancement through education.[59] Birmingham was renowned as a town of opportunity, offering the prospect of well-paid employment to anyone prepared to work hard. The perception that average wages for skilled workers in Birmingham compared favourably with other industries and trades, such as textiles and mining, appears to be correct, but it was also the case, perhaps unsurprisingly, that the wages earned by skilled workers were considerably higher than the earnings of unskilled workers and labourers. Newly arrived families who did not possess the necessary skills required for well-paid employment in Birmingham were therefore likely to rely on the supplementary earnings of their children. It also appears to be the case that families with young children below the age of ten were those most likely to be surviving on low incomes. Families with older children, such as Moses Howlett's family, were likely to do better, since young workers between the ages of 14 to 20 were in high demand. By the time of the Birmingham Education Society survey in 1867, average wages for skilled workers in Birmingham were approximately 30s per week, with some workers earning 40s or 50s per week, or more. However, the average earnings of more than 15,000 families included in the survey were only 20s per week, just two-thirds of the average earnings paid to skilled workers. This disparity in incomes suggests that many Birmingham families were reliant on their children's earnings because of low pay, but the financial situation of individual families may have improved when adult workers acquired additional skills and older children entered the workforce. The society's report that almost 1,000 children were 'too poor to be helped by a free school place' because of insufficient clothing indicates the extent of absolute poverty in some families living alongside more prosperous families in nineteenth-century Birmingham.

Differences in children's experiences are further emphasised by the accounts provided by George Holyoake and Will Thorne in their respective autobiographies. Holyoake was able to attend school and work in the evenings

---

58   *Ibid.*, p. 221.

59   Hopkins, *Birmingham*, pp. 158–61.

during the 1820s, after persuading a small tradesman to employ him. His earnings of 3s 6d per week were undoubtedly an important addition to the family budget, but perhaps not vital, as his father was a skilled worker in regular employment. Will Thorne's childhood experiences in the 1860s were much harsher because of the loss of his father. In effect, he became the family breadwinner from the age of seven, working full-time in the brickyards after a long walk to work. Nevertheless, he recalls his mother's insistence on his leaving the brickyards for the sake of his health, even though the family would suffer from the drastic loss of income. Some parents, at least, were more concerned about the well-being of their children than about earnings from their labour. These experiences illustrate the differing economic circumstances of labouring families in Birmingham and the impact of poverty on children: many families had no choice other than to rely on the earnings of their children.

6

Education, industrialisation and child labour

Introduction

Children in Birmingham faced a variety of experiences closely dependent on the economic circumstances of their families. A survey by the Birmingham Statistical Society in 1838 found that only 25 per cent of children were attending school either during the day or in the evening. In addition, successive government enquiries revealed low levels of literacy among Birmingham children, citing the early age of starting work as a major barrier to education.[1] George Jacob Holyoake's experiences during childhood, however, offer an alternative view of working-class approaches to schooling and child labour. The Holyoakes were a large family of 11 children living with their parents in back-to-back housing in the centre of Birmingham. The young Holyoake was fascinated by the sight of a tinman making lanterns in his workshop nearby. After some time the workman agreed to employ Holyoake 'when the afternoon school was over, to work through the evening soldering the handles on lanterns'.[2] What stands out from this description is the inclusion of the phrase 'when the afternoon school was over', indicating that from a contemporary perspective it appeared quite normal for a boy from a large working-class family to attend school every day, followed by work in the evenings. Holyoake did not mention which school he attended, but it may have been the Royal Lancasterian School in Severn Street, which was very close to his home in Inge Street. He also regularly attended Sunday school at Carr's Lane Congregational Church, another typical route into schooling for working-class children.[3] Holyoake's combination of school with part-time paid work raises questions about the availability of schooling for working-class children in the nineteenth century and challenges the traditional perception that Birmingham labouring families did not value formal education for their children.[4]

This chapter argues that working families in Birmingham adopted a variety of strategies to enable their children to access basic schooling while also

---

1   Royal Statistical Society, 'Report on the State of Education in Birmingham', *Journal of the Statistical Society of London*, 3/1 (1840), pp. 25–49; BPP, 1843, 430, XIII, p. 167.

2   Holyoake, *Sixty Years*, p. 19.

3   *Ibid.*

4   Hopkins, *Birmingham*, p. 158.

making contributions to the family income through paid work. It highlights the tensions between middle-class perceptions of the role of education in socialising children and the use of flexible schooling opportunities by members of the working class, and suggests that early forms of mass schooling in which older children worked as monitors and pupil teachers responsible for teaching younger children could also be interpreted as examples of child labour. The relationship between education, industrialisation and child labour in eighteenth- and nineteenth-century Birmingham is examined, addressing three main questions. First, how did changes brought about by industrialisation and rapid population growth impact on access to schooling? Second, how did working families view and experience the costs and benefits of schooling? Third, to what extent did families adopt strategies that enabled their children to combine schooling with paid work?

Access to schooling for children of working families in Birmingham

Early eighteenth-century Birmingham was served by a single endowed or charity school, the King Edward VI Free Grammar School in New Street, established in 1551 to provide education for 170 boys from artisan families. It was joined in 1722 by the Blue Coat School, a boarding school for poor parish children offering 150 places for boys and 50 places for girls. An additional 55 places for girls were provided by the Crowley's Charity School and the Protestant Dissenting Charity School.[5] Birmingham's population increased from 11,400 at the beginning of the eighteenth century to 52,250 by 1785, but six small additional schools for working-class boys provided by the King Edward VI School added only another 300 places. This relatively limited educational provision for the lower classes in Birmingham was supplemented by an undocumented number of privately run schools, plus 59 Sunday schools offering free instruction in religious education, reading and writing by 1786.[6]

The growth and popularity of Sunday schools from the 1780s onwards was one of the important educational changes taking place in England before the Education Act of 1870. Sunday schools provided by Anglican or dissenting churches were significant in providing education for the masses even as industrialisation, poverty and the rising demand for child labour prevented most children from having access to day schools. At Sunday school child workers could be provided with basic literacy skills without any loss of earnings. As Keith Snell points out, huge numbers of adults and children attended Sunday schools, far outnumbering those at day schools, and rising

---

5   Royal Statistical Society, 'Report on the State of Education in Birmingham'.

6   Hopkins, *Birmingham*, p. 159.

nationally from 425,000 in 1818 to 2,600,000 by 1851.[7] Sunday schools attracted large numbers of children in Birmingham: 16,757 children in 1838.[8] Apart from the advantage of free instruction, Sunday schools were important to working families, as intimated above, because they did not interfere with their children's ability to undertake paid work. Furthermore, attendance was not compulsory: children could move in and out of Sunday school instruction or from one Sunday school to another according to their family circumstances. The importance of flexibility, lack of compulsion in attendance and the power of working families to retain control over their children's time also provide an explanation for the popularity of dame schools among Birmingham's labouring classes.

The 1838 survey of education estimated that there were 45,000 children in Birmingham between the ages of five and 15, of whom 48 per cent were receiving instruction at either day schools or Sunday schools. A total of 14,480 children were attending day schools: 3,900 at dame schools, 4,280 at common day schools, 3,331 at charity or voluntary schools and 2,166 children at 'superior' private schools.[9] Dame schools were 'very numerous in Birmingham', with an average of 14.6 pupils per school, a lower figure than in comparable dame schools in Manchester, Bury, Salford, Liverpool and York.[10] Birmingham's dame schools also occupied more appropriate premises than schools in Manchester or Liverpool, with none held in cellars and 'very few in garrets or bed-rooms'. But dame-school teachers were notoriously poverty stricken: 'some were found suffering extreme privation and nearly the whole complained of their inability to provide a sufficient number of books.'[11] The Birmingham report found that 44 per cent of children at dame schools were below the age of five, yet the investigators dismissed the possibility that these children were too young for formal instruction: 'they are more open to judicious cultivation at this period than any other, habits being then formed, tastes acquired, associations and impressions received, and principles inculcated.'[12] The tone of the report suggests its authors considered that small local schools were failing to meet middle-class educational standards and values, issues that may not have been of concern to families sending their children to dame schools.

---

7   K.D.M. Snell, 'The Sunday-School Movement in England and Wales: Child Labour, Denominational Control and Working-Class Culture', *Past and Present*, 164 (1999), pp. 122–68.

8   Royal Statistical Society, 'Report on the State of Education in Birmingham', p. 27.

9   *Ibid.*, p. 27.

10   *Ibid.*, p. 29.

11   *Ibid.*, p. 30.

12   *Ibid.*, p. 30.

Working-class families chose to send their children to local dame schools because they offered flexible and affordable childcare combined with schooling, facilitating the household arrangements of mothers who needed to go out to work or were over-burdened in some respect, such as by chronic illness. According to the report, a major problem with dame schools was the poor quality of teachers: 'they are generally taken up by persons destitute of every qualification for teaching, and who have no other object in view than obtaining a subsistence.'[13] It added that dame-school mistresses were frequently unhappy with their earnings and many combined running a school with additional work, such as taking in laundry. The views of the parents were not included, but it seems unlikely they would have found fault with the school premises, since they were living in similar properties themselves. Most working families supported the teaching of letters and basic reading skills to very young children, and they also understood the need for people to make a living as best they could. Eric Hopkins has commented that dame schools in Birmingham 'hardly deserve to be dignified by the name of school',[14] and while this may be a fair comment in terms of educational provision it should also be recognised that dame schools provided a valuable service for local working-class families that more closely resembled a childminding service or nursery school.

Children attended dame schools from the age of three until six or seven, perhaps followed by enrolment at a common day school, a charity school or a voluntary school. The 177 privately run common day schools established in Birmingham by 1838 provided places for more than 4,000 children, but these schools were severely criticised in the report on education for overcrowding and poor methods of instruction. It found, for example, that children were expected to memorise lessons without understanding what was being taught: '[i]nstead of the master exerting himself to teach, the scholars are expected to learn.'[15] Common day schools focused on teaching the basics of reading, writing and arithmetic, with the addition of lessons in needlework for girls. Despite the alleged shortcomings of these establishments, the report recognised that teachers faced numerous barriers to effective learning, including family poverty amongst children, irregular attendance of pupils and the removal of children from school at an early age by their parents in order for them to begin paid work. In addition to the places provided by common day schools in Birmingham, a further 3,331 places were available in charity schools and voluntary schools. An important development in early nineteenth-century schooling for working-class children was the introduction of monitorial

---

13   *Ibid.*, p. 30.

14   Hopkins, *Birmingham*, p. 160.

15   Royal Statistical Society, 'Report on the State of Education in Birmingham', pp. 34–5.

Table 6.1 National Society and British Society Schools in Birmingham.

Year est.	School	No. of places	Fees (weekly)	Location
1809	Royal Lancasterian	400		Severn St
1812	Bham National	650	1d	Pinfold St
1812	Handsworth National	195	1d	Handsworth
1813	Erdington National	132	1d	Erdington
1826	Lancasterian Girls	110	1d	Ann Street
1829	Christchurch National	180	1d–3d	Pinfold St
1831	St Mary's National	101		Bath St
1834	Wesleyan School		2d–4d	Cherry St
1834	St Bartholomew's	350		St Bart's Sq
1834	St Peter's RC	160	1d–4d	Broad St
1834	St George's National	90	2d–4d	Gt Russell St
1839	Erdington British Sch	159	1d–6d	Erdington
1839	Legge St British Sch	160		Legge St
1843	St Philip's National		2d–3d	Lichfield St
1843	Hebrew National	180	1s	Hurst St
1844	Carr's Lane British	400		Carr's Lane
1845	St Peter's National	145		Moor St

Source: VCH, *A History of the County of Warwick, the City of Birmingham*, pp. 501–48.

schools by the British and Foreign School Society and the National Society (Table 6.1).[16] These voluntary schools added considerably to the number of places already available at the Free Grammar School and the Blue Coat School. Monitorial schools were founded by the Quaker schoolmaster Joseph Lancaster, who visited Birmingham in 1808 to give two public lectures promoting his method of affordable schooling for children from the lower classes. This visit was quickly followed by the formation in Birmingham of a Lancasterian School committee, dominated by members of Quaker families such as the Lloyds, Galtons and Sturges and Unitarians such as William Beale. A plot of land was acquired in Severn Street in the town centre and the Royal Lancasterian School opened in 1809.[17] Although mainly supported by leading nonconformists, the

---

16   W.B. Stephens, *Education in Britain 1750-1914* (Basingstoke, 1998); Michael Sanderson, *Education, Economic Change and Society in England 1780–1870* (Cambridge, 1995); Humphries, *Childhood and Child Labour*; Victoria County History, *The City of Birmingham*; M.B. Frost, 'The Development of Provided Schooling for Working Class Children in Birmingham 1781-1851', MLitt thesis (University of Birmingham, 1978).

17   Frost, 'The Development of Provided Schooling', pp. 167–8.

school was open to children of all denominations and attracted a number of Anglican subscribers. However, the Anglican clergy in Birmingham refused to support the new school, preferring to open their own National School in 1812, based on the Madras monitorial system promoted by Dr Andrew Bell.[18]

The cost of running this new type of school was minimised by an innovative teaching method: a single schoolmaster was employed to teach up to 1,000 children through the medium of monitors chosen from the oldest and most able pupils. The monitors were instructed by the schoolmaster, and then taught the lesson to a group of around ten younger pupils.[19] James Bonwick was a pupil at the Borough Road British School in Southwark who became head monitor and later a qualified teacher.[20] The Borough Road schoolroom accommodated up to 500 pupils, with a raised platform at the entrance for the master. The youngest children were placed at the 'sand desk', where the monitor held up a board with a printed letter for children to copy on the sand using a stick. The other seven classes were placed in semi-circular groups or 'drafts', with a monitor heading each group of pupils, who stood with hands behind their backs reading from printed cards.[21] Each day around 50 monitors gathered at the schoolmaster's platform to read lessons from the scriptures: 'At times, at our noon gathering, a sudden and wild burst of applause would rise from the class at some extra fine rendering.'[22] The monitorial system extended access to schooling for poor children because of the low expenditure involved, but the education of the monitors suffered. Senior monitors were selected for training as schoolmasters before being sent to open their own schools. Bonwick trained as an assistant master for three months before working as a temporary schoolmaster in Ipswich at just 15 years of age. The issue of discipline was clearly prominent when he was introduced 'to about a hundred of rough-looking Suffolk boys, to whom my London pale face and delicate appearance presented a decided contrast.'[23] The boys tried to leave, but Bonwick swiftly locked the door and ordered them to continue with their studies: 'not the slightest insubordination ever afterwards appeared and we were good friends till the Master returned to the school … .'[24]

---

18 *Ibid.*, p. 169.

19 Phillip McCann, 'Popular Education, Socialization and Social Control: Spitalfields 1812–1824', in Phillip McCann (ed.), *Popular Education and Socialization in the Nineteenth Century* (London, 1977), pp. 1–40 at 12–13.

20 Burnett, *Destiny Obscure*, pp. 169–75.

21 *Ibid.*, pp. 169–75.

22 *Ibid.*, pp. 169–75.

23 *Ibid.*, pp. 169–75.

24 *Ibid.*, pp. 169–75.

Bonwick's first-hand account of the monitorial system provides invaluable insights into early mass education for children in England, illuminating the extent to which working-class children were taught by other children from a similar background. It shows that parents of children at monitorial schools were likely to have been highly motivated, with a willingness to forego the possibility of paid work for their children. In addition to providing tuition in reading, writing and arithmetic, the Borough Road School offered lessons in geography, grammar, geometry, science and singing, but this was perhaps unlikely to have been typical of other schools. However, a major problem of the system was that monitors were disadvantaged by the requirement to teach. Thomas Dunning, a monitor at Newport Pagnall National School in 1820, recalled that when he was appointed to teach the younger classes he had very little time for his own writing or arithmetic and none at all for grammar or geography.[25]

When the first Lancasterian School opened in Birmingham in 1809, Joseph Lancaster appointed as schoolmaster 19-year-old John Veevers from the Borough Road School, indicating the close links between the development of monitorial schooling in Birmingham and Lancaster himself.[26] The Anglican Church in Birmingham responded to the popularity of the Lancasterian School by opening the National School in Pinfold Street in 1813. The original plan of providing 500 places was revised upwards to 1,000 places when large numbers of applications were received by the school committee. The school was in a two-storey building with the boys' school on the ground floor and girls' school on the first floor. Teaching was undertaken by child monitors, as at the Lancasterian School, with the addition of religious instruction to the curriculum.[27] However, initial enthusiasm for the National School did not continue and attendance declined from 750 pupils in 1817 to fewer than 200 pupils in 1825. The Lancasterian School in Severn Street was more successful in retaining pupils, although its original intake of 400 boys fell to 300 from 1821 onwards.[28] The reasons behind the decline in numbers remain unclear, but it is possible that lack of support for the National School was linked to the spread of political radicalism in Birmingham at this time. A series of gatherings protesting against economic conditions in the town was held on Newhall Hill in 1817, under the leadership of George Edmonds, which attracted the support of thousands of working men. Such potentially explosive radicalism was condemned by the local Anglican clergy, notably by the vicar of Christ Church, who made his views clear in a sermon entitled 'The Duty of Obedience to Established

---

25   *Ibid.*, p. 144.

26   Frost, 'The Development of Provided Schooling', p. 173.

27   *Ibid.*, pp. 183–5.

28   *Ibid.*, pp. 194–8.

Government'.[29] While the number of children attending schools in Birmingham tended to vary with periods of economic expansion and contraction, as parents withdrew their children to take advantage of opportunities for paid child labour, variations in attendance for this reason were equally likely to have affected the Anglican National School and the nonconformist Lancasterian School. It seems possible, therefore, that parents of children at the Pinfold Street National School withdrew their children as a response to criticism of their political beliefs and activities by the Anglican clergy. Birmingham was an intensely radical town at this period, and political events might easily have affected the numbers of children enrolled at a particular school.

National Schools and Lancastrian British Schools were advised by their respective societies at a national level, but they were managed by local school committees who raised funds through subscriptions and school fees. The decline in children attending the Pinfold Street National School was matched by a substantial increase in the number of private schools in Birmingham. In the two decades from 1820 a total of 41 schools for boys and 108 schools for girls opened, together with 245 new dame schools.[30] Regardless of the criticisms aimed at these establishments, these new private schools indicate that working families were not only willing to send their offspring to school, but also to pay the school fees. Moreover, it suggests that families wished to maintain independent control over their children's education and future working lives. In short, they were not prepared to submit to pressure from the Anglican Church or from employers seeking a subordinate and compliant workforce. This tension between middle-class and working-class attitudes towards the provision of schooling in the nineteenth century was not confined to Birmingham: a similar pattern emerged at schools in the Spitalfields and Bethnal Green areas of London. Phillip McCann has suggested that the main cause of low attendance at schools was 'the conviction, shared by many of the poor, that the schools had been provided *for* them by the middle classes, and were thus in some way alien to the interests of the labouring population'.[31] As McCann points out, better paid members of the working class were willing to pay school fees to support local dame schools and common day schools rather than send their children to free schools maintained and controlled by middle-class subscription. Independent-minded working-class families in the east end of London and in Birmingham thus shared very similar attitudes towards schooling.

By 1837 the number of children admitted annually to Pinfold Street School had fallen to 175, with children spending an average of just ten months enrolled

---

29   Victoria County History, *The City of Birmingham*, pp. 270–97.

30   Royal Statistical Society, 'Report on the State of Education in Birmingham', p. 27.

31   McCann, 'Popular Education', p. 29.

there. At the Lancasterian School 233 children were admitted in 1837, staying an average of sixteen months.[32] Even though a number of National and British Schools opened across Birmingham during the 1820s and 1830s there were clearly problems with the system of voluntary school provision. One of the issues identified in the 1838 report was that teaching was limited to reading, writing and arithmetic, plus sewing and knitting in girls' schools. It was also acknowledged, however, that monitorial schools achieved more than could be expected 'from persons furnished only with the means of teaching the greatest number at the least possible expense'.[33] The report thus recognised a need for the provision of low-cost schooling but failed to address the shortcomings of a system that relied on child monitors to teach other children. In effect, the children responsible for teaching in monitorial schools were undertaking the same work as teachers in private sector schools who were severely criticised for being unqualified. Supporters of the system may have favoured monitorial schools as a way of providing affordable schooling, but it could be argued that the teaching relied on a form of unpaid child labour. Clearly, some working-class families recognised the limitations of the system, sending their children for short periods of time to take advantage of basic schooling and then removing them as soon as they were old enough to obtain paid employment at the age of eight or nine.

The duration of schooling

Jane Humphries has identified a dip in the duration of schooling during the intensive years of industrialisation in the late eighteenth and early nineteenth centuries. Evidence drawn from working-class autobiographies suggests that the average years of schooling fell from 4.2 years in the 1760s to 2.37 years in the 1830s, and then increased again over the following decades.[34] Humphries suggests that the average time spent at school in the early nineteenth century was 'a nadir associated with social and economic conditions',[35] but Hopkins suggests that in Birmingham it was even shorter, at two years or less, and was linked to an inability or unwillingness to pay school fees together with the loss of children's earnings from paid work if they attended school.[36] The 1838 report shows that children spent an average of 1.15 years at Birmingham schools, with the shortest time, 0.25 years, at St George's National School in Great Russell Street. Children typically spent 1.58 years at the Wesleyan School

---

32   Royal Statistical Society, 'Report on the State of Education in Birmingham', p. 36.

33   *Ibid.*, p. 37.

34   Humphries, *Childhood and Child Labour*, p. 314.

35   *Ibid.*, p. 315.

36   Hopkins, *Birmingham*, p. 160.

and 1.17 years at St Bartholomew's National School. In contrast, children attended the Birmingham Blue Coat School for 4.58 years because of the strict regulations for acceptance at the school. However, these figures represent only the average length of time children spent at particular schools, as opposed to the actual length of schooling each child might have received overall. Large numbers of working-class children began their schooling at the age of three or four at a dame school, acquiring basic reading skills. They then attended a monitorial school, a common day school or perhaps a Sunday school. It is quite possible, therefore, that Birmingham children had received four to five years of intermittent and flexible schooling before beginning work, and that parents regarded this as sufficient preparation for the manual or domestic roles the majority of boys and girls were destined to follow.

It was certainly the case that Birmingham employers expressed a preference for young workers with some education, although they focused on the qualities of discipline and respectfulness acquired at school rather than skills in literacy. In his report to the Children's Employment Commission of 1843, Sub-Commissioner Grainger emphasised that employers found the better-educated mechanics 'more valuable to their employers and more trustworthy'; they were 'more respectful in their behaviour to their superiors than the opposite class', 'more accessible to reason and willing to conform' and overall 'more refined in their tastes and more guarded in their language than the uneducated'.[37] In the workshops of Birmingham many children and young people interviewed by the Sub-Commissioner could read, but were apparently unable to sign their names. Among those employed at Wallis's Mill in Dartmouth Street, Charles Tinney, aged 12, attended school every Sunday but was still learning his letters; Joseph Childs, aged 9, also attended Sunday school and knew the alphabet but could not sign his name; and John Chadwick, aged 14, could not yet read or write but was attending the Wesleyan Sunday school for five hours per week.[38] These examples highlight the importance of Sunday schools for working children and their desire to learn, despite the long hours at work. In view of the continual large influx of people moving into the town, it is possible that many working children had spent their early years elsewhere, and the literacy rate in Birmingham compared reasonably well, in fact, with those in other manufacturing regions. In 1846, 71 per cent of bridegrooms and 53 per cent of brides in Birmingham signed their names on the marriage register.[39] For comparison, in Lancashire the literacy rates of bridegrooms were 67 per cent and brides 41 per cent, and in the West Riding of Yorkshire the figures were 71 per cent and 49 per cent

37   BPP, 1843, 431, XIV, p. 38.

38   *Ibid.*, pp. 158–60.

39   Hopkins, *Birmingham*, p. 161.

respectively. For the county of Warwickshire as a whole, female literacy rates were higher than in Birmingham, with 71 per cent of bridegrooms and 62 per cent of brides able to sign their names on the register.[40]

From 1839 voluntary schools were provided with financial aid by the state and were subject to government inspections, which in effect created a public elementary school system. In addition to the monitorial schools provided by the National Society and British Society, the voluntary sector included church schools established by nonconformists, Roman Catholics and Anglicans that were not associated with the societies.[41] The new process of inspection evidently created some problems for the monitorial system by highlighting the deficiencies of its heavy reliance on the goodwill and dedication of child monitors. William Chell, master of Pinfold Street National School, explained his views on the difficulties: 'it is a great evil in this system that the master is obliged to judge of the progress of the scholars more by the reports of the monitors than his own observations.'[42] Chell's doubts about the accuracy of progress reports stemmed from his belief that monitors might be bribed by other pupils. As master of the school, he was responsible for any discrepancies in standards found by school visitors or inspectors, so the age and unpaid status of monitors had clear implications for the reputation of the school and hence for the master.

Similar problems were faced by William Chell's wife, who was the mistress of Pinfold Street Girls' School. Few children attended the school for more than a year, most of them leaving at eight or nine to begin work in factories or help with domestic duties at home. Many of the girls attended for just two or three months and could not derive much benefit in such a short time. The girls were taught sewing at the school but most of them left at such a young age 'they cannot make a garment, only learning plain sewing and marking.'[43] Children who had attended infant schools before enrolment were 'more playful and volatile' than other children and could read well, understood what they read, knew their tables and were generally well informed: 'On the whole, they are much quicker than those who have not been to school.'[44] However, the Children's Employment Commission found that teachers in National and British Schools were 'generally uneducated and untrained; they are acquainted with no other than the monitorial system; the teaching in almost all instances is

---

40   Stephens, *Education in Britain*, pp. 29–30.

41   *Ibid.*, p. 5.

42   BPP, 1843, 431, XIV, p. 197.

43   *Ibid.*, p. 197.

44   *Ibid.*, p. 197.

of a mechanical kind.'[45] Highlighting these inadequacies in the existing school system contributed towards the reorganisation of elementary schooling in England that followed. The pupil-teacher system introduced in 1846 gradually replaced monitors in elementary schools with pupil teachers. Under this new system 13-year-old pupil teachers were required to undertake five and a half hours of teaching each day and received seven and a half hours of instruction per week. This placed a considerable burden of hard work and commitment on these young people, but the system also offered the possibility of a Queen's Scholarship and training at a specialist college after five years as a pupil teacher, allowing them to become fully qualified teachers.[46]

The National Education League reported in 1871 that Birmingham had almost 65,000 children between the ages of five and 13 years, of whom 43 per cent were attending school.[47] The number of children at day schools in Birmingham had increased since 1838, yet remained relatively low. However, the intermittent and flexible nature of working-class attendance at school needs to be taken into account. Children in Birmingham typically experienced schooling on an irregular basis, subject to the changing economic demands of their families and the local economy. They attended school in times of prosperity, but were withdrawn by their parents when circumstances changed and their economic contribution was required. When family circumstances improved, children might be returned to school or combine paid employment with Sunday school or evening school. Further insights into schooling are provided by a door-to-door survey of families conducted by the Birmingham Education Society in 1867.[48] This large survey of 23,052 boys and 22,004 girls between the ages of three and 14 found that 19.8 per cent of boys and 21.09 per cent of girls aged five and above had never attended school. The findings thus indicated that approximately 80 per cent of working-class children in Birmingham were receiving some schooling even before the 1870 Act. The National Education League, the successor to the Birmingham Education Society, was formed to campaign for universal education, citing 'the poverty of parents' and 'their apathy and indifference to education' as barriers to schooling in Birmingham. The National Education League suggested that in Birmingham 'parents are aggrieved by any interference with their right to the earnings of their children.'[49] Educational reformers and some Birmingham employers believed that many parents were interested only in the earnings potential

---

45   *Ibid.*, p. 34.

46   Sanderson, *Education*, p. 15.

47   BAH, MS 4248.

48   BAH, LB.48, p. 3.

49   BAH, MS 4248.

of their children, sending them to work at the earliest opportunity.[50] An alternative interpretation might be that parents were determined to maintain control over their children's schooling and work, rather than submit them to the control of others. The costs and benefits of schooling for each working-class child had to be carefully considered by parents within the constraints of the family economy. Whereas the costs of schooling were relatively easy to determine, the economic benefits of schooling for children in a nineteenth-century manufacturing town were perhaps less obvious.[51]

The costs of schooling

The direct costs of schooling to be considered by working families were school fees, suitable clothing and shoes – costs which could be substantial for families, depending on their level of income and the number of children in the family. The indirect costs were much larger, however, as these represented the opportunity cost of the child's potential earnings. The establishment of the Blue Coat School in early eighteenth-century Birmingham aimed to remove the burden of the direct costs of schooling from poor parish families, but the number of places at the school was limited to 200 children with restricted access. One of the sermons preached by the Reverend Thomas Bisse at St Philip's Church emphasised the benefits of educating poor children 'to root out by degrees that race of idle vagrant poor, that sore evil and burden to this nation … that generation therefore of vagrant poor, which swarm in our streets and infest the land, are not born such, but bred up to it'.[52] This sermon, given on the opening of the school in 1724, was intended to persuade the wealthy parishioners of St Philip's to subscribe to the charity in order to solve the perceived threats of idleness, crime and vagrancy: 'Instead of the idle it brings forth the industrious; instead of the ignorant, the understanding, instead of the mischievous, the useful.'[53] The Blue Coat School aimed to prepare poor children for their allotted station in life by providing schooling up to the age of 14 and then placing them as trade apprentices or domestic servants. Nevertheless, free school places at the Blue Coat and other charity schools in Birmingham were very limited, providing around 300 school places in 1838 for a town of 45,000 children.[54]

More than 8,000 children were enrolled at dame schools or private common day schools in 1838, for which their parents covered the full fees. A further

---

50 BPP, 1864, 3414, *Third Report*, Appendix B, pp. 84–5.

51 Humphries, *Childhood and Child Labour*, p. 316.

52 Thomas Bisse, *Publick Education, Particularly in the Charity Schools*, pamphlet (London, 1725).

53 Bisse, *Publick Education*.

54 Victoria County History, *The City of Birmingham*.

3,000 children attended monitorial schools, which were partly supported by subscribers and partly fee-paying.[55] The average weekly fees at a dame school in Birmingham were 3d to 4d per week, with a small number of schools charging only 2d per week and 19 schools charging 6d per week. The fees for children attending common day schools in Birmingham were between 6d and 1s per week, with an average of 9d per week for boys and 8d per week for girls.[56] School fees for monitorial schools were substantially lower, ranging from 1d to 4d per week.[57] National School fees varied according to the location and efficiency of the school: St Paul's school in the jewellery quarter of Birmingham had a three-tier system, charging 9d per week for children of manufacturers and shopkeepers, 6d for journeymen's children and 3d for children of other working men.[58] A child's place at a monitorial school depended on recommendation by a subscriber; parents were thus placed in the position of having to make a request to their employer or other subscriber. One example is revealed in a list of requests to the firm of Boulton & Watt for recommendation to the National School at Handsworth, dated 14 January 1813 (see Appendix, table 8).

The list of requests to Boulton & Watt indicates that children attending monitorial schools in Birmingham were likely to be from families of relatively well-paid working men who could forego the potential earnings of their children. Some parents, however, disliked the notion of paying school fees for their children to be taught by other children, preferring instead to pay the higher fees at private common day schools. The Children's Employment Commission report in 1843 noted that at schools in the Staffordshire potteries

> monitors are appointed over each class. Boys, as well as girls, as soon as they arrive at eight, nine or ten years of age, are sent to work … parents even of the church have a strong objection to pay the weekly 2d, 3d or 4d for their children to be made the monitors of others, or to their receiving instruction from others as such.[59]

For other families, the inability to provide the clothing and shoes required by school rules was a major barrier to attendance. The Unitarian mission in Birmingham noted that the 'usual causes' for non-attendance at day schools were sickness and 'want of clothes' due to the extreme poverty of the parents.[60] The direct costs of schooling in the form of school fees and clothing were

---

55   Royal Statistical Society, 'Report on the State of Education in Birmingham', p. 27.

56   *Ibid.*, pp. 41–2.

57   Victoria County History, *The City of Birmingham.*

58   Frost, 'The Development of Provided Schooling', p. 370.

59   BPP, 1843, 431, XIV.

60   Frost, 'The Development of Provided Schooling', p. 369.

important to family budgets, but for some families they were less significant than the loss of children's earnings, which were for a Birmingham family's son around 3s 1d per week and for a daughter around 2s 5d per week, based on average rates of pay.[61] The availability of paid work for children in Birmingham meant that these direct and indirect costs represented significant disincentives for families to keep their children at school beyond the age of nine. How, then, were the benefits of schooling viewed and understood by working families?

The benefits of schooling

For the families of children sent to the Blue Coat School, the benefits included not only a child's upkeep, clothing and schooling but also the opportunity of a future apprenticeship in a respectable occupation. Blue Coat School boys in eighteenth-century Birmingham were apprenticed to trades such as engraver, gun-maker, brass-caster, cordwainer, brass-founder, baker and tailor. Prominent local industrialists had important connections with the school: for example, James Brown was apprenticed by the school in 1751 to John Baskerville to learn the trade of japanning and in 1766 George Craven was apprenticed to Matthew Boulton as a watch-chain-maker. In the following year, 1767, Matthew Boulton became treasurer of the Blue Coat School Charity.[62] Whereas boys were apprenticed to local artisans in the trades mentioned above, girls from the school were placed as domestic servants in tradesmen's households.

Children at endowed charity schools benefited from their school's links to apprenticeships and service placements in middle-class households, yet whether they obtained any improvement in social status is an issue debated by historians.[63] There is some evidence, however, to suggest that children benefited from attending schools with links to local employers, such as the Handsworth National School. Young workers employed at Boulton, Watt & Co.'s Soho Engine Manufactory included Thomas Wilkinson, aged 18, who had attended the Handsworth National School for more than three years and spent one year at Sunday school. He was apprenticed at 14 and worked as a fitter, earning 11s to 12s per week. William Harley, aged 20, had also attended the Handsworth National School for three years and Sunday school for four years.[64] Although the firm of Boulton, Watt & Co. was not exclusively connected with the Handsworth National School, many of their workmen's children attended

61   BPP, 1843, 431, XIV, p. 21.

62   BAH, MS 1622/2/1/1 Blue Coat School, Register of Pupils, 1724–83.

63   Alysa Levene, 'Charity Apprenticeship and Social Capital in Eighteenth-Century England', in Nigel Goose and Katrina Honeyman (eds), *Childhood and Child Labour in Industrial England: Diversity and Agency, 1750–1914* (Farnham, 2013), pp. 45–70.

64   BPP, 1843, 431, XIV, p. 163.

the school and the firm's proprietors contributed towards it.[65] The social capital acquired by pupils attending the school provided opportunities for them to become apprentices at the company. Moreover, it seems that education was viewed as an ongoing process by these employers, who encouraged apprentices to continue learning alongside employment: 'wages of apprentices are ample to allow them to subscribe to the evening schools and other institutions for their instruction, of which the greater number avail themselves.'[66] Some Birmingham employers established their own night schools for employees, such as brass-founders Winfield Brass Works in Cambridge Street and William Tonks and Sons of Moseley Street. From the employer's point of view, providing a night school created good relations between master and workers. As J.F. Winfield wrote in 1857: 'Your people become attached to you. They serve you from a love to you, because they feel you care for their best interests … . We have no strikes, no disorder.'[67] Winfield's paternalist approach illuminates the underlying motives of employers in creating a workforce that was educated, loyal and disciplined. At the same time, however, the willingness of young workers to attend evening classes after the working day highlights their desire for self-improvement through education.

For those children from the most destitute families, the industrialist William Chance founded Birmingham's first ragged school in 1845 at Windmill Street, near the town centre, with places for 280 children.[68] This example was followed by the opening in 1846 of St Philip's Ragged School in Lichfield Street and St Martin's Ragged School in Well Lane in 1848, offering school places to children from the most destitute families, those unable to afford either school fees or suitable clothing for their children. In fact, many working-class families in Birmingham went to great lengths to obtain some level of schooling for their children, the level of demand indicated by the wide range of schools established before the introduction of compulsory education. Parents typically sought a basic grounding in reading and spelling for their offspring, with the possibility of acquiring skills in writing and arithmetic at a later date, adopting a pragmatic approach in preparing their children for a lifetime of manual work. For the majority of people, access to flexible schooling that could accommodate the economic requirements of the family was the most important consideration. This approach to schooling contrasted with the views of school committees, who were confronted with the problems of irregular attendance and a high

---

65   *Ibid.*

66   *Ibid.*

67   Dennis Smith, *Conflict and Compromise: Class Formation in English Society 1830–1914: A Comparative Study of Birmingham and Sheffield* (London, 1982), p. 133.

68   Victoria County History, *The City of Birmingham.*

turnover of school pupils. Comments on poor school attendance made by the Reverend Wigram of Lambeth in 1835 illustrate the differences in perception:

> the evil complained of arises much more extensively from the indifference of parents to their children acquiring anything more than an ability to read and write. When this is once obtained, they have got the chief thing they want, and they do not choose to be under any restraint or to conform to the discipline arising out of settled rules.[69]

Reverend Wigram added that fluctuations in wages presented particular problems for school attendance; when wages were good 'the parents become high in their manners and difficult to manage' and during periods of low employment children were removed from school because they were needed at home or for 'the want of clothes'.[70] This view shows an awareness of working-class families' aspirations for their children in terms of acquiring basic literacy, but does not appreciate why earning a living or supporting the family in domestic duties took precedence over schooling. Moreover, it does not recognise the way in which families utilised a variety of strategies to access schooling for their children.

Strategies for combining schooling with child labour

One of the main strategies adopted by working families was to begin schooling as early as possible, before the age when children could obtain paid employment. From three years of age children could attend a local dame school, often run by a single schoolmistress in the living room of her own house. For a small fee of 2d to 3d a week mothers could leave their children 'out of harm's way', allowing them the freedom to undertake paid work either within or outside the home. The women running dame schools were unlikely to have formal teaching qualifications, but focused on teaching the alphabet and basic reading plus craft skills such as knitting and sewing. A toleration of absences and flexibility of hours at these local schools suited the needs of working families, but dame schools were strongly criticised by officials because of the teachers' lack of qualifications.[71] Despite this, many children appear to have received a good grounding in reading. Charles Shaw, born in Staffordshire in 1832, recalled attending 'old Betty W's school' from the age of three or four, where he learned to read: 'though she never taught writing, her scholars

---

69 Beryl Madoc-Jones, 'Patterns of Attendance and their Social Significance: Mitcham National School 1830–39', in Phillip McCann (ed.), *Popular Education and Socialization in the Nineteenth Century* (London, 1977), pp. 41–66 at 60.

70 Madoc-Jones, 'Patterns of Attendance and their Social Significance', p. 60.

71 Royal Statistical Society, 'Report on the State of Education in Birmingham'.

were generally noted for their ability to read while very young. I know I could read my Bible with remarkable ease when I left her school, when seven years old.'[72] Shaw's teacher may have been more proficient than some dame-school mistresses, but the schooling working-class children received at dame schools provided a base enabling them to progress to lessons in writing and arithmetic at Sunday school or night school. Shaw himself was a Sunday school pupil and credits his success at Sunday school with his early schooling: 'old Betty's teaching me to read so early and so well, placed me in front of much bigger boys, and by the time I was six years of age I was in a Bible class.'[73] As this example suggests, dame schools provided a valuable service for the working classes, offering a combination of childminding and nursery school services.

Families also used Sunday schools to secure schooling for their children without limiting their ability to contribute to the family economy. Working-class families may have followed the same route as wealthy Birmingham industrialist and philanthropist, Sir Josiah Mason, a self-made man whose schooling was a combination of dame school and Sunday school similar to that of Charles Shaw. Josiah Mason was born in Kidderminster, Worcestershire, in 1795, and attended a dame school next to his own house before beginning work at around the age of eight.[74] At this early age the young Mason became a street trader, buying cakes and rolls from a bakery and selling them from door to door for a small profit. He subsequently trained as a shoe-maker and learned to write at the Unitarian Sunday School in Kidderminster. He also attended the Wesleyan Sunday School 'for the purpose of making pens for the use of learners of writing, which was then commonly taught in Wesleyan Sunday Schools'.[75] Mason's Sunday school attendance not only taught him to write but possibly provided the inspiration for his highly successful steel-pen-making business, established in 1828. After moving to Birmingham in 1816 to work in his uncle's gilt-toy business Mason attended the Wesleyan Chapel and taught at the Wesleyan Sunday School in Erdington, where he later founded the Josiah Mason Orphanage in 1858.[76] The growth of Sunday schools during the late eighteenth century and early nineteenth century, particularly in the industrial towns, thus provided an important way for children to obtain further schooling beyond the age of seven or eight without any loss of earnings. The Sunday schools established by dissenters in Birmingham were more successful than Anglican Sunday schools in attracting increasing numbers of pupils because

---

72   Charles Shaw, *When I Was a Child: Autobiography of Charles Shaw* (London, 1903), p. 3.

73   Shaw, *When I Was a Child*, p. 5

74   John Thackray Bunce, *Josiah Mason: A Biography* (Birmingham, 1882), pp. 4–5.

75   Bunce, *Josiah Mason*, p. 8.

76   *Ibid.*, p. 17.

Table 6.2 Occupations employing the largest number of children and average age of starting work, Birmingham Educational Association Survey, 1857.

Boys aged 7 to 13			Girls aged 7 to 13		
Type of employment	*No.*	*Age of starting work*	*Type of employment*	*No.*	*Age of starting work*
Brass foundry	43	9 yrs 7 months	Button-making	34	9 yrs 2 months
Errands	31	9 yrs 5 months	Service	25	10 yrs 3 months
Button-making	23	9 yrs 1 month	Warehouse girls	8	11 yrs 6 months
Gun-making	11	9 yrs 1 month	Paper-box-making	6	10 yrs 7 months
Jewellery	11	9 yrs 10 months	Guard-chain-making	4	9 yrs 10 months
Glass-cutting	11	10 yrs 1 month	Pin-making	3	11 yrs 3 months

Source: BPP, 1864, 3414, *Children's Employment Commission 1862, Third Report*, Appendix B, 160.

they were prepared to teach writing and arithmetic on Sundays. Indeed, some of the Anglican clergy believed this practice encouraged parents to transfer their children to take advantage of the free lessons in writing and arithmetic.[77] This provides a further example of the strategies adopted by families to ensure their children could gain educational skills without interfering with their availability for paid work.

The Birmingham Educational Association survey of 1857, which involved 1,373 children between the ages of seven and 13, found that 42 per cent of children in the age group were attending day schools, 32 per cent were employed and 25 per cent were 'unemployed' or unoccupied. Sunday schools were attended by 63 per cent of children in the survey, confirming that they were an important source of schooling for a majority of children. Perhaps surprisingly, Sunday school attendance was higher among employed children than 'unemployed' or unoccupied children of the same age, possibly reflecting a lack of suitable clothing for children from the poorest families.[78] Of children aged between nine and ten 24 per cent were employed and 46 per cent were at school. By the ages of 11 to 12 years, 61 per cent of children were employed and 26 per cent at school, showing that by 1857 a majority of Birmingham children had been withdrawn from school to begin work, relying on Sunday schools to further their education. Birmingham industries employing the largest numbers of children included in the 1857 survey are shown in Table 6.2.

A further strategy used by families to maximise schooling opportunities without losing children's earnings was the selective use of private and voluntary

---

77   Frost, 'The Development of Provided Schooling', pp. 34–7, 205.

78   BPP, 1864, 3414, *Third Report*, Appendix B, p. 158.

THE INDUSTRIOUS CHILD WORKER

schools for children over the age of seven. Private common day schools expanded rapidly in Birmingham during the 1820s and 1830s, providing places for 4,280 pupils in 1838 compared with 3,331 pupils at the voluntary schools. The Birmingham Statistical Society for the Improvement of Education reported that common day schools were overcrowded, with poor teaching methods and a lack of moral instruction.[79] Nevertheless, private schools for the working classes in Birmingham continued to attract pupils until at least the 1870s. The Fitch Report identified 260 dame schools and common day schools in 1870 that were attended by 2,623 children over the age of five.[80] By this date there were 25,203 children enrolled in publicly aided elementary schools in Birmingham, indicating that state control over schools had been established, but differences of opinion about who should be in control of children's attendance and duration of schooling were yet to be resolved.

The popularity of private schools for working-class children for much of the nineteenth century was due largely to the amount of control parents were able to exert. Like dame schools, common day schools were located in working-class areas and, unlike the voluntary schools, they were not under the control of church or state authorities. Parents who could afford to pay the fees preferred to buy the services of a schoolmaster or mistress at a small local school, rather than send their children to a large voluntary school.[81] Private schools were willing to accept irregular attendances for children who might be needed for domestic or work reasons, thus fitting in with working-class lifestyles. They were lenient with regard to children's appearance and offered the type of schooling working families preferred: basic skills in reading, writing and arithmetic, and an absence of religious and moral instruction. Families also preferred private schools because they were perceived as more genteel, but in the absence of regulation many such schools were allegedly run by individuals with no knowledge or experience of teaching. An 1861 enquiry into popular education was particularly scathing about private schoolteachers in working-class areas of London: 'none are too old, too poor, too ignorant, too feeble, too sickly, too unqualified in any or every way, to regard themselves and to be regarded by others, as unfit for school-keeping.'[82] Birmingham schools were not included in the 1861 report, but the Fitch report detailed his visit to a private school in Birmingham:

79   Royal Statistical Society, 'Report on the State of Education in Birmingham', pp. 33–4.

80   BPP, 1870 (91) LIV 54, *Return of Schools for Poorer Classes of Children in Municipal Boroughs of Birmingham, Leeds, Liverpool and Manchester: Report on Quality of Education which Schools Provide*, p. 48.

81   Sanderson, *Education*, pp. 14–15; Stephens, *Education in Britain*, p. 82.

82   BPP, 1861, *Report of Commissioners into the State of Popular Education in England*, Vol. 1, p. 93.

I found 40 boys in the upper apartment of a mean and very dirty house … It is half past ten in the morning and the master is downstairs in his own sitting-room … it seems to be the normal state of the school that three-fourths of boys remain sitting at a time in complete idleness.[83]

Fitch concluded that qualifications of teachers in private schools in Birmingham were 'of the lowest order … teaching in the true sense of the word is almost unknown in the private schools … But the most striking characteristic of these humble private schools is the extraordinary idleness which prevails in them.'[84]

Although still popular with working-class families, the quality of private schools had remained unchanged over the decades, whereas elementary schools had improved with the introduction of state funding, trained teachers and the replacement of monitors by pupil teachers. A majority of school pupils were enrolled at public elementary schools by 1870, but in the absence of compulsion working-class parents failed to ensure regular attendance and persisted in removing children early. The average number of children actually attending elementary schools was 16,053, even though 25,203 children were enrolled. Furthermore, less than 50 per cent of pupils undertook the end of year examinations, with an average of 8,753 children successfully passing exams in reading, writing and arithmetic at the appropriate standard for their age group.[85] Following the implementation of the Revised Code in 1862, school funding operated on a payment-by-results system, making it essential for pupils to put in sufficient attendances and undertake the examinations. A school log book entry for a National school in Leeds highlights the extent to which schools depended on the attitudes of parents: 'the mistress asked all those children who were afraid of the Examination to put up their hands – the only hands held up were the Teachers.'[86] Publicly funded schools were under pressure to ensure that children attended regularly and were not withdrawn from school before taking the examination, putting teachers in conflict with parents over attendance, rules of behaviour, punishments and the school curriculum.[87] The situation in Leeds appears to have mirrored that in Birmingham elementary schools, where only a third of enrolled pupils passed the examinations on which school funding depended.

---

83 BPP, 1870 (91) LIV 54, p. 50.

84 *Ibid.*, p. 55.

85 *Ibid.*, p. 30.

86 Simon Frith, 'Socialization and Rational Schooling: Elementary Education in Leeds before 1870', in Phillip McCann (ed.), *Popular Education and Socialization in the Nineteenth Century* (London, 1977), p. 86.

87 Frith, 'Socialization and Rational Schooling', p. 85.

One final parental strategy for combining schooling with child labour was to lengthen the possible years of schooling by taking advantage of classes at evening schools. Children who received only intermittent schooling because of the economic circumstances of their family were able to enrol at evening schools without any loss of earnings. The 1838 Statistical Society survey identified 36 evening schools in Birmingham with 563 registered students.[88] Most of these schools were run by masters of common day schools and offered instruction in reading, writing and arithmetic, with some offering additional classes in grammar, geography, drawing and mathematics. Fees ranged from 3d to 1s per week, depending on the subject. Some working-class parents were highly ambitious for their children, seeking opportunities via trade apprenticeships followed by promotion within manual work. Children with basic schooling in reading, writing and arithmetic were thus able to extend their skills by studying additional subjects at a later date.[89] Evening classes in specialist subjects were provided by the Birmingham and Midland Institute, which in 1855 offered classes in physics, chemistry and physiology.[90] Around 39 per cent of students enrolled at the Institute were recorded as artisans, rising to 45 per cent of students in 1868, by which time the number of classes had risen to 14 and included writing, algebra, geometry, practical mechanics, French and German. The Institute offered 'penny classes' in arithmetic that proved so popular that teachers complained of overcrowding, indicating that young people in Birmingham were anxious to improve their prospects at work.[91]

The arithmetic class at the Birmingham and Midland Institute was included in Fitch's inspection of Birmingham schools in 1870: 'I saw the room inconveniently crowded with 154 young people, boys, girls and young men up to the age of 25, who formed the lower arithmetic class.'[92] Fitch was surprised to find so many young working people 'were ready to come on a winter's night into an inconvenient room, and sit for an hour solemnly listening to an explanation of the mysteries of compound multiplication, evidently as if the subject were quite new to them.'[93] The popularity of the penny class in arithmetic and other subjects showed evidence of young workers' desire for knowledge, yet Fitch viewed their enthusiasm as proof of the inadequate quality of schooling in Birmingham. This viewpoint was reinforced by a visit to the night school at the Winfield Brass Company for workers aged 13 to 18. In a class of 24

88 Royal Statistical Society, 'Report on the State of Education in Birmingham', p. 27.

89 Humphries, *Childhood and Child Labour*, pp. 329–30.

90 Smith, *Conflict and Compromise*, p. 146.

91 *Ibid.*

92 BPP, 1870 (91) LIV 54, p. 69.

93 *Ibid.*

boys who were tested by Fitch, only six reached the appropriate Revised Code school standard in reading and writing and only three in arithmetic.[94] These examples shine a light on how evening schools were perceived in two different ways: on the one hand, working-class families saw attendance at evening school as an alternative route into additional learning without impacting on paid employment. On the other hand, officials such as Fitch who wished to promote universal schooling viewed the demand for evening classes in literacy and arithmetic as evidence of the poor quality of existing schooling.

Conclusion

This chapter has examined the relationship between education, industrialisation and child labour, considering the question of how working-class families in Birmingham were able to access schooling for their children without any consequent loss of earnings from children's work. It began with the example of George Jacob Holyoake, one of 11 children from a working-class family in Birmingham. For children from families such as the Holyoakes, opportunities for schooling developed steadily over the nineteenth century. By the mid-century a variety of low-cost schools existed in Birmingham, from dame schools for the youngest children through to evening classes and penny lectures. Economic circumstances forced working-class families, especially those with numerous children, to weigh up the costs and benefits of sending their children to school. The direct costs of school fees, clothing and shoes were important considerations, but probably less significant than the opportunity cost of forfeiting children's earnings. In a manufacturing town such as Birmingham, where there was a high demand for child labour, the opportunity costs of schooling were greater than in market towns or county towns where there were fewer employment opportunities for children. On the other hand, the benefits of additional schooling beyond basic skills in literacy and arithmetic were more difficult to identify for children who were destined for manual labour.

This chapter has argued that Birmingham families adopted strategies to enable their children to access schooling on a flexible basis, facilitating children's availability for work. This might include beginning schooling at the age of three at a neighbour's dame school, followed by one or two years at a voluntary school or common day school before finding employment in a button manufactory or brass foundry at nine years old. After three or four years of schooling with a focus on reading and writing, children could attend school on Sundays or in the evenings after work. An important point to consider is that literacy skills were likely to be rapidly forgotten if children

---

94   *Ibid.*

did not continue to practice them after entering the workforce. This may partly explain why working children appeared to have been inadequately schooled when interviewed for official enquiries. In addition, children under pressure of questioning by a visitor on behalf of an Employment Commission would naturally be nervous and not respond well. The middle classes viewed education as desirable because it socialised children and controlled behaviour, producing more compliant employees. In contrast, working-class parents wished to retain control over their children, prioritising schooling that was appropriate for manual work with the expectation that children might contribute to the family income as early as possible. The evidence in this chapter demonstrates that differences of opinion over the form, duration and function of schooling were central to debates about child labour that continued throughout the nineteenth century.

7

The health and ill-health of child workers

Introduction

It seems self-evident that children's health must have been damaged by starting work at a very young age, but how far was this true? George Jacob Holyoake began his early working life making buttons in his mother's Birmingham workshop, where he was exposed to the dust from horn button-making and used a press, cutting shears, hammer, vice and file.[1] As a schoolboy he progressed to lantern-making using a soldering iron before beginning full-time work at the Eagle Foundry, where the dangers from molten iron and heavy machinery were ever present. Holyoake recounts the story of a workman whose leg was torn off when he was caught in a machine, and how he almost lost his own life as a child when he came close to being strangled in an accident at work. Fortunately, his calls for help were heard by a workman who 'stopped the machinery, and unwound me, just as the "chock" was beating into my throat … '.[2] Will Thorne also had a varied career as a child worker in Birmingham, beginning with the rope-works at six years old, followed by the brickyards, work as a plumber's mate and a role as a collector of cow and pig hair. By the age of 14 he was employed at a metal-rolling works with the task of removing metal bars from furnaces and placing them in an acid solution.[3] Thorne particularly recalled the scars he received from the 'brutalising' work of taking metal bars to be placed in 'pickling tubs' of acid solution: 'This biting acid would splash my hands and eat the flesh to the very bone … my clothes suffered badly from this solution: boots, trousers and shirts were attacked and eaten.'[4] Given the hazardous nature of these different jobs and the potential threats to health, questions arise about whether they were typical experiences for child workers in Birmingham and the extent to which the nature of children's roles in employment changed over time.

The relationship between early work and health has received relatively little attention from historians of child labour.[5] Some studies have utilised data on

---

1   Holyoake, *Sixty Years*, p. 19.

2   *Ibid.*, p. 24.

3   Thorne, *My Life's Battles*, p. 21.

4   *Ibid.*

5   Humphries, *Childhood and Child Labour*; Honeyman, *Child Workers*; Goose and Honeyman, *Childhood and Child Labour in Industrial England*.

stature as a measure of health in specific communities: a landmark study by Floud, Wachter and Gregory in 1990 found average heights of British males increased between 1740 and 1840, then decreased between 1840 and 1850, before increasing from 1850 onwards. This evidence, based on heights of military recruits, highlighted regional differences whereby men from Scotland and the north of England were taller than those from London and the south-east, and men from rural areas were taller than those from urban areas. The authors concluded that early industrial growth resulted in improved health and welfare among the working classes in general, but the impact of urban expansion tended to erode those benefits, leading to an overall decrease in average heights.[6] Further studies have found the heights of both rural and urban workers fell from 1780 and offer a number of explanations: a lack of adequate nutrition, adverse environmental conditions, chronic childhood disease and greater work effort.[7] These studies have identified a greater fall in urban living standards than rural ones during the early years of industrialisation, with a consequently more significant impact on children's health in urban districts.[8]

Concerns about the impact of factory work on children's health were identified in the 1833 Factories Report, with one physician, Dr Loudon, noting that factory children presented with 'stunted growth, relaxed muscles and slender conformation'.[9] This view was supported by Dr Hawkins of the Lancashire District, who reported on 'the lowness of stature, the leanness, and the paleness which present themselves so commonly to the eye at Manchester, and above all among the factory classes'.[10] Recent work by Peter Kirby has offered new perspectives on ill-health among child workers in textile mills through an interdisciplinary approach that places the health of child workers within the context of social, industrial and environmental change. He

---

6   R. Floud, K. Wachter and A. Gregory, *Height, Health and History: Nutritional Status in the United Kingdom, 1750–1980* (Cambridge, 1990); Roderick Floud and Bernard Harris, 'Health, Height and Welfare: Britain 1700–1980', *National Bureau of Economic Research*, 87 (1996), pp. 91–126.

7   John Komolos, 'Shrinking in a Growing Economy? The Mystery of Physical Stature during the Industrial Revolution', *The Journal of Economic History*, 58/3 (1989), pp. 779–802 at 793–5; Floud and Harris, 'Health, Height and Welfare', pp. 48–9; Pamela Sharpe, 'Explaining the Short Stature of the Poor: Chronic Childhood Disease and Growth in Nineteenth-century England', *Economic History Review*, 65/4 (2012), pp. 1475–94; Sara Horrell and Deborah Oxley, 'Bringing Home the Bacon? Regional Nutrition, Stature, and Gender in the Industrial Revolution', *Economic History Review*, 65/4 (2012), pp. 1354–79; Peter Kirby, 'Causes of Short Stature among Coal-Mining Children', *Economic History Review*, 48/4 (1995), pp. 687–99.

8   Stephen Nicholas and Richard H. Steckel, 'Heights and Living Standards of English Workers During the Early Years of Industrialization', 1770–1815, *Journal of Economic History*, 51/4 (1991), pp. 937–57 at 955.

9   BPP, 1833, 519, *Factories Inquiry Commission, Second Report*, Appendix 3, p. 5.

10   *Ibid.*, p. 6.

suggests, for example, that children from industrial towns were suffering from poor health and deformities such as rickets before beginning employment.[11] Potential risks to children's health at work included exposure to hazardous materials, such as dust and fumes; deformities caused by repetitive tasks; injuries resulting from accidents; and violence or ill-treatment of child workers by adult workers.[12] This chapter uses a similar approach to investigate whether links can be identified between child labour and ill-health in Birmingham and the West Midlands, utilising reports produced by the factory inquiries together with local medical records and newspaper reports. First, it addresses the question of how far children's health was affected by long hours of work and poor working conditions. Second, it examines the significance of children's exposure to hazardous materials and processes in the workplace. Third, it explores the experience of ill-treatment and violence against child workers.

Working conditions and child health

The first systematic account linking ill-health with occupation was Bernardino Ramazzini's *De Morbis Artificum Diatriba* (*A Treatise on the Diseases of Tradesmen*), published in English in 1746. This was based on his personal experiences when visiting workplaces in Italy to investigate workers in more than 50 occupations, including gilders, tinsmiths, glass-makers, printers, coppersmiths and brick-makers.[13] Regarded as the father of occupational medicine, Ramazzini identified the dangers of inhaling dust and fumes, exposure to excessive noise, heat, cold or humidity and musculo-skeletal disorders resulting from repetitive or restricted movements. In Birmingham and the West Midlands, meanwhile, differences of opinion emerged between local medical practitioners about the potential dangers of work in industrial environments. The Birmingham workhouse surgeon Thomas Tomlinson expressed the view in 1774 that 'the air and situation of Birmingham was very healthful', adding that 'the employment of the working people does not expose them to diseases or accidents, but is rather a means of their preservation from both.'[14] The exceptions were those whose employment involved the use of mercury and lead, such as gilding and painting, but these were 'a very small proportion comparatively with the rest'.[15]

A different view of occupational health was taken by Birmingham surgeon William Richardson, who wrote in 1790:

---

11 Kirby, *Child Workers and Industrial Health*.

12 *Ibid.*, pp. 27–35.

13 G. Franco, 'Ramazzini and Workers' Health', *The Lancet*, 354 (1999), pp. 858–61.

14 Thomas Tomlinson, *The Medical Miscellany* (Birmingham, 1774), pp. 203–07.

15 *Ibid.*, p. 203.

In the application of metals to the different arts, the persons employed are often injured to a great degree, by some of the particles entering their bodies; either in consequence of being swallowed along with the spittle, drawn in along with the breath, or absorbed by the pores of the skin.[16]

In addition to mercury and lead, Richardson identified processes involving copper, iron, tin and arsenic as potentially hazardous to the health of Birmingham artisans. To take the example of those who worked with copper: 'The makers of verdigrise and verditer, painters who grind and mix this last preparation with oils, and braziers, but in a slighter degree, are liable to take in some cupreous particles, which disorder the constitution somewhat in the same manner as lead.'[17] Richardson noted that these workers presented with sallow skin and green hair and spit and that they aged prematurely, with trembling limbs. In a second example, Richardson found that workers employed in forging and hammering iron were likely to suffer from eye injuries, recommending that specks of iron were removed by washing the eye with water or 'picking out the object with a needle. But these methods sometimes fail, in which case recourse must be had to the magnet, which will frequently succeed.'[18] In addition to accidental injuries, workers employed in the polishing and grinding of metal were likely to be affected by stomach and bowel illnesses caused by dust from the grinding stones. Richardson's 1790 account did not specifically mention any impact on the health of child workers. However, as each Birmingham workman traditionally employed one or two child assistants it seems inevitable that these children would also be at risk from exposure to dust, fumes or airborne particles.

William Richardson's investigation was one of a number undertaken by members of the medical profession linking industrial trades and occupations to illnesses. James Johnstone and Charles Hastings investigated lung diseases among needle pointers in Worcestershire, Thomas Percival studied lead poisoning and Arnold Knight focused on lung diseases of metal-grinders.[19] These studies were followed in 1832 by Charles Turner Thackrah's *The Effects of the Principal Arts, Trades and Professions and of Civic States and Habits of Living, on Health and Longevity*, in which he compared the relative health and life expectancy of industrial workers with agricultural workers and estimated that 50,000 people per year died from the effects of industrialisation

---

16   William Richardson, *The Chemical Principles of the Metallic Arts* (Birmingham, 1790), p. 189.

17   Richardson, *The Chemical Principles*, p. 190.

18   *Ibid.*, p. 192.

19   P.W.J. Bartrip, *The Home Office and the Dangerous Trades: Regulating Occupational Disease in Victorian and Edwardian Britain* (Amsterdam, 2002), pp. 14–15.

in Great Britain.[20] Thackrah's work was praised by the medical press, but state involvement in protecting workers from industrial illnesses was slow to emerge, with recognition of the 'dangerous trades' embodied in legislation only towards the end of the nineteenth century. The Factory and Workshop Act of 1895 was significant in identifying workers employed in trades involving lead, phosphorous, arsenic and anthrax as working in dangerous trades. These workers were typically from the poorest and least powerful sectors of society, and often included a high proportion of women and young people.[21] In the same way that industrial workers in the nineteenth century accepted long hours and poor working conditions, there was also a general acceptance that industrial illnesses were an inevitable part of earning a living. As well as changes in physical appearance, such as the greenish tint acquired by brass and copper workers, the common use of terms such as 'black spit' (miner's asthma), 'potter's rot' (potter's asthma) or 'Monday fever' (brass-founder's ague) illustrate the extent to which occupational ill-health was regarded as part of everyday working-class life.[22]

Legislation concerned with the health and safety of children working in industrial settings began with the 1802 Health and Morals of Apprentices Act, followed by the Factories Acts of 1833 and 1844. Early state intervention, however, focused on restricting hours of work for children employed in textiles mills and preventing accidents with textile machinery. Consequently, health and safety measures did not extend to child workers in industries such as the metal trades. The adverse effects of early work on children's health in Birmingham were recorded by a Birmingham physician, Dr John Darwall, in his published thesis *Diseases of Artisans*, presented to the University of Edinburgh in 1821.[23] Darwall was born in Birmingham and educated at the Free Grammar School before training as a surgeon, and was thus familiar with the main trades and methods of working in the town. He visited the Asylum for the Infant Poor in 1820, observing that children from the age of seven were employed in work that adversely affected their health: 'The power and ability of movement are completely lost and the height is obviously reduced. The knees too are often bent inwards and become weak.'[24] Based on personal observations, Darwall suggested that children were deformed by long hours of work in a sedentary position. Furthermore, he linked a range of diseases

---

20   *Ibid.*, p. 17.

21   *Ibid.*, pp. 267–89.

22   Anthony S. Wohl, *Endangered Lives: Public Health in Victorian Britain* (London, 1983), p. 264.

23   A. Meiklejohn, 'John Darwall and "Diseases of Artisans"', *British Journal of Industrial Medicine*, 13/2 (1956), pp. 142–51.

24   *Ibid.*, p. 144.

in adult workers to their occupations in local industries. Workers likely to suffer from pulmonary phthisis (tuberculosis), for example, were frequently employed in japanning, needle-pointing, sword pointing, gunbarrel-grinding, pearl- and horn-button-making and metal-grinding.[25]

A majority of child workers at the Birmingham infant asylum were employed in pin-making, with smaller numbers employed at straw-plait- and lace-making. These boys and girls were from pauper families admitted to the workhouse, and so were likely to be under-nourished, short in stature and perhaps in poor health before admittance to the asylum. It seems quite possible this particular group of children may fit the theory that child workers' health had already been already damaged before they started work by the environment and living conditions typical of industrial towns.[26] Their economic and social circumstances may have been similar to those of the London parish apprentices shipped in large batches from overcrowded workhouses to northern textiles mills. The Birmingham pin industry had a reputation for employing children from the most destitute families, a distinction that remained unchanged into the 1840s.[27] Elizabeth Dace, an overlooker at Phipson's pin manufactory, said:

> About half of the headers appear to have enough to eat, and are pretty well clothed; the other half don't ever know what it is to have enough to eat; some often come without breakfast … None but the poorest would like to send their little children to work at this trade.[28]

Sub-Commissioner Grainger found that many children in the Birmingham metal trades were very pale and weak in appearance, attributing the 'stinted growth' and general ill-health among workers to long hours of confinement in unhealthy conditions.

Boys apprenticed to small tradesmen in the metal manufacturing district of Willenhall in Staffordshire were in similarly poor physical health, suffering from overwork and adverse working conditions. Sub-Commissioner Horne's report to the Children's Employment Commission in 1843 cited innumerable cases of workers with distorted joints caused by long hours of working with hand tools and standing at a vice. These working practices caused malformations of the hands, wrists, shoulders and knees, so that the majority of older men in Willenhall were notable for their prominent knuckles, twisted

---

25   *Ibid.*, pp. 146–7.

26   Kirby, *Child Workers and Industrial Health*, pp. 36–53.

27   BPP, 1843, 430, XIII, p. 121.

28   *Ibid.*, p. 122.

wrists and deformed knees.[29] Excessively long hours, including night shifts, were also worked by children employed in the carpet industry at Kidderminster in Worcestershire. Eleven-year-old Homer Williams gave evidence to the 1843 Commission that after working through the night on the regular 12-hour shift he was 'hardly able to crawl along the streets to get home'.[30] Likewise, Elizabeth Taylor, aged 16, revealed she sometimes worked for 31 hours during a 36-hour period, with only one meal break and three hours sleep. And Louisa Jaff, aged 14, complained that working at nights as an assistant to a carpet-weaver had led to her becoming ill with a fever and inflammation of the chest. Given the excessive and unreasonable hours worked by children and young people in the Kidderminster carpet industry, it is hardly surprising that the Sub-Commissioner found them to be 'haggard, dirty and worn out'.[31]

The perception that child workers in Birmingham were generally weak and unhealthy was supported by medical evidence from Dr E.T. Cox, a surgeon with ten years' experience of examining military recruits enlisted in the region. Dr Cox recorded that recruits previously employed in agriculture were taller, stronger and healthier than mechanics from the manufactories, who were 'shorter, more puny and altogether inferior in their physical powers'.[32] Many potential recruits from Birmingham were rejected because they were below the standard height of 5ft 6 inches required to enlist in the marines. Additional evidence from Lieutenant Herbert, the recruiting officer for the district, confirmed that men formerly employed in manufacturing industries were frequently rejected due to poor physical build, lack of height and diseases caused by their occupation. In a list of 60 Birmingham men rejected for military service on medical grounds, 19 applicants were rejected by the Military Surgeon for 'want of stamina'.[33] Furthermore, Serjeant H. Buchan of the 82nd Regiment stated that he rejected three or four applicants each day in Birmingham because the general height of men in the town was around 5ft 4 inches or 5ft 5 inches – 'shorter than in any town he has known' – whereas men from the neighbouring country districts were 'generally taller and stouter'.[34]

This evidence of below-average growth and poor physical condition among workmen in industrial Birmingham confirms the findings of studies that have highlighted urban–rural differences in military recruits and convicts

---

29   BPP, 1843, 432, XV, Appendix II.

30   BPP, 1843, 431, XIV, Appendix I.

31   *Ibid.*

32   BPP, 1843, 430, XIII, p. 175.

33   *Ibid.*, p. 175.

34   *Ibid.*, p. 176.

facing transportation.[35] It seems reasonable to suggest that early work and long hours of labour in unhealthy working environments were significant factors contributing to the general ill-health and short stature typically found in Birmingham workmen. Sub-Commissioner Grainger concluded from his investigation that agricultural workers enjoyed better health, appearance and stature than the manufacturing population due to 'exercise in the pure air, moderation in the hours of work, and absence of night work'. In addition, he noted that children from country areas were 'better fed' than children from urban districts.[36] Child workers in Birmingham and the West Midlands were thus vulnerable to a combination of factors likely to have an adverse effect on their physical growth and general health, most notably long hours of work at a young age, poor nutrition and an unhealthy urban environment.

Environmental conditions in Birmingham workplaces that contributed to health problems included a lack of effective ventilation, contaminated air, excessive heat or cold and sedentary occupations. By contrast, the Commission found that Birmingham had a good water supply and an impressive availability of housing for individual families, as opposed to the shared accommodation typical of other industrial towns:

> There can be no doubt that the fact of each family having a distinct and usually comfortable dwelling has a most beneficial influence; it is probable that there is no large town in the kingdom where proportionally there are so many comfortable residences for the labouring population.[37]

However, such a favourable view of the state of working-class housing was not shared by all. Chadwick's report of 1842 on sanitary conditions in Birmingham found that 'the supply of water is ample, and pumps are to be seen in almost every court', but was less complimentary about the state of older housing and drainage in the town: 'The old courts are for the most part narrow, filthy, ill-ventilated and badly drained; … the privies in the old courts are in a most filthy condition.'[38] Courts in Birmingham consisted of back-to-back housing for up to 20 families sharing a wash-house, ash-pit and privy. Although the system of drainage and sanitation was poor, the report suggested that 'the comparative exemption of the inhabitants of this populous town from contagious fever may be in some measure owing … to the circumstance of almost every family

---

35   Floud et al., *Height, Health and History*, p. 20; Nicholas and Steckel, 'Heights and Living Standards', pp. 945–7.

36   BPP, 1843, 430, XIII, p. 42.

37   *Ibid.*, p. 101.

38   Chadwick's Report, 1842, pp. 193–4.

having a separate house … .'[39] Because families were unlikely to be living in shared housing they were less susceptible to contagious fevers such as typhus. In the year ending 30 June 1839, for example, the proportion of deaths in Birmingham from fever was one in 27 of all deaths, compared to one in 13 deaths in London and Liverpool and one in 12 deaths in Manchester. On the other hand, the proportion of deaths in Birmingham from pulmonary diseases was far higher than in these towns.[40]

The high rate of pulmonary diseases in Birmingham suggests the causes were related to its industrial base, however Chadwick's report identified 'only a few processes' as harmful, such as white-lead manufacture, gilding and dry-grinding of metal. It drew attention also to the dust produced in pearl-button-making, fumes in brass foundries and the unhealthy process of lacquering. Despite this, the report concluded that small, damp and poorly ventilated workshop premises were more detrimental to health than the actual work processes, and that employment in Birmingham industries could not be linked to any specific disease 'with the exception of those we have already noticed'.[41] Yet this latter category included metal-grinding and brass-foundry industries, representing some of the largest sources of employment in the region. The report also maintained that workers with a 'predisposition to disease' unfairly attributed their illnesses to 'harmless occupations', while more disease and death was caused by the poor lifestyle choices of workers, notably excessive consumption of alcohol, than by manufacturing occupations.[42]

It seems rather surprising that the 1842 report on the state of public health in Birmingham, which was produced by a committee of local physicians and surgeons, failed to make any clear links between ill-health and industrial occupations. It also denied the existence of employment of children under ten years of age in industry, other than in the pin industry, despite evidence from schools that children in Birmingham usually began work at the age of eight or nine years old. These conclusions suggest that members of the medical profession may have been wary of offending the town's wealthy industrialists, who were also the main subscribers and supporters of the voluntary hospitals. Hospitals in Birmingham, as elsewhere, were funded through voluntary subscriptions and support of fund-raising events, such as music festivals held in the Town Hall – that held in 1826 produced profits of £4,500 for the General Hospital, more than twice the annual income received from individual

39   *Ibid.*, p. 196.
40   *Ibid.*, p. 202.
41   *Ibid.*, p. 217.
42   *Ibid.*, p. 216.

subscribers.[43] Doctors were thus dependent on the goodwill of the Birmingham manufacturing elite to support them in establishing specialist hospitals such as the eye and ear hospitals, the children's hospital and the women's hospital. Their financial support and the strength of the local manufacturing economy placed Birmingham in a leading position for hospital provision when compared with other towns.[44]

Two decades later the extent of unhealthy working conditions in Birmingham workplaces was highlighted in the Children's Employment Commission Report of 1862. This enquiry identified overcrowding, lack of ventilation, poor lighting and insanitary conditions in numerous workplaces, including 'some of the establishments of the highest standing in Birmingham'.[45] It noted that large numbers of workshops were 'merely adaptations of common street houses', whereas some of the large button manufactories were so overcrowded that girls were 'creeping in under the women's legs and the benches' to join 'rows of little girls sitting back to back on common benches'.[46] William Aston's button factory employed 100 girls between the ages of seven and 13, a further 200 girls aged 14 to 18, and 300 women.[47] Overcrowding and lack of ventilation together with gas lighting contributed to the unhealthy working environment. Many of the younger girls interviewed at this factory complained of suffering from headaches and sore throats due to their work.

In some of the smaller workshops the working environment for children was even worse. Three young boys and a girl were employed at Cope's button workshop, where the manufacturing process involved boiling bones for bone buttons, which gave off an offensive smell, and where sacks full of bones were lying about.[48] Bone and vegetable ivory buttons were made using steam power at Lepper's button works, where the workshop was very dirty and there were with strong smells from the bones and vibration from the machinery. Three young boys – Thomas Hughes, aged 11, William Billingsley, aged 8, and Henry Hands, aged 9 – were found squatting on the floor in their task of cracking the ivory nuts.[49] As these examples illustrate, child workers in Birmingham were employed in unhealthy working environments throughout the nineteenth century. Moreover, although legislation in the 1830s and 1840s restricted the

---

43 Jonathan Reinarz, 'Industry and Illness: Investing in Health and Medical Provision', in Carl Chinn and Malcolm Dick (eds), *Birmingham: The Workshop of the World* (Liverpool, 2016), p. 243.

44 Reinarz, 'Industry and Illness', pp. 256–7.

45 BPP, 1864, 3414, *Third Report*, p. 53.

46 *Ibid.*, p. 53.

47 *Ibid.*, p. 91.

48 *Ibid.*, p. 99.

49 *Ibid.*, p. 101.

employment of children in mining and textile factories, children were not prohibited from other trades harmful to health, such as metal-grinding and the brass industry.

Industrial diseases and chronic conditions

Workers in the metal trades of Birmingham and the West Midlands risked damaging their health when exposed to fine dust particles. File-makers, metal-grinders, metal-polishers, pin-makers and gunbarrel-makers were just some of those who developed respiratory complaints. These typically began with a tightening of the chest and shortness of breath, followed by a persistent cough and eventually chronic bronchitis and the lung disease called 'grinder's asthma' or 'grinder's rot'. This condition was extremely well-known in Sheffield, where Dr Arnold Knight traced the origins of grinder's asthma in the cutlery trade back to the mid-eighteenth century, when some workmen became solely employed as grinders as a result of division of labour in the trade.[50] Dr Knight reported that from a total of 2,500 grinders in Sheffield in 1819 only 35 had survived to the age of 50, and none of the 80 fork grinders in Sheffield were above the age of 36 years. A further survey conducted into the deaths of 61 fork-grinders in Sheffield in 1843 established that 47 had died before reaching the age of 36, and none lived beyond the age of 50.[51] Following a visit to a Birmingham gunbarrel workshop that left him with a troublesome cough, Dr John Darwall focused his attention on the effects of dust as a cause of respiratory illnesses.[52] Yet Darwall's hypothesis on the dangers of exposure to dust and long hours of sedentary work to the health of young child workers in the pin industry was not taken into account by the Factories Inquiry Commission of 1833. Inspectors who visited Phipson's pin manufactory reported there was no evidence of ill-health, noting only that children were crowded together and spent long hours sitting down at work. Similarly, at Ledsam's button factory, where 87 children were employed, they found no signs of ill-health among child workers, describing the work as 'light'.[53]

The stated intention of the Children's Employment Commission of 1843 was to examine 'the influence of occupations upon the health of the artisan population of Birmingham'. It concluded that pearl button-making, lacquering, dry-grinding and brass-foundry work were unhealthy industries for workers[54]

---

50 Arnold Knight, *Observations on the Grinder's Asthma*, Medical and Surgical Society of Sheffield (Sheffield, 1822), pp. 5–8.

51 Wohl, *Endangered Lives*, p. 271.

52 Bartrip, *The Home Office and the Dangerous Trades*, p. 17.

53 BPP, 1833, 450.

54 BPP, 1843, 430, XIII.

and that large numbers of children were employed in button manufacturing, frequently starting employment from the age of seven as assistants to adult button-makers. Children usually worked from 8am to 7pm with breaks for meals, but when trade was brisk they were expected to work from 6am to 9pm alongside the adults. The child workers' task of 'putting in' or arranging the buttons for the stamper was a relatively simple process and because the normal working day was less than ten hours the Commission did not consider the work damaging to children's health. Nevertheless, the enquiry reported that some occupations for child workers were more hazardous than others even within the same industry. Large button factories were described by inspectors as spacious, light and airy, but small workshops that specialised in the manufacture of pearl, bone and horn buttons involved dusty processes that were clearly unhealthy for both adult and child workers.[55] At Thomas Bullock's horn- and bone-button factory in Cleveland Street, the bone-button workshops were 'very small, dark and close' with 'a great quantity of dust from cutting out the bones'. One young girl had the task of working at a machine for shaking buttons, which produced large amounts of dust, and some of the children were so small they were given stools in order to reach the lathe used for cutting and shaping buttons.[56] Very young children were employed in the pearl button trade 'as soon as they are in any way tall enough to reach the lathe' even though adult workers considered it an unhealthy trade because of the amount of dust. William Tonks, a pearl-button-maker who employed three children as assistants, remarked that the dust from pearl-buttons caused 'sickness and cough' and said he had known 'several who were not accustomed to it who have died from it'.[57]

Children working in small metal-polishing workshops alongside adult workers were also at risk from the effects of dust. At Wallis's Mill in Dartmouth Street, five metal-polishers employed a number of women, boys and girls in crowded workshops with 'a most noxious smell' and dust that 'makes the eyes smart'.[58] Some of the spoon-polishers routinely worked with their mouths covered by handkerchiefs to protect them from the lime-dust they used. Sixteen-year-old Elizabeth Thompson initially worked at making Florentine (fabric covered) buttons, but when that trade declined she became a spoon-buffer at Wallis's Mill. The spoons were polished with pumice and sand and finished with lime-dust that was known to give workers stomach complaints. Elizabeth often felt ill and said the spoon-buffers frequently complained about the use of lime, but the worst and most dangerous task of 'lime-shaking' was

---

55   *Ibid.*, p. 138.
56   *Ibid.*, p. 138.
57   *Ibid.*, pp. 140–41.
58   *Ibid.*, p. 158.

given to the youngest children in the workshop.[59] Joseph Childs, aged nine, was an assistant to a spoon-polisher with the job of wiping the spoons after polishing. Joseph said he was tired at night but could not sleep well because he had a cough and was forced to sit up due to 'a belly-ache and pain in his back'.[60] Similar hazards were encountered by apprentices in the glassworks of the Stourbridge district in Worcestershire. Boys in this industry were exposed to dust from putty powder made from lead and tin oxide, known to be harmful substances and possibly fatal if swallowed.[61]

Even though spoon-polishing and many other trades were recognised as unhealthy trades by the workers employed in them, the risks to health appeared to be accepted by workers as an inevitable price to be paid in order to earn a living. Furthermore, no special consideration was given to the health of child workers, perhaps because the long-term effects of dust or fumes, in the form of progressive and irreversible pulmonary disease, took many years to become apparent. The long-term effects on health reflected the situation in textile industries, where inhalation of cotton dust led to high levels of pulmonary diseases among cotton workers. Workers such as spinners rarely remained in the occupation beyond the age of 30 or 40, and it was commonly accepted that the development of asthma and other lung diseases was a normal consequence of the work.[62]

The 1843 Children's Employment Commission report identified the extent of pulmonary diseases such as chronic bronchitis in Birmingham, yet failed to make any link with occupations and trades in the town. The records of three Birmingham physicians covering the years from 1831 to 1835 indicated there were 7,220 cases of pulmonary disease, accounting for a sixth of the 45,951 patients treated. The number of deaths from pulmonary disease during this period was 678, representing a third of total deaths recorded in Birmingham. By comparison, there were 163 deaths from fever such as typhus and 286 deaths from contagious diseases such as smallpox and scarlet fever.[63] The report noted that pulmonary diseases were 'nearly twice as fatal as fevers in Birmingham', arguing that cases of fever were relatively low owing to the benefits of natural drainage, a good water supply and the availability of family housing in the town. The possible factors underlying high rates of pulmonary disease were not fully discussed, however, other than identifying certain occupations as 'producing injurious effects'. These more dangerous occupations

---

59   *Ibid.*, pp. 158–9.

60   *Ibid.*, pp. 158–9.

61   BPP, 1843, 432, XV, Appendix II.

62   Kirby, *Child Workers and Industrial Health*, pp. 78–86.

63   BPP, 1843, 430, XIII, p. 177.

included white-lead manufacture, gilding, dry-grinding, lacquering, pearl-button-making and brass foundry work.[64] Despite these caveats, child workers who spent long hours working in unhealthy industries were not included in the protective legislation introduced in the mid-nineteenth century.

High death rates in Birmingham from pulmonary diseases were again highlighted in the Fourth Report of the Medical Officer of Privy Council in 1861. The inquiry by Dr Greenhow found that for the period from 1848 to 1854 death rates from pulmonary disease of 8.38 per 1,000 males and 6.99 per 1,000 females were 'considerably in excess of the standard rate' for both adults and children.[65] Dr Greenhow attributed excessive deaths to local industrial occupations, most notably deaths of workers affected by dust and fumes, such as sword-grinders, edge-tool-grinders, pearl-button-makers, brass-founders and pin-pointers. Jewellers and goldsmiths were at risk of damage from the use of gas blow pipes, and workers in the button trade and steel pen trade suffered from over-crowding, lack of ventilation and excessive heat or cold. Furthermore, Dr Greenhow's report noted that 'young children of both sexes are employed at an earlier age, or for longer hours, than is permissible in factories worked under the restrictions imposed by the Factory Acts.'[66] Eight-year-old Daniel Thompson, for example, worked in a brass-casting workshop earning around 2s per week as an assistant to his father. When he first started work he 'felt short of breath and it hurt me in the chest and made me sick … coughed last night awful, and often cough here.'[67] Isaac Skivington had worked for 12 years as a brass-caster in a candlestick factory. Although only 25 years old, he was often ill with 'shivering' caused by inhaling the fumes and dense white smoke created by molten brass, and said: 'about 40 is the outside age a man works as a brass caster … casting is the worst job in Birmingham.' His assistant, 18-year-old Richard Marsh, had worked in brass-casting workshops from the age of nine. He had no symptoms of ill-health as yet, but always took the precaution of drinking milk for breakfast, 'it keeps the sulphur off your stomach. Have heard the casters say so.'[68]

There was a general recognition within the industry that brass-casting was an unhealthy trade, with several workmen confirming that very few brass-casters were still working at the age of 50 owing to ill-health. Nevertheless, many young boys from nine years of age upwards were employed in brass-casting workshops. The future health of these children was clearly at risk, as stated in

---

64   *Ibid.*, p. 181.

65   BPP, 1861, *Medical Officer of the Privy Council, Fourth Report*, p. 138.

66   *Ibid.*, p. 141.

67   BPP, 1864, 3414, *Third Report*, p. 66.

68   *Ibid.*, p. 68.

Dr Greenhow's report: 'Brass casters are almost unanimously said to be short-lived, and very liable to suffer from asthma.'[69] Similar hazards were faced by boys employed in the iron foundries and brass foundries of the Wolverhampton district, including the towns of Willenhall, Walsall, Tipton and Bilston.[70] The casting shops in iron foundries were generally lofty and open up to the roof, but they were still very hot and loaded with dust and vapour. The numerous brass-casting workshops in these districts were typically small and poorly ventilated, so that when metal was poured into the moulds the vapour was inhaled by the workmen and the boys assisting them. If the risks to health from casting were already well known within these industries, then why were so many young children employed?

The manufacturing and employment structure of Birmingham and West Midlands industries provides a number of possible explanations. The owners of factories and workshops in the region employed the adult workforce, often on a piece-work basis, but generally did not directly employ child workers. They could therefore deny any responsibility for the children on their premises. Rather, workmen typically employed one or two child assistants, without whom they could not complete their work. Moreover, as in the case of eight-year-old Daniel Thompson, workmen frequently employed their own sons as assistants, despite any potential risks. Additionally, the parents of child workers in these industries may have been unwilling to forego the wages children could contribute to family incomes where there was no immediate perceived threat to health. Child workers themselves seem to have been resilient in the face of potential injuries or ill-health. Henry Martingale, aged 11, was employed as a metal-polisher for a gun manufacturer and, although he suffered from a cough and sore throat from working with emery powder, he was more anxious to avoid the sparks that flew off the grinding wheel: 'sometimes they fly into my eyes. One piece stuck in the middle of it for a week, and at last the grinder got it out with his penknife.'[71] As this incident reveals, child workers and adult workers alike were faced with the serious and immediate threat of injuries or accidents at work, which were more urgent concerns than any possibility of future ill-health.

Some children in Birmingham were employed in industries that became officially identified as dangerous trades by the end of the nineteenth century, most notably those that involved work with lead, arsenic, mercury, phosphorus

---

69   BPP, 1861, *Medical Officer of the Privy Council, Fourth Report*, p. 145.

70   BPP, 1864, 3414, *Third Report*, Appendix A.

71   BPP, 1864, 3414, *Third Report*, p. 77.

or anthrax.[72] A century earlier, in 1790, the surgeon William Richardson had identified manufacturing processes using lead, arsenic and mercury in the Birmingham metal trades as dangerous to health.[73] The same threats were also discussed by Dr John Darwall in his thesis 'Diseases of Artisans with Particular Reference to the Inhabitants of Birmingham'.[74] White phosphorus was used almost exclusively for the manufacture of Lucifer matches, an industry in which, it was established in 1840, exposure to oxidising phosphorus vapour caused necrosis of the jaw.[75] Nonetheless, the Children's Employment Commission of 1862 recorded a number of Lucifer match factories in Birmingham where children of eight or nine were employed, including David Bermingham's factory in Aston Brook, Dowler's in Great Charles Street and Loder's in Hill Street.[76]

White lead was a common name for lead carbonate, a white powder used in the manufacture of paint and pottery glazes. Workers involved in the manufacture of white lead were at the greatest risk of lead poisoning, but painters and potters were also frequently affected through handling white lead and inhaling the dust or vapour when mixing the paints and glazes. The symptoms of lead poisoning included abdominal pains, anaemia, convulsions, paralysis and blindness, and in some cases proved fatal.[77] Edward Dayers, aged 14, was treated at Birmingham General Hospital as an urgent in-patient case in 1862, suffering from severe spasms. Edward had the tell-tale 'blue lead line' on his gums, confirming the diagnosis of lead poisoning brought on by his work as a painter of venetian blinds. He had been a painter for three years, working from 7am to 7pm in a workshop with little ventilation, with two younger boys working alongside him.[78] Work involving the use of lead or white phosphorus was known to be hazardous to health, yet these significant workplace threats continued to be ignored by employers. In addition, the evidence concerning children working in Birmingham's metal industries indicates that risks to child workers' health increased rather than decreased over the course of the nineteenth century as industries expanded to encompass new processes. To what extent was this indifference towards the health and well-being of children at work also reflected in attitudes towards accidental injuries and ill-treatment of child workers?

---

72 Bartrip, *The Home Office and the Dangerous Trades*, pp. 59, 137, 171, 233; Barbara Harrison, *Not only the 'Dangerous Trades': Women's Work and Health in Britain, 1880–1914* (London, 1996), pp. 55–7, 66–7; Wohl, *Endangered Lives*, pp. 265–70.

73 Richardson, *The Chemical Principles of the Metallic Arts*, pp. 193–9.

74 Meiklejohn, 'John Darwall and "Diseases of Artisans"', p. 147.

75 Bartrip, *The Home Office and the Dangerous Trades*, p. 177.

76 BPP, 1863, 3170, *Children's Employment Commission 1862, First Report*, pp. 91–4.

77 Bartrip, *The Home Office and the Dangerous Trades*, pp. 59–82.

78 BPP, 1864, 3414, *Second Report*, p. 146.

Industrial injuries and child workers

Accidents in Birmingham industries typically involved injuries to the fingers, hands, arms and legs caught in machinery; injuries to the eyes from dust and metal fragments; or burns from molten metal and explosions. The Chadwick Report of 1842 stated that accidents suffered by the manufacturing population of the town were 'very severe and numerous', identifying three main areas of concern: accidents caused by lack of fencing around machinery so that workers were dragged into machines by their clothing; accidents that resulted in severe burns and scalds; and accidents due to the inherent dangers involved in percussion-cap manufacturing.[79] However, the report did not specifically identify injuries to children and gave no details of industrial accidents. Records for the Birmingham General Hospital show that 29 working children below the age of 14 were admitted as urgent in-patients in the period 1840–48, yet none of these cases involved an accidental injury in the workplace.[80] These medical records suggest that accidents to children working in Birmingham factories and workshops were unlikely to have been of the serious nature indicated by the Chadwick Report. Most child workers in Birmingham at this time were employed to assist adults using intermediate technology such as the stamp and the press, and were thus more vulnerable to relatively minor injuries that did not require admittance into hospital.

Some injuries at work appear to have been fairly regular events accepted by children as an inevitable part of the job. William Hall, aged ten, worked at Ingram's horn-button factory, where he 'had many a crack on the head from the fly … has had a black eye from it'.[81] The 'fly' was a lever on the press operated by the button-maker and, since each button-maker employed two or three children, William's story suggests this type of accident may have been common among child workers. A serious accident occurred in 1840 at Clifford's rolling mill, where 13-year-old William Field was one of nine boys employed. William suffered severe injuries when his right hand was caught in the rollers, resulting in the loss of all four fingers on his right hand and one finger on the left hand as he tried to free himself. Charles Clifford, owner of the rolling mill, claimed the accident was due to the boy's carelessness in cleaning the rollers from the wrong side, which caused him to be pulled into the machine. Clifford denied that cleaning the rollers was a dangerous procedure for children.[82] Despite hearing this type of evidence from the Children's Employment Commission of 1843, no government action was taken to protect child workers in towns such

---

79   Chadwick's Report, 1842, p. 208.

80   BAH, HC GH/4/2/15, Birmingham General Hospital, Urgent Medical In-patients, 1839–48.

81   BPP, 1843, 430, XIII, *Second Report*, p. 139.

82   *Ibid.*, p. 157.

as Birmingham from dangerous machinery. Nevertheless, steps were taken by the government in the 1844 Factory Act to protect workers by the compulsory fencing of flywheels, gearing and shafts in textile mills to reduce the very high number of accidents. In 1849 factory inspectors reported 2,021 accidents in textile mills over a six-month period, involving 109 amputations and 22 deaths.[83] The failure to extend safety legislation to factories in Birmingham and other similar industrial towns may have been due to the relative absence of heavy machinery from Birmingham's industries at this time. Attitudes towards the health and safety of workers remained complacent, with employers typically blaming industrial accidents on the workers themselves, regardless of their age or experience. Official attitudes towards industrial safety, however, began to change over the following two decades.

The possibility of accidents caused by industrial machinery in Birmingham increased considerably over the following years as industries expanded to employ 19,500 young people under the age of 20, including 2,000 children below the age of ten in 1862.[84] The Children's Employment Commission highlighted the dangers of shafts and bands used for turning lathes and wheels, particularly in screw manufactories, where a large proportion of employees were female. The long skirts and loose shawls worn by women and young girls were a particular hazard near machinery. While noting that serious accidents to child workers were relatively rare, it suggested that this was due only to chance, citing the case of a woman factory worker who had recently been killed after becoming entangled in a shaft. The Commission's report included the details of a number of children and young people attending the General Hospital in 1862 as surgical in-patients: Robert Kelly, aged ten, was injured during metal-rolling, resulting in the amputation of his hand; Thomas Brand, aged ten, had a fractured forearm caused by a mill-band; William Inman, aged 9, had a wound on the sole of his foot after treading on waste metal in a workshop; Edward Cartwright, an 18-year-old moulder, had a burn on his foot from a hot iron; William Matthews, aged 14, had severe burns of the arms and legs from an accident with liquid metal during brass-casting; and Mary Kennedy, aged 18, suffered severe lacerations described as 'probably fatal' after being caught in cogwheels at a penholder works.[85] At the same time, less serious accidents involving injuries to fingers and thumbs from the use of stamps and presses were extremely common. A well-known saying among workers in Birmingham was that 'a person cannot be a good stamper till he has lost two or three

---

83   Kirby, *Child Workers and Industrial Health*, p. 98.
84   BPP, 1864, 3414, *Third Report*.
85   *Ibid.*, p. 147.

Table 7.1 Industrial injuries at Birmingham General Hospital, April–June 1862.

M/F	Age	Occupation	Part injured	Cause
M	13	Guns	Finger	
M	12	Guns	Finger	
M	10	Guns	Forearm	Chisel
M	10	Firewood		Resin burn
M	13	Press	Finger	Press
M	13	Clogs	Finger	
M	11	Guns	Arm	
M	11	Stamping	Finger	Stamp
F	13	Cutler	Thumb	Press
M	12	Buttons	Finger	
M	11	Guns	Hand	Bayonet
M	11	Finisher	Finger	Wood
M	10	Brass	Finger	Press
M	12	Gilding	Foot	Sulphuric acid
F	12	Press	Finger	Press
M	9	Brass	Finger	
M	12	Buttons	Finger	Press
M	10	Saws	Finger	Saw
M	12	Shears	Finger	Shears
M	12	Guns	Finger	
M	13	Guns	Thumb	
F	10	Press	Finger	Press
M	12	Files	Abdomen	
F	13	Tin-work	Thumb	Shears
M	10	Hinges	Finger	Machine
M	11		Hand	Press
M	13	Drilling	Finger	Hook
F	12	Press	Finger	Press
M	12	Printer	Finger	Press
F	13	Buttons	Finger	Press
M	11	Machine	Finger	Stamp

Source: BPP, 1864, 3414, *Children's Employment Commission 1862, Third Report*, p. 158.

fingers'.[86] The out-patient book at Birmingham General Hospital for the two months ending 19 June 1862 shows there were 31 injuries to children under 14 resulting from accidents at work (Table 7.1).

The potential danger from industrial accidents was made particularly clear to Assistant Commissioner White when a significant explosion occurred at Walker's percussion-cap factory in the centre of Birmingham just three days after his visit in 1862. Nine workers died in the explosion and at least 40 were injured, many of them young girls. Fatal injuries were suffered by ten-year-old Emily Holmes, who was employed in the warehouse, Rosanna Whately, aged 13, and Anna Maria Wood, aged 14. This accident was preceded by five or six previous explosions in Birmingham, including one in 1858 that resulted in the deaths of 19 people.[87] Birmingham's four percussion-cap factories were based in premises adapted from private houses and located in crowded residential streets. Hence, the Commission recommended that the dangerous processes of priming, mixing and drying should be moved to buildings separate from other workshops.[88] Unfortunately, these safety measures did not prevent a series of serious explosions at percussion-cap factories during the next decade.

The *Birmingham Daily Post* reported a large explosion on 17 November 1870 at Kynoch's ammunition manufactory at Witton on Birmingham's outskirts, the ninth such explosion to take place since the opening of the factory in 1862.[89] It resulted in eight deaths including those of five children: James Whiting, Eliza Hale, and Eliza Reeve, aged 12, and Elizabeth Bracey and Charles Matthews, aged 11. At least 20 other workers were injured by the explosion. The inquest held on 25 November revealed that James Whiting was admitted to the General Hospital with severe burns on his face, arms and body but died the following day. Eliza Hale died from burns three days later and Charles Matthews after seven days.[90] The tragedy at Kynoch's factory was followed just three weeks later on 9 December 1870 by a further large explosion involving fatalities at nearby Ludlow's cartridge factory.[91]

The evidence from these serious explosions, together with the other cases detailed above, illustrates that child workers in industry were at considerable risk from accidents in the workplace. The injuries they suffered ranged from relatively minor – damage to fingers, for example – to very serious, resulting in amputation of limbs, severe burns and the tragic loss of young lives. Although

---

86 *Ibid.*, p. 158.

87 BPP, 1863, 3170, p. 105.

88 *Ibid.*, p. 57.

89 'The Witton Explosion', *Birmingham Daily Post*, 26 November 1870.

90 *Ibid.*

91 'The Explosion at Messrs Ludlow's, Witton', *Birmingham Daily Post*, 22 December 1870.

steps were taken to protect children working in textile factories and mines in the 1840s, the health and safety of child workers in other industries appears to have been seriously neglected until decades later.

Ill-treatment of and violence towards child workers

Peter Kirby has argued that any analysis of the ill-treatment of children in the workplace should be set within a wider social context, as children in the eighteenth and nineteenth centuries were routinely exposed to violence as part of everyday life. Not only was physical discipline commonplace in schools and at home but children were likely to have witnessed drunken fights, the ill-treatment of animals for sport or violent industrial disputes. Furthermore, violence towards child workers was linked to their social background rather than occupation, so that the children most likely to suffer severe violence in the workplace were parish apprentices and illegitimate children sent to work at an early age.[92] Birmingham industries did not employ large groups of parish apprentices in the same way as cotton mills did, but the numerous young children in pin-making were known to be drawn from the most destitute families. Sub-Commissioner Grainger visited the premises of Phipson's pin factory at 7.45pm on 8 December 1840. The adult workers had finished for the day, leaving the children at work supervised by a female overlooker who carried a cane. By chance, the Sub-Commissioner arrived in time to witness the woman striking one of the children with the cane.[93] This was evidently not an isolated event, as overlooker John Field confirmed that children were sometimes 'corrected' with the cane on the head or back. The female overlooker concerned, Elizabeth Dace, said if the work was not done properly she gave the child 'a tap with the cane on the back, has never struck a child over the head or face'. Mary Bowling, who had worked at Phipson's since the age of seven stated that Elizabeth Dace often used the cane on the children, especially at night when they became tired.[94] This evidence suggests that overseers in the impoverished pin trade resorted to violence to keep tired young children working at night after the adult workers had left. It demonstrates that children from the lowest end of the social scale were likely to be ill-treated by supervisors or overseers, even when they were not living away from their homes and families. It also supports the contention that socially deprived children were those most likely to be the targets of workplace violence by revealing that ill-treatment was not restricted to parish apprentices. There is additional evidence, however, to show that parish children were routinely subjected to harsh punishment from their employers in many West Midlands industries.

---

92   Kirby, *Child Workers and Industrial Health*, pp. 124–8.

93   BPP, 1843, 430, XIII, p. 119.

94   *Ibid.*, pp. 121–2.

Children from Coventry, Tamworth and Walsall were frequently apprenticed by their parishes to metal-workers in the south Staffordshire town of Willenhall. The 1843 Commission reported that these apprentices were 'shamefully and most cruelly beaten' by their employers 'with a horsewhip, a strap or a stick'.[95] Sub-Commissioner Horne witnessed boys with fresh bruises, sores and scars caused by beatings with hammers, files, iron tongs and other tools used by the workmen, and stated: 'The treatment of the apprentices is atrocious and no care whatever is taken of them.'[96] In a similar example, children hired annually by the nail-makers of the Sedgley district in south Staffordshire were also treated with great cruelty. These boys were sometimes beaten with red-hot irons or showered with white-hot sparks from iron bars taken straight from the forge. In one incident reported to the sub-commissioner a workman punished a boy for poor workmanship by hammering a nail through his ear.[97]

Parishes sent large numbers of children as apprentices in the south Staffordshire coalfields, where they were controlled by contractors, or butties. The Bilston colliery alone had 200 to 300 apprentices, although some parishes refused to send their children to the area because of its reputation for the harsh treatment of child workers. William Gove, a mine agent, stated that apprentices were forced to work in coal seams where the men themselves would not work. This information was endorsed by a miner, John Greaves, who added that most of the men wore a leather strap which they readily used against the boys.[98] Violence towards child workers was also widespread in the carpet industry at Kidderminster, in Worcestershire. Boys working as assistants to carpet-weavers were routinely subjected to physical attacks by being kicked or beaten with a wooden rod.[99] Young girls employed in the carpet industry were also ill-treated, becoming the victims of sexual abuse when working alone at night with a male weaver. The Commission heard from parents that the lives of hundreds of girls in Kidderminster were ruined in this way, with the result that numerous illegitimate children were born to young females working in the carpet trade. A letter received by Sub-Commissioner Scriven highlighted the problem in Kidderminster of 'the frequent seduction by married men because of solitary night-working with draw-girls … girls become mothers at the earliest age'.[100]

Incidents of violence towards children in the Birmingham button industry were reported by some of the adult workers. Daniel Baker described boys who were

95   BPP, 1843, 432, XV, Appendix II.
96   *Ibid.*
97   *Ibid.*
98   BPP, 1842, 380, Appendix.
99   BPP, 1843, 431, XIV, Appendix I.
100 *Ibid.*

'severely beaten' by the men who employed them, including a boy struck with iron tongs. Button-stamper John Harrold said that men often worked rapidly to make up for lost time and if the boys could not keep up with them 'they were ill-used and knocked about. Has seen little boys, 7, 8, or 9 years old, seriously beaten.'[101] Statements provided by child workers themselves indicate that they accepted certain levels of violence as part of the harshness of everyday life. Thirteen-year-old William Chaplin, who was employed at a button factory, reported: 'Gets a box (on the ears) if he neglects his work'; William Hall, aged ten, who was working at Ingram's Horn Buttons, said: 'Gets a rap now and then, has never known any lad seriously beaten'; Benjamin Bradley, aged seven, a japanner, was 'never beaten, except a box on the ear, which does not hurt him'; and spoon-buffer William Lawless, aged nine, said: 'When the boys neglect their work the master corrects them, he beats them with the strap, he does not hurt them much but frightens them.'[102] These statements explain that children accepted and perhaps expected to receive some physical punishment from the workmen who employed them. However, since the children were interviewed in the workplace it seems unlikely that they would have complained about excessively harsh treatment for fear of the consequences. Punishment from adults was therefore typically described as a 'rap' or 'tap', which 'did not hurt much' and was quickly dismissed.

Child workers may have adopted a brave front when interviewed, but it was not necessarily the case that they were hardened by everyday violence and thus immune to acts of ill-treatment in the workplace. The premier of New South Wales, Sir Henry Parkes, never forgot his own experience of being subjected to violence as a child worker in Birmingham, despite his later success and rise to political prominence.[103] Born in 1815, Henry Parkes was the son of a tenant farmer on the Stoneleigh estate in Warwickshire. His family fell on hard times during an economic downturn and they later moved to Birmingham when the father was imprisoned for debt. At the age of 11 Henry found work in a rope works, where, on one particularly memorable occasion, he was attacked by an overseer with a crowbar, leaving him unconscious.[104] This attack clearly left a strong impression that remained with him throughout his life. Similarly, the trade union leader and MP Will Thorne also remembered the violence he received when employed in a brickyard at the age of nine. Working to support his widowed mother and sister, he had to walk the four miles to work from home. The brick-maker worked very quickly and, if kept waiting, 'he would give me a sharp tap on the head with a piece of wood used for levelling the clay at

---

101   BPP, 1843, 430, XIII, pp. 128–9.

102   *Ibid.*, pp. 138–58.

103   Stephen Dando-Collins, *Sir Henry Parkes: The Australian Colossus* (Sydney, 2013), pp. 8–11.

104   Dando-Collins, *Sir Henry Parkes*, pp. 8–11.

the top of the brick mould.' By the age of 14 Thorne was working at a metal-rolling mill, where he was given the task of keeping the metal straight and tight on the rollers, 'otherwise it became spoilt and I received many a sharp knock or blow from my overman, Jack Groves'.[105] Will Thorne and Sir Henry Parkes remembered for decades their ill-treatment as children at the hands of adult workmen, underlining the fact that childhood experiences of violence had long-term psychological as well as physical effects that were not easily forgotten.

The Birmingham Association for the Suppression of Climbing Boys began campaigning in the 1830s against the use of climbing boys by chimney-sweeps. A series of Acts passed in 1788, 1834 and 1840 aimed at preventing chimney-sweeps from employing climbing boys, yet a lack of enforcement meant the legislation was continually ignored. The Birmingham campaign was headed by prominent business leader John Cadbury and supported by chimney-sweep Richard Bennett, who was a former apprentice climbing boy. Bennett recalled being forced up chimneys two or three times a day as a child.[106] Despite the efforts of the Birmingham Association in funding prosecutions against sweeps who disobeyed the law, there were still 25 climbing boys employed in Birmingham in the 1860s.[107] The practice eventually ceased after the introduction of the Chimney Sweepers Act in 1875, which required sweeps to be licensed and made it a duty of police to enforce all previous legislation. The history of the campaign against climbing boys illustrates that even national campaigns and government action failed to protect vulnerable children from exploitation by unscrupulous adults in the absence of legislation backed up by enforcement.

A second group of young people who were at particular risk of abuse and in need of protection were the girls and young women who were drawn into prostitution, a problem that was widespread in 1840s Birmingham and perceived by the police to be linked to early employment. Police records show that in 1840 Birmingham was home to 200 brothels, 110 'houses of ill-fame' and 187 'houses where prostitutes lodge'.[108] The keeper of Birmingham prison, George Redfern, reported that prostitution had greatly increased in the previous few years, adding that it was so common 'as to be regarded as a not unusual mode of obtaining money, like other employments'.[109] Redfern and local police officers believed that many country girls from Worcestershire and Shropshire arrived in Birmingham to find work as servants, before

---

105 Thorne, *My Life's Battles*, pp. 18–22.

106 BAH, MS 466/253 Richard Bennett, A Few Extracts from Memory to the Association for the Suppression of Climbing Boys, 1858.

107 BPP, 1863, 3170, lxxxiv.

108 BPP, 1843, 430, XIII, pp. 172–3.

109 *Ibid*, pp. 172–3.

turning to prostitution to earn a living. But, more significantly, they stated that 'promiscuous mingling' of boys and girls in local manufactories resulted in girls taking the first steps to prostitution at the age of 13 to 15. Police constable John Upton, who had been given the specific task of obtaining information about juvenile prostitutes and thieves, believed that boys and girls working together in factories formed close personal relationships in which girls were seduced and then abandoned, subsequently leading them into prostitution. In Upton's words, 'Girls who are seduced in this way frequently become prostitutes. They rarely marry the party who is the seducer.'[110] Upton added that prostitution amongst factory girls had increased partly because of 'shortness of trade' and that 'in general the girls employed in the manufactories of this town are not virtuous.'[111] Police Inspector William Hall said that in the lodging houses and brothels of the town, there were many juvenile prostitutes who worked in manufactories during the daytime. Several of these girls between the ages of 13 and 15 were suffering from venereal diseases. He added that many of them 'fall into this condition in consequence of the vicious habits of the parents. Sometimes from the drunkenness of the father; sometimes from the second marriage of the mother, leading to disputes and strife.'[112] It could be argued that these nineteenth-century police attitudes towards factory girls who had turned to prostitution have parallels with modern-day cases involving the grooming and sexual abuse of teenage girls. Cases brought before the English courts in 2015 and 2016 revealed that police officers and social workers had failed to intervene on behalf of the girls involved because they believed the victims had made 'a lifestyle choice.'[113]

Similar views on prostitution were held by middle-class female reformers who established charities in the later decades of the nineteenth century. Women from prominent nonconformist Birmingham families focused on poverty as a major cause of prostitution, joining organisations such as the Ladies Association for Friendless Girls and setting up Reform Homes for young women convicted of prostitution.[114] Birmingham was not unusual in this respect: juvenile prostitution during the nineteenth century was widespread in London and in ports such as Liverpool.[115] One of the issues contributing to the sexual exploitation of children

---

110 *Ibid.*, p. 173.

111 *Ibid.*

112 *Ibid.*

113 'Rochdale grooming trial', *The Telegraph*, 8 May 2012; 'Rochdale grooming case', *The Guardian*, 8 April 2016; 'I exposed the Rochdale scandal', *The Guardian*, 15 May 2017.

114 Paula Bartley, 'Moral Regeneration: Women and the Civic Gospel in Birmingham, 1870–1914', *Midland History*, 25/1 (2000), pp. 143–61 at 146–8.

115 James Walvin, *A Child's World: A Social History of English Childhood, 1800–1914* (Harmondsworth, 1982), p. 144.

was the legal age of consent, which remained at 12 years for much of the period. Research by Sarah Toulalan into trials for rape and sexual assault at the Old Bailey between 1694 and 1797 has found that approximately half of the cases involved child victims aged 14 and under.[116] From a total of 109 girls involved in these trials, only 17 were between the ages of 12 and 14, indicating that allegations of rape and sexual assault were more likely to be brought to court where girls were below 12. Government intervention increased the age of consent from 12 to 13 years in 1875, and to 16 years in 1885 under the Criminal Law Amendment Act, which also gave police the powers to close down brothels. As was the case with climbing boys, juvenile prostitution required legislation and enforcement to tackle the problem of the sexual abuse of young girls.

Interviews with child workers in Birmingham for the Children's Employment Commission enquiry of 1862 differed from the 1843 enquiry in that none of the children mentioned acts of violence or ill-treatment in the workplace. There may be a number of possible explanations for this. First, it seems likely that children in 1862 were not directly questioned about violence towards them, and as interviews were held in the workplace it is unlikely that such information would have been volunteered. Second, it is possible that attitudes towards child workers had changed since the 1840s. There was a great demand for child labour in Birmingham and few young children were apprenticed. They were therefore free to leave any employer who was violent towards them and find employment elsewhere. Third, by 1862 there were no large groups of very young children in a single industry, as had been the case with the pin industry of the 1840s. On the other hand, child workers were likely to be punished for working too slowly by adult workers dependent on piece-work payment. Some insights can be gained from interviews conducted with young workers who had been admitted as in-patients to Birmingham General Hospital.

Joseph Hood, 17, was admitted to hospital suffering from heart disease brought on by rheumatic fever. He had been employed in the glass industry for four years, working six-hour shifts by day and at night. As Joseph disclosed, 'The men are not very kind to you in a glass-house; they're rough brutes there.'[117] Boys were beaten on the head with iron pinchers or were kicked and sworn at for making small mistakes. They did not report this behaviour to the glass-house master, or they would be beaten again by the workmen. Boys were often knocked down to the ground and kicked, and in one incident a 12-year-

---

116 Sarah Toulalan, 'Child Sexual Abuse in Late Seventeenth and Eighteenth-Century London: Rape, Sexual Assault and the Denial of Agency', in Nigel Goose and Katrina Honeyman (eds), *Childhood and Child Labour in Industrial England: Diversity and Agency, 1750–1914* (Farnham, 2013), pp. 23–44 at 24.

117 BPP, 1864, 3414, *Third Report*, p. 145.

old boy was hit 'on the back of his head with the blowing iron, which had some glass on the end of it, and cut his head open'.[118] Joseph Slater, 14, had worked in a foundry from the age of ten, and was admitted to hospital with acute rheumatism. He also revealed that boys were regularly hit and kicked by the workmen: 'One man kicked me on the bottom of the spine so that I could not bend my back for two or three days.'[119] A third hospital patient, ten-year-old George Ingram, was left at the hospital by his two employers. The doctors reported that George was at 'the point of death from English cholera', but had been abandoned on a bench by the men 'without a word of information or concern'.[120] The callous treatment of George Ingram and the violence described by Joseph Hood and Joseph Slater suggests there had been little change in attitudes towards the ill-treatment of child workers in the two decades from 1840 to 1860. It seems likely that children interviewed in the workplace by the Commission were not questioned on this topic, perhaps in order to avoid any reprisal from the workmen. It also appears that children working in certain industries were subjected to routine violence from adult workers in the form of beatings, kicks and blows to the head. Kirby argues that most punishments in the workplace 'tended to be moderate' and were closely related to safety in the workplace: for example, the role of child trappers in opening ventilation doors in mines was essential for safety.[121] While this may have been the case in some circumstances, Kirby's conclusion that 'the beating of child factory workers was extremely rare'[122] is not supported by the evidence of children in Birmingham and West Midlands industries.

Conclusion

Thousands of children were employed in Birmingham and West Midlands industries during this period, yet first-hand accounts of children's work are rare. The danger from accidents and violence in the workplace described by George Jacob Holyoake, Will Thorne and Henry Parkes provide small but significant insights that are reinforced with evidence from the factory enquiries and newspaper reports. Holyoake's memories of his near-fatal accident at work remained with him during his lifetime, as did Thorne's memories of working at Abraham's metal-rolling and ammunition works.[123] In addition to accidental injuries or injuries from violence, children were exposed to numerous risks to

---

118   *Ibid.*, p. 145.

119   *Ibid.*, p. 145.

120   *Ibid.*, p. 146.

121   Kirby, *Child Workers and Industrial Health*, p. 142.

122   *Ibid.*, p. 150.

123   Holyoake, *Sixty Years*; Thorne, *My Life's Battles*.

their health, such as the dust and fumes that could lead to serious pulmonary disease. Ramazzini's work linking ill-health and occupations, which was available in English from the 1740s, was followed in 1790 by William Richardson's detailed analysis of the health risks related to specific Birmingham metal industries.[124] Despite the existence of this scientific evidence, and indeed the acceptance by workers themselves that occupations such as metal-grinding and brass-founding were injurious to health, children continued to be employed in these industries throughout the nineteenth century. The effect on children of exposure to these hazards is particularly difficult to establish, as the chronic damage done to health became apparent only many years afterwards. However, the high death rates from pulmonary disease reported in Birmingham in the 1840s and 1860s indicate that child workers were being placed at risk of long-term ill-health.[125] Measures to combat these problems were not addressed until the implementation of the 1867 Factory and Workshops Acts, which required factories and workshops producing dust to install extraction fans. The 1867 Acts also restricted employment to children of at least eight years of age, raised to ten years of age in 1878.

Industrial injuries to children and young people were frequent but often relatively minor, perhaps involving fingers caught in a stamp or press. The expansion of Birmingham industries over the course of the nineteenth century, however, resulted in increased threats of harm to child workers from large-scale machinery, such as metal-rolling machines, and from industrial processes involving acids, molten metal and explosives. Reports of serious burns and fatal injuries to child workers in percussion-cap-factory explosions between 1862 and 1870 further highlight the increased risks children faced when compared with the earlier years of industrialisation. Moreover, the ill-treatment of child workers in factories and of climbing boys illustrates the violence children could experience from adults in the workplace.

Will Thorne had worked from the age of six, yet his memories of Abraham's metal-rolling and ammunition works offer a graphic and disturbing description of dangerous working conditions: 'The roar and the rattle, the steam and the heat of that inferno remains vivid in my memory, and many times I have dreamt of the place, waking up in a cold sweat of fear.'[126]

---

124 Richardson, *The Chemical Principles*, p. 190.

125 BPP, 1861, *Medical Officer of the Privy Council, Fourth Report*, pp. 138–50.

126 Thorne, *My Life's Battles*, p. 21.

8

Set adrift: Birmingham's child migrants

Introduction

Eleven-year-old Mary A. of Dale End was sent to the Birmingham workhouse for seven days' 'correction' in January 1878 after being caught stealing. Mary's mother was imprisoned for receiving the stolen goods, leaving a younger daughter Elizabeth, aged ten, to fend for herself. The girls' mother had been separated for some time from their father, allegedly 'a fearful drunkard', and had given birth to a child by another man who had also abandoned the family.[1] This family was part of a poverty-stricken underclass that existed in Birmingham below the level of the poor but hard-working and respectable working-class. The family's dire situation came to the attention of John Stead, a visitor for the Middlemore Emigration Homes, who recommended Mary and Elizabeth for admittance to the Girls' Emigration Home. From the perspective of the Birmingham philanthropist John Middlemore, these two young sisters were exactly the type of children who needed to be saved from the threat of sinking into a life of crime and juvenile prostitution. They would be housed, fed, clothed, educated and trained for a few months in the home, before being shipped out to a new life with a Canadian farming family.[2] In the same way, thousands of children removed from the overcrowded slum dwellings and lodging-houses of nineteenth-century Birmingham were transported across the Atlantic by Middlemore's emigration charity. Younger children were sent for adoption by families, but children aged ten and above were sent overseas by the charity to work as farm-hands and domestic servants in rural Canada. The migration of poor Birmingham children to Canada thus represents a further dimension of nineteenth-century child labour that has been largely unexplored.

This chapter intends to capture the experiences of some of these children before and after migration from Birmingham to Canada, exploring the issues around practices that today might be described as child trafficking. What were the attitudes of middle-class philanthropists, such as John Middlemore, towards the numerous deprived children found in towns such as Birmingham and commonly referred to as 'gutter children' or 'street

---

1   BAH, MS 517/245 Middlemore Homes Application Book, 1877–78.

2   BAH, MS 517/245.

arabs'? To what extent were child migrants to Canada drawn from so-called criminal or immoral families that put them at risk? Were migrant children welcome in Canada purely as a source of cheap labour for Canadian farms and rural settlements? And what were the actual experiences of child migrants who were sent overseas?

Child saving

The Middlemore Emigration Homes were founded in 1872 by John Throgmorton Middlemore (1844–1924), the son of a wealthy Birmingham businessman.[3] From the age of 20, Middlemore spent four years in the US and Canada, where he was impressed by the equality of opportunity and healthy rural lifestyles these countries seemed to offer. On his return to Birmingham he resolved to set up an emigration scheme for deprived and seemingly abandoned children living on the streets, convinced that they would have a better life as 'helpers' with farming families in Canada. The first home for boys opened in Edgbaston in 1872, and over the next five decades more than 5,000 Birmingham children made the journey on board ships bound for Canada.[4] Middlemore was one of the pioneers of child migration schemes, along with evangelical child savers such as Maria Rye and Annie Macpherson. Rye began work by forming the Female Middle-class Emigration Society in 1862, arranging for groups of middle-class women to emigrate to Australia and New Zealand. By 1868 she was escorting young women and girls to Canada to work as domestic servants, followed in 1869 by child migrants to be placed with farming families. At around the same time Macpherson opened homes for poor children in London's East End before taking a group of boys to Canada in 1870.[5] A number of child-saving activists and philanthropists subsequently became involved in child migration to Canada, including Father Nugent in Liverpool, Louisa Birt in London and William Quarrier in Scotland.[6] The well-known Barnardo's Homes became involved in child migration a few years later in 1882, and eventually became the largest provider of child migrants to Canada, sending 24,854 children between 1882 and 1915.[7]

3   Ian Cawood, 'Middlemore, Sir John Throgmorton, first baronet (1844–1924)', *Oxford Dictionary of National Biography* (Oxford, 2013) <http://www.oxforddnb.com/view/article/97843>, accessed 21 August 2017.

4   BAH, MS 517/63 One Hundred Years of Child Care. The Story of Middlemore Homes 1872–1972, pp. 1–7; Roy Parker, *Uprooted: The Shipment of Poor Children to Canada, 1867–1917* (Bristol, 2010), p. 31; Roger Kershaw and Janet Sacks, *New Lives for Old: The Story of Britain's Child Migrants* (Kew, 2008), p. 74.

5   Parker, *Uprooted*, pp. 10–21.

6   *Ibid.*, pp. 25–30.

7   *Ibid.*, p. 67.

From the point of view of the child savers, children were being rescued from the moral and physical dangers of Victorian Britain's crime-ridden slums to enjoy a healthy life in rural Canada. It is important to recognise, however, that from the start of the emigration movement Maria Rye was aware that Canadian families were willing to welcome young migrants on the basis that they would undertake farm or domestic work in exchange for board and lodgings.[8] It seems clear, therefore, that Canadian families viewed the migration arrangements rather differently from the organisers of the schemes. Rather than offering homes to children from impoverished backgrounds, Canadian farmers were seeking cheap labour to work on their farms. Those involved in child migration schemes promoted the idea of a 'rural idyll' by looking back to pre-industrial England, when pauper children were traditionally apprenticed as farm servants to live as part of a family and receive training in agriculture. But, at the same time, there was a contradiction in attitudes towards families and family life. Evangelical activists and philanthropists such as Middlemore proclaimed a strong belief in the importance of family life, yet they focused their greatest efforts on breaking up families, separating the most vulnerable children from parents and siblings.[9] Instead of assisting families who might have been experiencing temporary difficulties, such as lack of employment or the loss of a parent, the promoters of child migration schemes separated children from their own 'inadequate' families and placed them with unknown Canadian farmers.

Attitudes towards child labour were also somewhat contradictory. In general, the middle classes regarded child labour as a form of exploitation and children as dependants in need of protection. Yet child migrants were handed over to families in Canada who needed the physical labour of farm-hands and servants. The lives of children from the slums and courts in large towns such as Birmingham were far removed from middle-class concepts of childhood; hence little distinction was made between street children who may have lived within a family and had regular work and children who fended for themselves and lived in lodgings.[10] For example, eight-year-old James B. was admitted to the Middlemore Emigration Homes with the comment; 'Father dead. Boy got his living by singing in the street', and George D., aged 12, was admitted on the grounds of: 'Father drunkard, turns children out of house

---

8   Kershaw and Sacks, *New Lives for Old*, p. 21.

9   Joy Parr, *Labouring Children. British Immigrant Apprentices to Canada, 1869–1924* (Toronto, 1994), p. 11.

10   Anna Davin, 'When is a Child not a Child?' in H. Corr and L. Jamieson (eds), *Politics of Everyday Life: Continuity and Change in Work and the Family* (London, 1990), pp. 37–61 at 42–3; Anna Davin, *Growing up Poor: Home, School and Street in London, 1870–1914* (London, 1996), pp. 160–64.

at night, boy hawks mussels'.[11] From this information, it is not clear whether these boys were actually living on the streets or simply working to earn money as best they could. Furthermore, it is unclear whether the Middlemore Homes adopted a policy of actively searching the streets of Birmingham in pursuit of ragged children, a policy that was followed by philanthropist Thomas Barnardo in London.[12]

Although the supporters of child migration schemes included wealthy and prominent members of society, such schemes were not without critics. Andrew Doyle was sent to Canada by the British government in 1874 to examine all aspects of the selection and follow-up care of child migrants. His report, published in 1875, was highly critical of the methods used by Macpherson and Rye, describing emigration as 'schemes for providing cheap labour for Canadian farmers'.[13] Doyle visited several hundred children and became particularly concerned about the lack of supervision following placements, which left children at risk of mistreatment and overwork. Consequently, the Local Government Board temporarily suspended any further emigration of children from the workhouses.[14] Other critics of child migration included George Cruikshank, the well-known illustrator and temperance campaigner, whose 1869 cartoon *Our 'Gutter Children'* depicted hordes of small children being swept up from the streets into a cart, with Maria Rye supervising the operation.[15] As Cruikshank highlighted in his drawing, the use of language such as 'gutter children' and 'street arabs' by the leading figures such as Rye revealed their attitudes towards the most destitute in society and a lack of concern for the wishes of the children themselves.[16]

John Middlemore used similar language to describe the Birmingham children he was determined to save. In fact, his first published report of 1873 was headed 'Gutter Children's Homes. First Report with List of Subscribers'.[17] Similarly, an article published in the *Morning News* in November 1872 was headed 'Birmingham Emigration Home for Gutter Children' and described the newly opened home as intending 'not to relieve distress but to save from prison, and consequently only children of the street-arab class are admitted into it'.[18]

11   BAH, MS 517/471 and MS 517/472 Middlemore Homes Entrance Books, 1875–78.

12   Ellen Boucher, *Empire's Children: Child Emigration, Welfare and the Decline of the British World, 1869–1967* (Cambridge, 2014), p. 36; Lydia Murdoch, *Imagined Orphans: Poor Families, Child Welfare and Contested Citizenship in London* (New Jersey, 2006), pp. 17–20.

13   Kershaw and Sacks, *New Lives for Old*, pp. 35–43.

14   Parker, *Uprooted*, p. 50.

15   Parr, *Labouring Children*, p. 31; Kershaw and Sacks, *New Lives for Old*, p. 22.

16   Kershaw and Sacks, *New Lives for Old*, p. 22.

17   BAH, MS 517/463 Middlemore Homes Reports, 1873–79.

18   BAH, MS 517/93 & 93A Middlemore Homes Newpaper Cuttings Book, 1872–1929.

By the time the second report was published in 1875, however, the boys' home in St Luke's Road and the girls' home in Spring Street, both located in the wealthy suburb of Edgbaston, had been renamed the 'Children's Emigration Homes', indicating that the term 'gutter children' was soon regarded as unacceptable.[19] From the outset, Middlemore made it clear that his intention was not to provide a children's home for destitute children in Birmingham but to accommodate them for a short period in preparation for emigration to Canada. In some cases children were transported in a matter of weeks rather than months. Furthermore, he stated clearly in the first report that 'Children are not taken to Canada because they are poor, but to save them from their bad companions, to whom, if they remained in Birmingham they would always be tempted to return.'[20] In this respect, the Middlemore Emigration Homes differed from other charitable organisations, such as Macpherson's Revival Homes in London, Quarrier's Homes in Scotland or Barnardo's Homes, as these also offered food and shelter to orphans or destitute children who were not necessarily destined for emigration.

When the Middlemore Homes first opened in 1872 there were relatively few alternatives available in Birmingham for the residential care of vulnerable children. The provision for pauper children at the Asylum for the Infant Poor had closed in 1852 and children's accommodation had been transferred to the workhouse at Winson Green. Secondly, the orphanage founded by Josiah Mason in 1860 was able to accommodate approximately 300 children, but its strict admissions policy meant that places were offered only to children who were orphaned rather than abandoned or abused. Thirdly, Birmingham's industrial schools provided a total of 70 to 80 residential places, a small number when compared to industrial schools in other large towns, which housed up to 1,000 children. For children living in Birmingham at this time whose families were unable or unwilling to provide for them, it seems, then, that there were few alternatives to life on the streets other than the workhouse or migration to Canada. Accounts of childhood experiences of life in the workhouse suggest that they were often used as a form of temporary relief by families under the old Poor Law, but this changed under the harsher New Poor Law regime, which limited eligibility.[21] John Munday recalled that at the age of ten he preferred a life on the streets to entering the workhouse,

---

19   BAH, MS 517/463.

20   *Ibid.*

21   Jane Humphries, 'Care and Cruelty in the Workhouse: Children's Experiences of Residential Poor Relief in Eighteenth- and Nineteenth-Century England', in Nigel Goose and Katrina Honeyman (eds), *Childhood and Child Labour in Industrial England: Diversity and Agency, 1750–1914* (Farnham, 2013), pp. 115–34 at 122–3.

where food was inadequate and inmates were subjected to regimentation and corporal punishment.[22]

Between 1850 and 1900 the number of institutions providing residential child-care places increased substantially in many districts. New institutions included residential industrial schools under the Poor Law, such as the Swinton Schools in Manchester, correctional institutions or reformatories to accommodate young offenders and private children's homes run by voluntary organisations such as Barnardo's or the Waifs and Strays Society.[23] The apparent lack of places in these types of residential institution in Birmingham, relative to the town's population, may have been a factor in the numbers of children admitted to the Emigration Homes and their subsequent migration to Canada. In John Middlemore's view, Birmingham was a town in which 'a multitude of children are not only born and bred in crime, but that from the mere coercion of circumstances, they have little other than an idle, vagrant and criminal life open to them.'[24] To what extent, then, were children who were admitted to the Emigration Homes drawn from these allegedly criminal and vagrant families?

Admission to the Birmingham Emigration Homes

The entrance books show that 67 boys and 38 girls were admitted to the Emigration Homes in Birmingham during 1878 and 1879. Among these children, 50 boys and 32 girls were migrated to Canada.[25] The stated policy of the Emigration Homes was to admit children below the age of ten (for adoption) or at around 13 years of age (for employment).[26] The three youngest children admitted in 1878 and 1879 were just one year old, and four children were 13 years old, but none were above 13, indicating that they were either refused admission or were unwilling to enter the home.[27]

Further analysis of the admissions records for 1878 and 1879 suggests that few of the children were orphans, although many were illegitimate or from single-parent families (Table 8.1). One-year-old Annie B. was described as 'child illegitimate, mother prostitute', as were Elizabeth M. (six) and her sister Catherine (four). Emily F. (six) had no parents or relatives and was living with 'Mrs Goodwin'. William R. (five) was described as 'illegitimate,

22 Humphries, 'Care and Cruelty', pp. 127–30.

23 Nicola Sheldon, '"Something in the place of home": Children in Institutional Care 1850–1918', in Nigel Goose and Katrina Honeyman (eds), *Childhood and Child Labour in Industrial England: Diversity and Agency, 1750–1914* (Farnham, 2013), pp. 255–76 at 258–62.

24 BAH, MS 517/463, First Report, 1873.

25 BAH, MS 517/471 and MS 517/472.

26 BAH, MS 517/463, First Report, 1873.

27 BAH, MS 517/471 and MS 517/472.

father absconded, has been in prison, police now in search of him', while the admission record for Abraham M. (11) stated: 'father deserted, mother keeps a brothel'.[28]

As the records above indicate, many of the children were too young to be involved in criminal or delinquent behaviour themselves, but they were likely to be at risk if the descriptions of family backgrounds are accurate. Steven Taylor's study of child migration to Canada from Manchester and Salford Boys' and Girls' Refuge between 1871 and 1891 found that only 19 per cent of children came from backgrounds regarded as 'criminal' or 'bad'. In one such case, 'Richard J.' was admitted for emigration just before the death of his mother on the grounds that his elder brothers and sisters 'had all gone wrong'.[29] In contrast to the Manchester study, a number of children admitted

Table 8.1 Reasons for admittance to the Birmingham Emigration Homes, 1878–79.

Main reason given for admittance	Number	% of total
Father dead	18	17
Mother dead	10	10
Orphaned	6	6
Deserted by father	9	9
Deserted by mother	8	8
Ill-treatment by stepfather	5	5
Ill-treatment by stepmother	1	1
Neglected by father/mother	2	2
Parents very poor	4	4
Illegitimate and neglected	14	13
Father in prison	6	6
Mother in prison	2	2
Child truants/runs wild	8	8
Father a bigamist	2	2
Mother a prostitute	2	2
Mother insane	3	3
No reason recorded	5	5
Total	105	

Source: BAH, MS 517/471 and MS 517/472 Middlemore Homes Entrance Books, 1875–78.

---

28   BAH, MS 517/471 and MS 517/472.

29   Steven Taylor, 'Poverty, Emigration and Family: Experiencing Childhood Poverty in Late Nineteenth-Century Manchester', *Family and Community History*, 18/2 (2015), pp. 89–103 at 89–94.

to the Birmingham Emigration Homes appear to have been from unstable or violent families. Joseph M. was admitted at the age of eight when his father was 'sentenced to 14 years penal servitude for attempting the life of the woman with whom he lived'. Charles G. (seven) was admitted because his 'mother deserted, father a drunkard, boy a typical Arab'. Ten-year-old Frederick C.'s record stated: 'Father dead, one brother in reformatory, two in workhouse, mother frightful drunkard, cruel to children'. Of Elizabeth S. (11), whose father was dead, it was said that 'girl runs the streets ie. Wharf Street, man in jail for committing rape upon her'. Elizabeth ran away from the home after just one night and did not appear in any further records. In another case, eight-year-old Sarah E. was an orphan living with her uncle when she was brought to the home after witnessing a murder committed by him.[30] These children were clearly in need of care and protection, but the details explaining the reason for each child's admittance to the home are regrettably brief. In most cases there is no information about the full circumstances leading up to the child entering the Emigration Home, or about wider family members who may have been potential carers.

The Manchester study of child migrants found examples of children considered to be in physical or moral danger from contact with their parents, but there were no cases of children involved in criminal activity and only 3 per cent of cases involved disruptive behaviour.[31] Among children admitted to the Birmingham home in 1878 and 1879 there was a similar lack of criminal or disruptive behaviour, at least for those children migrated to Canada, possibly because many of them were very young. Three-year-old Sarah H. was brought to the home because her mother had been 'kicked to death' and her father was a brothel-keeper. Seven-year-old Mary Jane D.'s mother had been 'again and again in prison', taking Mary Jane to prison with her. Only one girl admitted to the home showed evidence of disruptive behaviour. The record for Elizabeth B. (13) states: 'parents living, runs the streets, seeking her own ruin'.[32] Elizabeth was not one of the children migrated to Canada and no information was recorded about when she left the home or whether she returned to her parents. The admission records for boys show that they were more likely to be disruptive. Michael M. (12) 'stops out at night'; John M. (11), 'truant, runs away from home a fortnight at a time'; Thomas K. (12) had 'parents living', but was an 'incorrigible truant'; Frederick C. (11) 'slept out at night and ill-treated his mother'. In two cases there are descriptions of alleged criminal behaviour: Arthur H. (10) had 'set house on fire, landlords won't have boy in the house';

---

30   BAH, MS 517/471 and MS 517/472.

31   Taylor, 'Poverty, Emigration and Family', p. 93.

32   BAH, MS 517/471 and MS 517/472.

and John B. (7) was described as 'a thief'.[33] In the last two cases both boys were migrated to Canada, suggesting that Middlemore viewed them as young enough to be saved from a life of criminality by removing them from their families. Five boys whose behaviour was disruptive did not go to Canada, however, possibly because they ran away from the emigration home or because they were deemed too difficult to control.

When ten-year-old Elizabeth A. was taken into the Birmingham Emigration Home in early 1878, the entrance book recorded: 'Mother in prison, girl utterly wild and untamed. Springs out of bed, shouts and screams, strikes other girls.'[34] Elizabeth's views are not known, but it seems plausible that she refused to be quiet and obedient because she was extremely unhappy at being placed in the home. She had been separated from her older sister Mary, who was sent to an Industrial School in York, and from her mother, who was imprisoned. The loneliness, isolation and fear experienced by a child suddenly removed from her family to an emigration home 'for her own good' can only be imagined. In a second case, nine-year-old Edward C. was admitted to the home in 1878 with the remarks: 'Boy cursed and swore at his mother when she was apparently on her death bed.'[35] From this information it seems likely that Edward was terrified at the thought of his mother leaving him and was aware she would never return. In the event, Edward did not make the journey to Canada but was removed from the home in December 1878, perhaps claimed by his father or another family member. A third case concerns 11-year-old Annie B. The entrance book reveals that Annie was living in lodgings 'provided by Miss Ickfield' and reported: 'Mother dead, thoroughly filthy man, details too vile to record'.[36] These very brief comments tell us virtually nothing about the circumstances of this child, but she appears to have been removed to lodgings for her own safety. Numerous entries for other children refer to parents who were neglectful, thieves, drunkards, prostitutes, bigamists and even murderers, so it appears there may have been cases of possible abuse where the details remained unrecorded. For a child who had been abused by an adult, the prospect of being sent to live with complete strangers in Canada must have been very frightening.

Taylor's study of the Manchester Refuge revealed that some children who were migrated to Canada had parents who were 'decent but poor'. In one case a boy was left in the refuge on a temporary basis during a crisis period, but was quickly sent to Canada without his father's knowledge or consent. Taylor

33   BAH, MS 517/471 and MS 517/472.
34   BAH, MS 517/471 and MS 517/472.
35   BAH, MS 517/471 and MS 517/472.
36   BAH, MS 517/471 and MS 517/472.

suggests that residential children's homes were used as a welfare resource by poor families, but in this case the coping strategies of the poor were being exploited.[37] It seems unlikely that parents in Birmingham would have used the Emigration Homes for temporary relief, but it may have been the case that some 'decent but poor' parents felt they had no choice but to agree to their child's emigration to Canada. Benjamin S. was admitted at the age of 11 in 1878, with the record: 'Father dead, mother and children starving',[38] and left for Canada in June 1879. Three brothers from Digbeth, Thomas H., aged ten, and William and Walter, both aged eight, were admitted to the home early in 1878. The brothers were living with their parents but the family was starving and the children were found begging on the streets at midnight.[39] Thomas was dispatched to Canada shortly afterwards, in May 1878, and his brothers followed two years later, in July 1880. This delay indicates that the Emigration Homes were retaining children for longer than previously, perhaps because children below ten were sent for adoption and there was a shortage of families wanting to adopt. Children of ten and above were placed as assistants with farming families looking for farm workers and domestic servants. The fifth report of the Emigration Homes, published in 1878, revealed that a total of 385 children had been received into the homes since opening, and 310 children had been taken to Canada. Only 17 children had been found placements in Birmingham.[40] The *Morning News* of 8 April 1875 reported that Middlemore had made efforts to settle children in Birmingham but with disastrous results: 'Out of six who were sent out and settled in situations, five got into prison immediately after; two were taken up for larceny, one for manslaughter, and one for burglary.'[41] This experience reinforced Middlemore's view that those children who were in danger of slipping into criminal and immoral lifestyles should be removed as far as possible from their families in Birmingham to prevent them from absconding. How, then, did children fare once they arrived in Canada?

Experiences of life in Canada

John Middlemore took his first group of 29 children to Canada in the early summer of 1873, despite having made no advance arrangements for their reception. Fortunately, he was able to persuade three charitable organisations in Toronto to accept the children and they were later placed in Toronto and

---

37   Taylor, 'Poverty, Emigration and Family', pp. 94–5.
38   BAH, MS 517/471 and MS 517/472.
39   BAH, MS 517/471 and MS 517/472.
40   BAH, MS 517/463, Fifth Report, 1878.
41   *Morning News*, 8 April 1875.

in the town of London, Ontario.[42] The older children were placed as servants with families and the younger children were adopted by childless families. However, three of the boys placed as servants in Toronto ran away, 'causing much trouble and anxiety', and consequently Middlemore resolved to place future migrant children with farming families in rural districts of Ontario so they would have no opportunity to abscond.[43] The majority of child migrants from all emigration organisations were placed on farms in rural areas to meet the Canadian demand for cheap farm labour. Around 80 per cent of the population of Canada lived in rural areas in 1871, but there was a continual movement to the urban centres by the sons and daughters of small farmers, resulting in a high demand for immigrant children from the 'old country' to work on farms as labourers and domestic servants.[44] The greatest demand was for children and young people between the ages of 12 and 16, but many farmers were willing to accept younger children if they appeared suitable. Children were likely to be returned to the distribution homes if they were not strong enough to undertake the work, and very young children typically spent much longer in the distribution homes waiting for adoptive families.[45] Placing children in rural areas was believed to provide fewer temptations and less moral danger than the towns and cities, yet the distribution homes did not interview prospective employers before sending children to live with them. Canadian applicants for child workers simply sent a description of their own family and the child required, together with one reference from a clergyman and a small fee. It appears that British charities took it for granted that child migrants would be safe with rural farmers.[46] In this respect the Middlemore Homes in Canada seem to have been particularly neglectful, as they had a local reputation for taking insufficient care over placements and poor supervision afterwards in comparison with other organisations.[47] After completing their placements in rural Canada, many British girls were keen to leave the countryside for towns and cities, where they found work in factories or shops.[48] More than 50 per cent of boys also gave up working on the land to become labourers or factory workers in the towns, leaving around 22 per cent in agricultural occupations and a further 23 per cent in industries such as logging, mining and fishing.[49]

---

42   Parker, *Uprooted*, p. 31.

43   BAH, MS 517/463, First Report, 1873.

44   Parker, *Uprooted*, pp. 129–31.

45   *Ibid.*, pp. 138–9.

46   Parr, *Labouring Children*, p. 47.

47   Kenneth Bagnell, *The Little Immigrants: The Orphans Who Came to Canada* (Toronto, 2001), pp. 185–8.

48   Parr, *Labouring Children*, pp. 126–7.

49   *Ibid.*, pp. 130–31.

The work undertaken by children on Canadian farms depended largely on their age, size and strength: a boy of nine was expected to fetch water and wood, gather eggs, feed pigs and bring in cows. Older boys worked in the fields, tended crops and brought in the harvest. The younger girls were given tasks such as child-minding, whereas older girls undertook domestic chores in the home and around the farm.[50] It was common for children to be moved between placements, as employers complained urban children were unsuitable for farm work: they were 'too small', 'too slow', 'disobedient', 'obstinate' or 'untruthful'. Even in cases where children had run away, this was reported by employers only when writing to request a replacement child worker.[51] In many ways, child migrants to Canada in the late nineteenth century were treated in a similar way to pauper children in eighteenth-century England, who were routinely apprenticed as farm servants by the parish in exchange for board and lodging. The difference was that children transported to Canada were totally isolated from everything familiar to them, unlikely to ever see their families again, and without even Poor Law officials to turn to for assistance. As Taylor points out, child savers and philanthropists in Britain promoted child migration as a route to a better life in Canada, but the expectation that children would work for their keep was contrary to nineteenth-century legislation aimed at limiting child labour and introducing compulsory education.[52] The employment of children in factories and workshops in England was restricted by the Factory and Workshop Act of 1878, which prohibited children below the age of ten from working. Children of ten to 13 years were permitted to work for half-days only and were required to attend school for half-days. These measures were reinforced by the 1880 Education Act, which made school attendance compulsory for all children up to the age of 13. Yet, at the same time, children removed from England to Canada were expected to undertake long hours of farm labour in harsh conditions from the age of ten, with few opportunities for schooling in remote rural areas.

The annual reports of the Middlemore Emigration Homes invariably suggested that children were doing well and were extremely happy in their new homes. Samples of children's letters included in these reports were chosen for their favourable comments, but even these extracts provide some insights into children's feelings about migration to Canada. Thomas G.: 'I am getting along pretty well at my trade, but my eyes, which are a little sore, make it hard for me … I like Canada pretty well, but I feel a little lonesome.'[53] Elizabeth W.:

---

50   *Ibid.*, pp. 82–3.

51   Parker, *Uprooted*, pp. 216–19.

52   Taylor, 'Poverty, Emigration and Family', p. 97.

53   BAH, MS 517/463, First Report, 1873.

'Please Mr Middlemore will you tell me how my sister Florence and my brother William is getting on. I hope you will bring them next year.' William L.: 'Please try to bring my sister to Canada.'[54] Henry N.: 'I thank you very much for the trouble you took with me. I am happy to tell you that I have got a good home. I will do my best to do what is right and good.' Sarah Ann E.: 'Please give my best love to all the children, and please think of me always trying to be your good little girl.'[55] None of the letters from the children mentioned being unhappy or disliking their placement, but they were full of enquiries about their brothers and sisters and other children from the emigration homes. Many of the letters were affectionate towards John Middlemore, the matron and staff of the home, sending love and saying they were very grateful and trying to do their best. As these letters indicate, the impact of separation from former family and friends was experienced even by children who appeared to be happily placed in welcoming new homes.

The Middlemore Homes settlement reports on individual children contain information about children's lives once they arrived in Canada at this time (1873–80). Details about six of the children from the 1878–79 intakes have been traced, including three girls aged four, ten and 11 years and the three Hughes brothers sent to Canada at the age of ten. Only the four-year-old girl was adopted, the other five children being placed with employers as farm assistants or servants within two weeks of arrival in Canada. This confirms that Birmingham children were sent to Canada as child workers at ten years old. Elizabeth A. (ten) was placed with Andrew Abra of Sydenham Mills on 4 July 1878 'as an assistant for one year' in exchange for accommodation, food and 'clothes washing'. The agreement was renewed in July 1879 and, according to an inspection report of September 1879, Elizabeth was in 'a good home' but her behaviour was 'not very satisfactory'. By August 1881 her behaviour had become 'very insufficient' and she was removed. Elizabeth was then sent to work for farmer N. Horton of Owen Sound, a port on Lake Huron, 'as a general servant' for the pay of '$3 per month plus food'. She was removed from this placement after five months and moved again in October 1882 when she was 14 years old to earn $4 per month as a general servant. No further reports were included in her file after the age of 14.[56] Elizabeth's views about her experiences and how she was treated by her employers remain hidden, but the evidence of her transfers between employers and reports of her poor behaviour suggest her experience of life as a child worker in Canada was difficult. From this, it is possible to speculate that Elizabeth missed her own family and

---

54   BAH, MS 517/463, Second Report, 1875.

55   BAH, MS 517/463, Third Report, 1876.

56   BAH, MS 517/253, Middlemore Homes Settlement Reports, 1873–81.

familiar surroundings and very probably disliked working as a farm servant. Resentment of her predicament and feelings of powerlessness inevitably resulted in the non co-operative behaviour typical of a child experiencing separation anxiety disorder.

Annie B. (11) arrived in Canada at the same time as Elizabeth and was immediately placed as an assistant with Phillip Odell of London, Ontario. A visit by an inspector two years later in July 1880 stated only that Annie was in good health, she was living in a good home and her behaviour was 'very good'. No further records about Annie were added to the file, perhaps because she had also reached the age of 14. Catherine M. was four years old when migrated to Canada in 1878, leaving behind a life as the illegitimate daughter of a Birmingham prostitute. She was adopted on 21 June 1878 by a Canadian who signed an agreement 'to treat her in all respects as his own child'. The family were visited annually by inspectors who recorded Catherine's 'good health', 'good home' and 'very satisfactory' behaviour. The final report was when Catherine was 15 years old, and recorded simply that she was 'happy' and her behaviour 'very satisfactory'.[57] The inspection reports for Catherine were again brief, but it appears that when young children were adopted more care was taken to visit them at least once a year. Whether an adopted child would have reported unhappiness or ill-treatment by the family on which she was totally dependent is unclear.

The H. brothers Thomas, William and Walter were all migrated to Canada at the age of ten. Thomas left England in May 1878 and was placed with Thomas Abbott on 12 June 1878 'as an assistant' to work in exchange for accommodation, food and clothes washing. The agreement was renewed in October 1879 and a report at the same time recorded Thomas was in good health and that his general condition was 'as a member of the family', but he was described as 'untruthful, otherwise satisfactory'.[58] The placement was clearly not successful, as Thomas was moved four months later, in February 1880, to Mrs H. Thompson 'as an assistant'. This placement lasted until August 1880, when Thomas was placed with John Ferguson, earning $40 per annum 'with food'. Three further employers were recorded in September 1881, November 1881 and finally July 1885, by which time Thomas was 17 years old and earning $8 per month 'with food'.[59] Thomas experienced six employers during his first seven years in Canada, indicating a worrying lack of security for a young boy who was being moved from place to place. This was not unusual, however; Parr's study of child migrants from the Barnardo's homes found that children

57 Ibid.
58 Ibid.
59 Ibid.

were frequently moved, as their economic worth increased with age and ability. The Barnardo's girls moved on average four times during their early years in Canada, and the Barnardo's boys moved three times on average.[60] Thomas's younger brother, William H., arrived in Canada in July 1880 and for the first year was placed with George Ferris on 30 July 1880 'as an assistant' for 'food, clothes washing and mending'. The agreement stated that William should attend Sunday school regularly and day school 'three months in the year at least'. The agreement was renewed for the next five years, and the report of a visit in 1883 found William's health 'good' and his behaviour 'very good'.[61] The Canadian census shows that at the age of 20, in 1891, William was employed as a farm labourer for farmer Stephen Cosens in the Ontario district of Huron East.[62] The third brother, Walter, arrived in Canada at the same time as William and was placed on 30 July 1880 with William Kirkpatrick. Walter's agreement was renewed for the following three years; a report dated 1883 described his health as 'good' and his behaviour as 'very satisfactory'.[63] Information from the Canadian census confirms that Walter was living in the household of William Kirkpatrick, a farmer, in 1881 as a farm servant. Ten years later, 21-year-old Walter was working as a farm labourer in the household of farmer Joseph Johnson.[64] The Middlemore settlement reports provide few details and are too brief to indicate the childhood experiences of the three brothers. However, a letter written to John Middlemore by Walter in 1899, when he was 29 years old, has been retained in the files and provides some insights into his childhood and life as a young man.[65] Walter had moved to the United States by 1899, and was living in a town on Lake Huron, Michigan, along with his elder brother Thomas. They were both married by this time, as was William, who was living in Manitoba. Even though the brothers had been separated as soon as they arrived in Canada and despite the years spent apart they had managed to remain in contact as a family. Walter had married 'a Scotch girl from one of the Glasgow orphan homes. She is a good steady quiet Christian woman one that I am quite proud of we get along very happy together.'[66]

The main purpose of Walter's letter to John Middlemore was to enquire about his mother, last heard from 12 years earlier. He was obviously anxious

---

60 Parr, *Labouring Children*, p. 88.

61 BAH, MS 517/253 Middlemore Homes Settlement Reports, 1873–81.

62 Canadian Census Reports, 1881 and 1891.

63 BAH, MS 517/253 Middlemore Homes Settlement Reports, 1873–81.

64 Canadian Census reports, 1881 and 1891.

65 BAH, MS 517/253 Middlemore Homes Settlement Reports, 1873–81; MS 517/253 Letter from W. Hughes to J. Middlemore, 18th September 1899.

66 BAH, MS 517/253 Letter from W. Hughes.

to gain help in tracing his mother, writing that he would never forget 'the kind Christian training' he received in the Middlemore Home, which had made him into 'a good Christian man', but he also revealed that after leaving the home he was 'treated very unkind by the man I was given out to … Mr William Kirkpatrick'. Walter continued his letter by stressing the importance of keeping in touch with children once they were placed on Canadian farms because 'some of them are used very rough and shameful'.[67] The comments in Walter's letter raise questions about the ill-treatment and over-work of child migrants by employers, even where follow-up inspections had reported arrangements were satisfactory. Walter's placement with farmer William Kirkpatrick continued for three or four years, yet his letter reveals he was ill-treated as a child by his employer. Moreover, he suggests that other children had similar experiences to his own, implying that incidences of mistreatment or harshness were well-known among former child migrants. Walter's letter is also significant in providing first-hand insights into the importance child migrants attached to maintaining family and community ties.

Walter had retained contact with his brothers in Canada, yet for other children whose siblings were in England such contact was less likely. It is apparent that Walter's attachment to his mother and to his home town of Birmingham had not diminished, even after 20 years. His marriage, too, suggests evidence of a sense of community between former child migrants. The desire among child migrants to maintain links to family, friends and place of birth was further demonstrated at the outbreak of the First World War, when 54 per cent of Middlemore boys in New Brunswick volunteered for military service with the Canadian Expeditionary Force.[68] The majority of Middlemore volunteers were employed in farming and lumbering and, with an average age of 22 years, they were younger than the national average age for volunteers, of 26. Many of those who volunteered were motivated in part by a desire to return to England, taking advantage of periods of leave to visit Birmingham.[69] This very strong desire to reconnect with family and the home country appears to have been an ongoing theme in the experience of child migrants to Canada.

Conclusion

On 16 February 2017 the House of Commons of the Canadian Parliament issued an official apology to child migrants, recognising 'the injustice, abuse and suffering endured by the British Home Children … who were shipped from

---

67   *Ibid.*

68   Curt Mainville, 'The Middlemore Boys: Immigration, Settlement and Great War Volunteerism in New Brunswick', *Acadiensis: Journal of the History of the Atlantic Region*, 42/2 (2013), pp. 51–74.

69   Mainville, 'Middlemore Boys', p. 69.

Great Britain to Canada between 1869 and 1948, and torn from their families to serve mainly as cheap labour once they arrived in Canada'.[70] This apology not only recognised the ill-treatment received by British child migrants to Canada but also made explicit that they were welcomed purely as child workers. The evidence in this chapter demonstrates that middle-class 'child savers' focused their efforts on removing pauper children from families perceived as inadequate or criminal, reflecting negative attitudes towards the poor and a fear of social disruption. Although these children were frequently depicted as orphaned 'gutter children' or 'street arabs', this study shows that many children were leaving behind various members of their family. They were almost certainly in need of some form of care or support, as families experienced problems of destitution arising from family breakdown, unemployment, illness or death. However, there is little evidence of criminal or disruptive behaviour among the children despatched to Canada. Moreover, it is not clear from the records why some parents, such as the family with three young sons, consented to their children's emigration to Canada rather than entering the workhouse for temporary relief. This raises further questions about the possible options, or lack of options, available to distressed Birmingham families in a period of civic improvement in the town during the era of Joseph Chamberlain, Mayor of Birmingham, and his successors.[71]

Children just ten years old were sent from the emigration homes in Birmingham to work for Canadian farmers as servants in exchange for board and lodgings. Although the Middlemore Homes claimed that children 'around the age of 13 years' were found work, the records show that much younger children were placed on isolated farms where they were regarded as live-in farm servants rather than members of the family. At around the same time, British legislators were attempting to reduce child labour by introducing compulsory education for all children up to the age of 13, a provision that did not extend to child migrants. In the later nineteenth century, children such as Elizabeth, Annie, Thomas, William and Walter should have been attending school instead of labouring on farms. It is paradoxical, too, that while for much of the nineteenth century families were drawn into Birmingham from the countryside to take advantage of industrial employment opportunities, by the 1870s some of the poorest children were being removed from urban streets to work on rural land overseas, where many experienced hardships and the agencies involved failed to ensure children's welfare during follow-

---

70   House of Commons Canada Debates, Hansard No. 142, Thursday, 16 February 2017.

71   Peter T. Marsh, 'Chamberlain, Joseph (1836–1914)', *Oxford Dictionary of National Biography* (Oxford, 2004); online edn 2013 <http://www.oxforddnb.com/view/article/32350>, accessed 22 August 2017.

up inspections. As this chapter demonstrates, once children had arrived in Canada, the requirements of farmers for cheap child labour took precedence over the education and well-being of child migrants.

9

Childhood redefined

Introduction

The later decades of the nineteenth century brought a number of changes and reforms that helped to reshape the lives of working-class children. The 1870 Education Act enabled locally elected school boards to provide elementary school places for all children, and was followed by further legislation that restricted child labour by making school attendance compulsory from 1880 and abolished the payment of school fees in 1891.[1] By the turn of the century children up to the age of 12 were thus legally required to be in full-time school rather than employment, although many children continued to work part-time outside school hours as errand boys, messengers, delivery boys or domestics and shop workers.[2] The state also became more involved in the lives of children perceived to be the most destitute and at risk of neglect or abuse, taking on 'child saving' activities that had previously been the preserve of philanthropists and voluntary agencies such as Barnardo's.[3] The 1880 Industrial Schools Amendment Act permitted children to be removed from premises frequented by prostitutes, and the Prevention of Cruelty to Children Act, introduced in 1889, gave the police new powers to prevent children from begging in the streets and to prosecute parents for neglect. Alongside these interventions the National Society for the Prevention of Cruelty to Children (NSPCC), also established in 1889, appointed inspectors who undertook much of the work involved in enforcing the new legislation in practice.

These legislative measures were partly a response to campaigns by middle-class social reformers, together with a more general recognition in society that even the poorest children were entitled to enjoy a carefree and innocent childhood that was free from exploitation, neglect or abuse by adults. This shift in attitudes to childhood encompassed the notion that attempts should be made to accommodate pauper children in family-type homes, ideally close to natural surroundings in the fresh air of the countryside, rather than confined in workhouses or other large institutions. In many areas Poor Law guardians began to build children's cottage homes in 'village' settings, often complete with

---

1   Cunningham, *Children and Childhood*, p. 157.

2   Hopkins, *Childhood Transformed*, p. 224.

3   Cunningham, *Children and Childhood*, p. 137; Sheldon, 'Something in the place of home', p. 261.

schools, infirmaries, bakeries and workshops. In the Birmingham area cottage homes for 420 children were opened by the Birmingham Union at Marston Green in 1880, the King's Norton Union built cottage homes for 80 children at Shenley Fields in 1887 and the Aston Union provided cottage homes for 368 children at Fentham Road in Erdington. The Wolverhampton Union built eight cottage homes on a 20-acre site at Wednesfield in 1890, providing accommodation for up to 240 children. How far were children's cottage homes in the Birmingham and Wolverhampton areas able to provide a 'homely' alternative to children's accommodation in the workhouse or residential district schools? An examination of the Wolverhampton Union's children's cottage homes at Wednesfield explores the issue of whether they offered poor children the semblance of a family home or merely a short-term solution to disruptive periods in their lives.

State involvement in children's lives

The 1880 Industrial Schools Amendment Act built on the original 1857 Act by permitting the removal of children from houses or premises frequented by prostitutes. In the 1850s Mary Carpenter and fellow reformers campaigned for the establishment of reformatory schools and industrial schools to counter the risk of juvenile delinquency among children described by Carpenter as from 'the dangerous and perishing classes'. Under the 1857 Act, children and young people up to the age of 16 who were already involved in crime and thus from 'the dangerous classes' were committed to reformatories. Children under 14 years of age found begging in the streets or neglected by their parents were from 'the perishing classes' at risk of criminal behaviour, and were sent to certified industrial schools.[4] The subsequent Amendment Act of 1880 was passed following pressure by reformers such as Ellice Hopkins, who was committed to the reform of prostitutes and the prevention of young girls from falling into prostitution.[5] This legislation made it a criminal offence for children under the age of 16 to reside in houses or lodging houses that operated as brothels. The police were given powers to remove children from such premises and place them in certified industrial schools alongside vagrant, destitute or disorderly children.

Over the course of five years before the Amendment Act, from 1868 to 1873, the Gem Street Industrial School in Birmingham admitted a total of 71 girls. Most were committed to the school for either vagrancy (30 per cent)

---

4   Pamela Horn, *The Victorian Town Child* (Stroud, 1997), pp. 203–04.

5   Peter Higginbotham, *Children's Homes: A History of Institutional Care for Britain's Young* (Barnsley, 2017), p. 229; Michelle Cale, 'Saved from a Life of Vice and Crime: Reformatory and Industrial Schools for Girls, c1854–1901', DPhil thesis (University of Oxford, 1993), pp. 47–52.

or theft (23 per cent), with smaller numbers committed for being destitute, uncontrollable, 'with no proper guardians' or 'frequenting the company of thieves'. Vagrancy, destitution and criminal behaviour were commonly viewed as routes into early prostitution for young girls, who were therefore regarded as in dangerous situations that left them at risk of sexual exploitation.[6] The 1880 Act thus represented a move towards greater state involvement in children's lives, which included the aim of controlling the moral behaviour of girls from destitute families. Ellice Hopkins and other middle-class reformers believed that working-class girls should be raised as 'modest, decent and obedient' daughters who were suitable for employment as domestic servants in middle-class households, rather than in well-paid but less respectable factory work.[7] Day Industrial Schools were introduced to provide elementary education and training for children whose education was being neglected by their parents, but without removing them from the family home. Wolverhampton opened a Day Industrial School in 1881 at Salop Street, providing non-residential places for up to 150 children between the ages of seven and 13 years. In theory, the children were to receive vocational training that would prepare them for respectable future employment, but in practice at the Wolverhampton school this training amounted to little more than chopping firewood for boys and housework or kitchen work for girls.[8] It appears, therefore, that even though the school may have been relatively successful in keeping children off the streets and out of trouble, it was very limited in the ability to provide training for employment.

A significant change in the relationship between the family and the state took place in 1889 with the passing of the Prevention of Cruelty to Children Act, which further increased state involvement in children's lives. Societies for the Prevention of Cruelty to Children were established in Liverpool and London during the 1880s with the objective of preventing the physical abuse of children, including the practice of sending children out at night to beg or hawk goods on the streets.[9] The 1889 Act introduced penalties for parents who mistreated or neglected their children and prohibited children from hawking on the streets, acting, singing or performing for payment at night-time between the hours of 10pm and 5am. These new restrictions applied to boys up to the age of 14, and girls up to the age of 16, while children under the age of ten were prohibited from these activities at any time of day or night, with parents fined or imprisoned for breaking the law. Inspectors were appointed

---

6   Cale, 'Saved from a Life of Vice', pp. 82–3.

7   *Ibid.*, p. 51.

8   WALS, D-EDS-168, Wolverhampton Day Industrial School.

9   Horn, *Victorian Town Child*, p. 120.

by the National Society for the Prevention of Cruelty to Children (NSPCC), which was established in the same year, with powers to investigate cases of ill-treatment or neglect and to remove children from abusive homes.

Well-known organisations such as Barnardo's and the Waifs and Strays Society were part of a substantial network of charities concerned with child welfare that were established in the second half of the nineteenth century. Many of these voluntary organisations were founded by middle-class female philanthropists who were particularly concerned with the protection and care of girls and young women. Louisa Twining, founder of the Workhouse Visiting Society, also opened a residential home in central London for unemployed young servant girls, providing them with an alternative to the workhouse. The home was unable to continue owing to lack of funding, but was replaced in 1875 by the Metropolitan Association for Befriending Young Servants (MABYS).[10] This organisation for the support of 'orphans and friendless young servants in London' was established at the suggestion of workhouse inspector Jane Nassau Senior. It attracted voluntary help from 800 to 900 ladies who visited and offered support to almost 7,000 young domestic servants employed in the capital. The Metropolitan Association provided a registration service for young servants seeking employment in London as well as hostel accommodation for girls. A similar organisation, the Girls Friendly Society, was founded in Warwickshire in 1875 by Mary Elizabeth Townsend, with the aim of supporting country girls who moved into towns and cities in search of work. The GFS established a number of branches around the country providing lodges, training homes and convalescent homes for young women and girls, as well as a workhouse visiting scheme. Girls who worked could join the society from the age of 12, but they were required to belong to the Church of England, a rule that did not apply to the young servants supported by MABYS.[11] A third organisation, the Ladies Association for the Care of Friendless Girls, was set up in 1876 by Ellice Hopkins with the aim of preventing young girls from falling into prostitution. Locally run associations promoted moral teaching, provided training homes and set up refuges for girls at risk. The Ladies Association was active in campaigns against prostitution, including lobbying for the 1885 Criminal Law Amendment Act, which increased the age of consent from 13 to 16 years.[12]

Social reformers Florence, Rosamund and Joanna Hill were active in debates over state provision for poor children who were left orphaned, abandoned, destitute or homeless. In the mid-nineteenth century a number of Poor Law

10   Florence Davenport Hill, *Children of the State* (London, 1889), pp. 119–23; Higginbotham, *Children's Homes*, pp. 226–7.
11   Hill, *Children of the State*, p. 128; Higginbotham, *Children's Homes*, pp. 227–9.
12   Cale, 'Saved from a Life of Vice', p. 48; Higginbotham, *Children's Homes*, pp. 229–30.

unions had joined together to build large residential district schools with the aim of reducing 'inherited pauperism' by separating children from adults in the workhouse. By the 1860s, however, social reformers had already recognised the problems commonly found in district schools and began to support the system of boarding-out of children with working-class families.[13] Florence Davenport Hill's book *Children of the State* advocated this method for orphaned and deserted children in England, following the lead of successful policies in Scotland and Ireland.[14] Large-scale institutions were notorious for the spread of contagious diseases, especially eye diseases, which were an ongoing problem for district schools. The schools were criticised both for their lack of individual attention to children and because the poor quality of training given to girls in domestic skills did not prepare them either for employment in domestic service or for lives as wives and mothers.

From Hill's perspective, children who were regularly admitted for short periods of time were a disruptive and negative influence over other children in the institution. The families known as 'ins and outs' entered the workhouse system with their children for a few days or a few weeks at a time, and then left again when casual work became available.[15] One family entered the St Pancras workhouse 17 times between July 1885 and December 1886, and a second family was admitted 24 times over a seven-month period in 1886. Hill described such families, who relied on intermittent and casual labour, as 'of the most degraded type, and shocking must have been the experiences the miserable children poured forth on their little companions at school'. In order to separate children who needed long-term care from the 'ins and outs', the ideal solution was to board out orphaned and abandoned children with respectable working-class families on a long-term basis. In this way they could become part of a family, experience a proper home life and attend school with local children.[16] The question remained, however, of how best to provide for the majority of poor children who needed support but were neither orphaned or abandoned and did not fit the criteria for boarding-out.

Children's cottage homes

The earliest children's cottage homes were built by charities in village settings: The Home for Little Boys in Kent opened in 1865, Princess Mary's Village Home for Little Girls in Surrey opened in 1870 and the Barnardo's Girls' Village Home in Essex opened in 1876. Following the success of these early homes and in

---

13   Horn, *Victorian Town Child*, p. 191.

14   Hill, *Children of the State*, pp. 141–74; Horn, *Victorian Town Child*, pp. 191–2.

15   Horn, *Victorian Town Child*, p. 187.

16   Hill, *Children of the State*, pp. 68–9.

line with changes in public attitudes towards childhood, many social reformers and Poor Law guardians began to support similar schemes to replace existing institutions. Children's cottage homes were built in self-sufficient communities, often around a village green, and were likely to include a school, chapel, workshops, bakery, laundry and sometimes swimming baths as well. Supporters of the system argued that family-type homes in the countryside, well away from towns and cities, were the ideal setting for pauper children to become good citizens and to learn a trade or become trained in domestic service. Even though children's cottage homes were popular with some reformers and Poor Law guardians, they were also the subject of much debate. Criticism of the cottage-homes system centred on the high capital expenditure and running costs, plus the isolation of children from normal working-class life.

In the Barnardo's Girls' Village Home each cottage was arranged in the same way as a small middle-class home, containing a living room, dining room, playroom or nursery, together with a kitchen and scullery. Girls living in the home became accustomed to this particular form of middle-class domestic life, and were trained in domestic skills that prepared them for service in a similarly arranged household.[17] The Kensington and Chelsea Union cottage homes at Banstead in Surrey, opened in 1880, provided a number of detached cottages, a school, a staff house for the teachers and a house with garden for the master and matron. Each of the girls' homes accommodated up to 26 children and the boys' homes up to 38, with baths in all the cottages plus swimming baths for the boys who 'all looked remarkably clean'.[18] The Kensington and Chelsea guardians dealt with the problem of disruption caused by the 'ins and outs' by opening a probationary home in Hammersmith. Children remained in this home until clear of any infectious disease, and were often removed by their parents before being transferred from London to the cottage homes at Banstead. The Birmingham Union children's cottage homes at Marston Green were built on a large well-planned site, but without a probationary home as a filter for new entrants. This resulted in a constant turnover of children in the Marston Green homes, with approximately 40 per cent of the children remaining for short-term stays only, and a consequent loss of any possible family atmosphere.[19] From a contemporary standpoint, Florence Davenport Hill concluded that although children's cottage homes were an improvement on workhouses and district schools, 'their studied neatness and affected homeliness does not give the *feeling* of home'.[20]

---

17   Murdoch, *Imagined Orphans*, pp. 61–4.

18   Hill, *Children of the State*, pp. 89–90.

19   *Ibid.*, pp. 91–2.

20   *Ibid.*, p. 90.

Hill presented the case for the boarding-out of children in terms of financial savings to the ratepayers, which involved average costs of 4s per week for each child. The cost of keeping a child in the workhouse was 3s per week, but with additional expenditure on staff wages and building expenses. Children in some Poor Law unions had been transferred to separate district schools, where the costs per child were higher at an average of 6s 4d per week. For children who were boarded out, there was the additional benefit to ratepayers of placing them in the homes of 'the respectable labouring classes' and thus breaking the cycle of pauperism.[21] Making an appeal to public opinion, Francis Peek, chairman of the Boarding-out Committee of the Howard Association, argued that children in the workhouse were raised as 'pauper outcasts', enduring 'a childhood of miserable monotony within its dull prison-like walls, without love and without hope'.[22] He added that district and industrial schools were an improvement on workhouses, but the children were left without home ties, received no domestic training and were forced to mix with the children of thieves and tramps. On the other hand, children who were boarded out formed strong ties with their foster parents, and 'fall into the habits of industry they see around them, and rarely turn out ill'.[23] Joanna Hill continued to press the case for boarding-out children with families in the local community. Writing in 1876, she highlighted the extent of eye disease in district schools, which affected 80 per cent of the children and could lead to blindness in the most serious cases.[24] Birmingham parish had the largest number of boarded-out children in England, incurring an average expenditure of £10 8s per annum for each child, a saving on the large sums spent on maintaining children in district schools. Orphaned and deserted children from Birmingham were placed with families of good character who undertook to treat the children as their own, providing 'the ordinary circumstances and surroundings of an every-day home among the best of the working classes'.[25]

Those opposed to boarding-out described the system as 'delightful in theory' but 'an inadequate means of dealing with the large number of children now maintained by the poor rates'. At the same time, the cottage-homes system was still unproven as an alternative to large-scale children's institutions.[26] One drawback of the cottage homes was the high cost of bringing up children

21   Florence Hill, 'The Boarding-Out System', *The Examiner*, 24 February 1872.

22   Francis Peek, 'The Boarding-Out of Pauper Children', *The Examiner*, 16 March 1872.

23   *Ibid.*

24   Joanna Hill, 'Our State Children "At Home"', *The Langham Magazine*, 1876, pp. 336–9.

25   Hill, 'Our State Children', p. 337.

26   Leigh Hunt, Albany Fonblanque and John Forster, 'Cottage Homes for Pauper Children', *The Examiner*, 21 October 1878.

in small groups, since equipping each cottage with kitchen, living room, laundry and bathroom facilities for 20 to 30 children was far more expensive than providing for several hundred children. A second drawback was the considerable expense involved in training and employing the large number of house parents needed to staff a children's village. Although cottage homes were recognised as preferable to large institutions in terms of improving the quality of children's lives, questions were raised about whether ratepayers should be asked to fund accommodation and facilities that were beyond the means of many ordinary hard-working families. Furthermore, critics of cottage homes argued that they were unaffordable because increases in the poor rate created greater unemployment, and consequently more paupers in need of assistance. Provision of children's cottage homes should therefore be left to charitable organisations rather than funded by ratepayers under the poor law.[27] Despite these disadvantages in terms of costs, the Birmingham guardians decided in 1878 to build cottage homes for pauper children on 16 acres of land in the Warwickshire countryside at Marston Green, a site that was extended to more than 80 acres by the turn of the century.

Birmingham also set up a Boarding-out Committee in 1879 to oversee long-term care arrangements for the relatively small number of children who were orphaned or abandoned. Joanna Hill, a member of the Boarding-out Committee in the neighbouring Kings Norton Union, argued that cottage homes housing up to 40 children were merely 'pseudo cottage homes' and quite different from boarding-out, where children were placed in real family homes.[28] Using Birmingham as an example, Joanna Hill pointed out that the Marston Green homes had housed an average of 381 children during the year ending in March 1886, but due to the large number of transient children a total of 680 children had passed through the homes over the period, and only 180 children had remained for two years or more. Whereas the proportion of new admissions to existing resident children in voluntary schemes was around 15 per cent, at Marston Green the proportion of new admissions amounted to 50 per cent, bringing 'insuperable difficulties' for creating the atmosphere of a real family home.[29] These statistics indicate that voluntary cottage-homes schemes were providing long-term care for children without families, as opposed to those needing temporary respite.

The focus on protecting orphaned or abandoned children from 'corruption' by children in need of short-term support reflected a contemporary middle-

---

27   *Ibid.*

28   Joanna Hill, 'The Pseudo and the Real "Cottage Homes" for Pauper Children', *Westminster Review* (1896), pp. 660–75.

29   *Ibid.*, pp. 663–4.

class perception that the offspring of 'ins and outs' were a threat to stability in children's institutions because they remained closely connected to their own families.[30] Lydia Murdoch has argued that children of the casual poor were often presented in the press or by charities such as Barnardo's as abandoned by their parents, but even though they were the most numerous in Poor Law institutions it was not usual for them to be left permanently. In most cases, families turned to the poor law for assistance in times of crisis, such as loss of employment, illness, or lack of housing. During these short-term emergencies parents were likely to place their children in an institution on a temporary basis, withdrawing them again at the earliest opportunity. The move towards family-type provision by the state, either in children's cottage homes or in foster homes, illustrates the growing influence of middle-class female reformers who stressed women's specialist expertise in childcare and domestic matters.[31] An emphasis on middle-class notions of domesticity, however, failed to reflect the harsh realities of life for families who were living in urban poverty. Evidence from the Wolverhampton archives, examined below, throws light on the experiences of children and parents from the poorest families who turned to the poor law for assistance.

Case study: Wolverhampton Union Children's Cottage Homes

The Wolverhampton Board of Guardians acquired a 20-acre site approximately three miles outside the town in Amos Lane, Wednesfield, with the intention of removing children from close proximity to adults in the workhouse. When opened in 1890, the Wednesfield Children's Cottage Homes consisted of eight cottages for up to 240 children, a school, an infirmary, swimming baths and a probationary lodge where children were initially housed for quarantine. The registration book indicates that a total of 258 children was admitted into the cottage homes over the year January to December 1897[32] – a number exceeding the residential places actually available. However, virtually all the children were short-term residents, remaining for periods of a few days to several months, with only two children remaining for more than a year. Approximately equal numbers of boys and girls arrived at the homes in 1897, ranging in age from two to 15 years old. Children were most frequently admitted to the Wednesfield cottage homes when their parents entered the union workhouse in Wolverhampton. The second most common reason was because one or both parents were in prison. In one case, a family of four children – two girls aged eight and two boys aged seven – were admitted because their father had

---

30   Murdoch, *Imagined Orphans*, pp. 49–51; Sheldon, 'Something in the place of home', pp. 256–7.

31   Murdoch, *Imagined Orphans*, pp. 65–6.

32   WALS, D-COT/2/1, Wolverhampton Union Cottage Homes, Register of Children.

been imprisoned and their mother was confined to an asylum. The children remained in the cottage homes for a period of three months before being claimed by their father. Similarly, a family of four brothers aged between four and 12 years arrived at the homes in November 1897 when their father was in the general hospital and their mother in an asylum. In this instance, the children remained in the homes for three months before being released into the care of an aunt.[33]

In most cases children left the Wednesfield homes to be returned to their mothers. Ten-year-old Fanny A., for example, was admitted in December 1897 because her mother was in the workhouse. Fanny remained in the cottage homes for ten months until returning to her mother in September 1898. Sarah A., aged five, also entered the homes in December 1897, in this case because her mother was in prison, but it was evidently a short sentence because Sarah was returned to her mother within a month. Nine-year-old Mary K. went into the cottage homes in May 1897 when her mother entered the workhouse, and she was readmitted in July, August and September for a few days each time, as her mother repeatedly returned to the workhouse. Girls who were above the age of 12 when arriving at the cottage homes were quickly found employment as domestic servants. Elizabeth B., aged 15, entered the homes on 6 March 1897 and was placed in service with the Reverend F. Sutherland a month later on 7 April 1897; Mary B., aged 14, who was admitted on the same day as Elizabeth, was placed in service on 29 March with Mrs Thomas of Brierley Hill, some ten miles away; and 13-year-old Mary Ann D. was placed in domestic service in Nuneaton, almost 36 miles from her home town of Wolverhampton.

The records indicate that relatively few boys above the age of 12 were admitted into the cottage homes, and there was a pattern of absconding among boys in this age group. Henry D. was a 13-year-old in 1897 who remained in the homes for four months before absconding. There is no further record of Henry in the register for that year, but it seems that there was no system of follow-up for children who absconded from the homes. Twelve-year-old James J. absconded from the homes after just one day, although a note on his record shows that his clothing was returned on the following day, suggesting that he may have gone to a family member who then returned the property. A third boy, George P., aged 11, lived at the homes for five months before absconding 'in Homes clothing', but with no record of his whereabouts. What seems clear from these cases is that the return of cottage homes clothing was an important issue for the guardians responsible for controlling finances, but the whereabouts of children who absconded was not recorded. In a further example, four brothers who arrived at the homes in July 1897 absconded two months later in September

---

33   WALS, D-COT/2/1.

1897. There is no indication of how Henry, aged ten, John, aged six, George, aged four, and two-year-old Albert were able to leave the homes by themselves, but it seems likely that they were collected by their family, since the clothing issued to them was recorded as returned.[34] Since clothing was a valuable commodity to families living in poverty, the fact that cottage homes clothing was invariably returned indicates that future assistance to families may have depended on it being safely handed back.

The Wednesfield cottage homes were provided with a school on the site as well as a number of workshops that offered training to boys in carpentry, shoe-making and metal-working. The school log book for March 1898 shows that 130 children were registered at the school, with a further 14 boys undertaking industrial training.[35] It seems unlikely, however, that children could have derived very much advantage from either the workshop training or the schooling in view of the brief length of time most children spent at the cottage homes. As Murdoch has highlighted, children were typically placed in institutions by their families when faced with short-term emergencies. When the crisis of unemployment, illness or homelessness was resolved, or the prison term served, then children were retrieved by their parents or another family member. This cycle of predicaments experienced by poor families resulted in the constant movement of children in and out of institutional care, including children's cottage homes. When compared with large institutions such as workhouses or district schools, the cottage-homes system offered obvious benefits to children in terms of their physical surroundings, healthcare and schooling, but the hope of providing pauper children with something resembling a family home proved more difficult to achieve in practice.

Conclusion

The nineteenth century saw the concept of childhood gradually redefined as a period of innocence and freedom from earning a living for most children, including the poorest. In the second half of the century the child-saving activities undertaken by individual philanthropists and voluntary agencies were joined by government legislation and the involvement of professionals. The Education Acts and Factory Acts ensured that by the turn of the century children remained in school until the age of 12, although many continued to work part-time outside school hours as errand boys and girls or street-sellers. Changes in attitudes to childhood and pressure from middle-class social reformers brought greater intervention by the state in children's lives, including the removal of children from abusive or neglectful families. Furthermore,

---

34 *Ibid.*

35 WALS, D-COT/1/1 Wolverhampton Union Cottage Homes, School Log Book.

these pressures combined to focus attention on the most appropriate type of institutional provision for children of the poor. Poor Law guardians began to seek out alternatives to children's accommodation in overcrowded workhouses and large district schools, considering options such as boarding-out in foster homes or children's cottage-home villages in the countryside. As middle-class women became increasingly involved in public life, they sought to establish their particular expertise in domestic matters and issues around childcare. Social-reform activists such as Florence and Joanna Hill favoured boarding-out with local families for children who needed long-term care because they had no family of their own. For the vast majority of children who needed relatively short-term care in the Birmingham and Wolverhampton districts of the West Midlands, cottage-home villages accommodating around 1,100 children in total were built between 1880 and 1890. The example of the Wolverhampton homes at Wednesfield shows that children typically spent a few weeks or months in the cottages, but almost none remained for longer than a year, demonstrating the agency of the poorest families in Wolverhampton in using the children's cottage homes in times of extreme necessity, such as homelessness or imprisonment, and allowing them to keep their families together in the long-term. The aim of providing a home-like environment for children proved difficult to achieve in view of the constant movement in and out of the homes, but the guardians were successful in their aim of isolating children from 'undesirable' adults in the workhouse.

10

Conclusion

Child workers were an integral part of the Birmingham and West Midlands' economy from the early years of industrialisation through to the latter decades of the nineteenth century, making significant contributions to expansion and industrial development in the region. Large numbers of children were expected to begin work from an early age, some, like Will Thorne in 1863, at just five or six years old. Parents regarded their children as potentially valuable contributors to the family economy and the availablity of work for children in manufacturing industries encouraged families to migrate from rural areas into towns. There was a greater intensity of child labour in the early decades of the nineteenth century, with the lengthening of working hours and increasing numbers of women and children in the workforce, while the prevalence of child labour extended beyond the classic period of industrialisation. And while poor families migrated from the countryside to towns in search of employment, middle-class 'child savers' sent children from the poorest families to Canada overseas to work as farm servants, separating them permanently from their families.

Child workers and the local economy

Child workers made important contributions to economic expansion in Birmingham and the West Midlands. Few parish children were apprenticed to Birmingham masters, even from the parish of Harborne, only three miles from the town.[1] Children bound in Birmingham were ten years of age or above, indicating that tradesmen were unwilling to accept very young children as parish apprentices. However, large numbers of pauper children were employed at the Birmingham Asylum for the Infant Poor, in effect a children's workhouse that put children to work at pin making, straw-plaiting, bead-stringing and glass-cutting.[2] In the coalfields of south Staffordshire and Warwickshire children began work between the ages of seven and nine, and in the Shropshire coalfields at just six years of age. Some of these boys were parish apprentices who received board and lodgings but no wages until the age of 21, even though they were forced to work in the most difficult and dangerous conditions in the mines.

---

1   WoCRO, 5498/9; 9135/38–41; BAH, EP 14/157; SCRO, D4383/6/5; D3773/5/1059–1251; WCRO, DRB0056/143–144.

2   BAH, GP B/2/1–5.

Non-apprenticed children were an essential part of eighteenth-century Birmingham's metal-button industry, which was dependent on a division of labour between skilled adult workers and child assistants.[3] In Birmingham and West Midlands' manufacturing industries children were directly employed by individual workmen rather than by the owners of firms, so that child workers were scattered throughout the numerous factories and workshops of the region. The methods of production and employment practices found locally meant that child workers in these industries were excluded from protective legislation contained in the Factory Acts of the 1830s and 1840s, although there was a high demand for child workers in a wide variety of industries, including button-making, brass-casting, lock-making, nail-making, tin-plating, carpet-weaving, glass-making and the gun trade. The average age for starting work in Birmingham was eight or nine years in 1841, and an estimated 2,000 children below the age of ten continued to be employed in Birmingham in 1862. The prevalence of child labour in manufacturing industries thus goes well beyond the mid-nineteenth century. Moreover, since the production of manufactured goods was largely dependent on the labour of low-paid child assistants, children working in these industries made a vital contribution to the local economy.

The importance of children's earnings

Children's earnings were of great importance for family incomes and parents made strategic decisions in order to maximise this supplement to the household economy. So, for example, children were removed by their parents from the Birmingham Infant Asylum once they were trained in pin-making and could obtain employment in the pin workshops, and Phipson's pin manufactory employed children from the poorest and most destitute families, whose wages were paid directly to their parents, often in the form of an advance payment. Children in the button industry also frequently worked to support their parents owing to poor trade conditions and low wages, and because the demand for child workers and young people in Birmingham was greater than that for adult workers. Average earnings for adults with skills in metal manufacture were higher than those in industries such as textiles or mining, and considerably higher than in agriculture. High wages and a strong demand for child workers contributed to population expansion in Birmingham and other industrial towns over the course of the nineteenth century. However, there was a wide gulf in economic circumstances between the families of skilled workers and those of unskilled workers, unemployed workers or with one parent absent. Will Thorne's autobiography provides a

---

3   Tucker, *Instructions for Travellers*, p. 34; Fitzmaurice, *Life of Shelburne*, pp. 274–7.

particularly vivid first-hand account of the type of hardships encountered by children following the loss of a parent.[4]

The impact of early work on education and health

Work patterns intensified during the nineteenth century, including for children: there was a general expectation that children would work for far longer than the normal ten-hour working day. Nine-year-old Benjamin Beach, for example, began work at 6am each morning to make advance preparations before his father's arrival at work between 7am and 9am, and children employed at Phipson's in 1840 were still at work at 8pm, an hour later than adult workers, who left at 7pm.[5] Children thus worked at least as many hours as adult workers in the mid-nineteenth century, an intensity of labour that clearly had implications for their education and health.

Working families in Birmingham chose to send their children to local dame schools at a very young age, making use of an affordable form of childcare that was easy to access and permitted mothers to return to paid employment. At the age of six or seven children moved to common day schools, charity schools or voluntary schools run on the monitorial system, typically attending for one or two years before beginning paid work at the age of eight or nine. They were thus likely to have received four or five years of schooling in reading, writing and religious instruction, perhaps supplemented by Sunday school. Labouring families adopted a number of strategies to ensure that their children received basic educational skills without losing earnings, but apparently considered that a few years of schooling were sufficient for children destined for manual labour or domestic work.

The hazardous nature of children's work to health was illustrated in the first-hand accounts of George Jacob Holyoake and Will Thorne. Children worked in poor environmental conditions at harmful industrial processes that produced dangerous fumes and dust, such as brass-founding, or were exposed to lead, arsenic, mercury and white phosphorus. They suffered from accidental injuries in the workplace, mainly to the head, eyes and fingers. These injuries seem to have been regarded as normal everyday events: losing a finger was part of the process of becoming an experienced workman. Additionally, they were often subjected to ill-treatment from adult workers in the form of beating and kicking. Children employed by metal-workers in Willenhall, by nail-makers in Sedgley and by coal-miners in the south Staffordshire coalfields were treated with exceptional cruelty by their employers. The risks to child workers' health increased quite significantly over the course of the nineteenth century as new

---

4   Thorne, *My Life's Battles*, pp. 15–16.

5   BPP, 1843, 431, XIV.

industrial processes and machinery were introduced. Accidents involving metal-rolling machines and fatal explosions in the percussion-cap industry are just two examples of these hazards. Finally, female child workers could be drawn into juvenile prostitution following failed sexual relationships with male co-workers, suffering sexual abuse as a result. Police officers in the nineteenth century made moral judgements about such girls, regarding them as morally corrupt and failing to perceive them as victims of exploitation. These attitudes are often echoed in the twenty-first-century police response to the grooming and sexual abuse of young girls by predatory males.

Changes in attitudes

In the eighteenth and early nineteenth centuries it was widely believed that children of the poor should be put to work at a very early age to discourage idleness and instil the habit of industriousness in the young. Children housed in the Birmingham Asylum for the Infant Poor were expected to earn their keep by working at repetitive manual occupations such as pin-making and lace-making. Concerns about health and education emerged in the 1830s, followed by decisions to abolish work for children under nine and limit work to six hours per day for those up to the age of 13 years, in line with the 1833 Factories Act.[6] These policies reflected changing attitudes in society towards childhood, placing a greater emphasis on the role of education for all children as a means of reducing pauperism and dependence on the poor rate.

With the introduction of the 1867 Factory Act and 1867 Workshops Regulation Act, children below the age of eight could no longer be legally employed, and those between eight and 13 years could work only half-time. Legal restrictions on child labour during the 1860s took place alongside the emergence of middle-class schemes to clear urban streets of poor children, often termed 'gutter children' or 'street arabs'.[7] Supporters of the Middlemore Emigration Homes in Birmingham were persuaded that slum-dwelling children would have a better life in rural Canada, far removed from the harmful influences of their own families. Children as young as ten were sent to work as farm servants on isolated Canadian farms, with little scrutiny of their future employers and even less inspection afterwards. Child migration schemes thus became a new form of child labour for the poorest children in the later decades of the nineteenth century, shifting children off the streets and out of sight across the ocean.

Examples of agency by child workers are relatively few, since decisions were usually made by adults on their behalf. In some instances children made a

---

6   BAH, GP B/2/1/3.

7   Parker, *Uprooted*, pp. 10–31.

choice to undertake paid work in preference to attending school, but most children did not have this option. However, child workers like George Jacob Holyoake shared a strong sense of family duty and were proud of their ability to earn a living and add to the family income.[8] By the age of 13 or 14 many young people began to use their own agency to make decisions about moving from one employer to another as they became more experienced workers in well-paid trades.

In the second half of the nineteenth century economic divisions within the working classes widened: on the one hand, families of skilled workers enjoyed rising levels of prosperity, particularly among families with adolescent children earning good wages while remaining in the family home; on the other hand, large numbers of families had fallen into poverty because of intermittent work, unemployment or family breakdown.[9] By the end of the century, when children were legally required to remain in education until at least the age of 12, new measures were aimed at protecting children from abuse and neglect. As middle-class women became more prominent in public life they took an active part in debates concerned with child welfare, including the boarding-out of children with foster families and the replacement of children's wards in the workhouse with cottage-home villages. While the latter may not have been successful in providing the 'homely atmosphere' intended, they were at least beneficial in allowing parents to keep their families together in times of crisis.

The issues explored here remain relevant to current events around the world. Only in the last few years has the extreme hardship and abuse experienced by child migrants despatched from the UK to Australia in the 1950s and 1960s been acknowledged, with a recommendation for compensation in 2018 by the Independent Inquiry into Child Sexual Abuse.[10] Moreover, the study of historical child labour is relevant to understanding the experiences of millions of child workers around the globe, from the brick-kilns and mica mines of India to the garment factories of Bangladesh, and from cocoa farms in Ghana to the cobalt mines of the Democratic Republic of Congo.[11] The close

---

8   Holyoake, *Sixty Years*, pp. 10–19.

9   BAH, LB.48.

10   Ben Macintyre, 'When Good Intentions Lead to Awful Crimes', *The Times*, 3 March 2018.

11   P. Bengtsen and L. Paddison, 'Beauty companies and the struggle to source child labour-free mica', *The Guardian*, 28 July 2016; M. Safi, 'Child labour "rampant" in Bangladesh factories, study reveals', *The Guardian*, 7 December 2016; '200 children found working in India brick kiln', *The Guardian*, 5 January 2017; A. Kelly, 'Children as young as seven mining cobalt used in smartphones, says Amnesty', *The Guardian*, 19 January 2016; P. Whoriskey and T.C. Frankel, ' Tech giants pledge to keep children out of cobalt mines that supply smartphone and electric-car batteries', *The Washington Post*, 20 December 2016; T.C. Frankel, 'Cobalt mining for lithium ion batteries has a high human cost', *The Washington Post*, 30 September 2016.

historical links between family poverty and child labour in Birmingham and the West Midlands resonate with the prevalence of child labour in countries around the world today, highlighting the significance of historical research for understanding current economic and political challenges.

Appendix

1. Occupations of parish apprentices in Birmingham, 1750–1835 (from nine sample parishes)

Occupation	Age									Total
	7	8	9	10	11	12	13	14	Not known	
Domestic service			4			1	2	2	5	14
Cordwainer		2	1	6	3	5	9	8	2	36
Chape-maker				1					2	3
Breeches-maker									1	1
Tailor			2				1	2		5
Mantua-maker				1				1		2
Peruke-maker		1			1		1	1	1	5
Basket-maker				1	1				1	3
Brush-maker		1						1	1	3
Cabinet-maker								3		3
Wood-turner				1	1		1	4	1	8
Locksmith				1	3		1	2	1	8
Gunsmith/finisher		1		2	2	2	4	1	1	13
Gunbarrel-borer	1	1		1			1			4
Blade-maker		1			1	1			1	4
Bayonet-forger								1	1	2
Polisher						1				1
Cutler									1	1
Brass-founder				1	2	1	1	3		8
Button-maker	1			1				2	6	10
Buckle-maker			1	2	4	2	2	2	7	20
Toy-maker				2		3		1	5	11
Pin-/wire-worker	1		1	1		2			1	6
Other trades			4	9	9	6	14	10	8	60
Factory manufacture										
Transport										
Building & timber				1			1	1	1	4
Retail, hostelries				1			1	3		5
Professional										
Totals	3	7	13	32	27	24	39	48	47	240

Source: parish apprenticeship certificates, SCRO, D3773/5/1059–1251; D4383/6/5; BAH, EP 61/7/8; EP 14/157; WCRO, DRBO100/107–109; DRB0056/143–144; DRB0019/83–89; WoCRO, 5498/9; 9135/38–41.

2a. Apprentices' occupations by gender – three Worcestershire parishes

Occupation	No. of boys	No. of girls
Agriculture husbandry/housewifery	400	319
Trades and crafts	137	14
Textile factories		1
Mining	24	
Domestic service		4

Source: WoCRO, 5498/9 Alvechurch Parish Apprenticeship Certificates; WoCRO, 9135/38–40 Bromsgrove Parish Apprenticeship Certificates.

2b. Apprentices' occupations by gender – three Staffordshire parishes

Occupation	No. of boys	No. of girls
Agriculture husbandry/housewifery	26	115
Trades and crafts	220	25
Textile factories	2	18
Mining	37	
Domestic service		1

Source: BAH, EP14/157; SCRO, D4383/6/5; SCRO, D3773/5/1059–1251, Parish Apprenticeships.

2c. Apprentices' occupations by gender – three Warwickshire parishes

Occupation	No. of boys	No. of girls
Agriculture husbandry/housewifery	125	129
Trades and crafts	345	55
Textile factories		18
Mining	2	
Domestic service		8

Source: WCRO, DRB0100/107–109; DRB0019/83–89; DRB0056/143–144, Parish Apprenticeships.

3a. Children apprenticed in Birmingham by three Warwickshire parishes

Years	No. to Birmingham	Average age	% of all parish children
1750–59	9		19
1760–69	7		11
1770–79	20	11.5	22
1780–89	16	12.1	16
1790–99	34	12.1	39
1800–09	46	11.6	25
1810–19	21	12.3	40
1820–29	22	13.2	56
1830–35	9	12.6	53

Source: WCRO, DRB0019/83–89 Tanworth in Arden Parish Apprenticeship Certificates; WCRO, DRB0100/107–109 Coleshill Parish Apprenticeship Certificates; WCRO, DRB0056/143–144 Knowle Parish Apprenticeship Certificates.

3b. Destinations of parish apprentices from three Warwickshire parishes

	Home parish	Birmingham & Aston	Warks., Worcs. or Staffs.	Other	Total	% to Birmingham
1750–59	5	9	33	0	47	19
1760–69	35	7	19	1	62	11
1770–79	55	20	15	0	90	22
1780–89	49	16	31	1	97	16
1790–99	29	34	20	4	88	39
1800–09	75	46	54	8	184	25
1810–19	5	21	26	0	52	40
1820–29	3	22	13	1	39	56
1830–35	0	9	8	0	17	53
Total	264	184	218	15	681	27

Source. WCRO, DRB0019/83–89 Tanworth in Arden Parish Apprenticeship Certificates; WCRO, DRB0100/107–109 Coleshill Parish Apprenticeship Certificates; WCRO, DRB0056/143–144 Knowle Parish Apprenticeship Certificates.

4. Payments to Shakespear family by Knowle Overseers, 1765–74

Date	Record of payment	Amount
12 Nov 1765	Gave Eliz. Shakespear	1s 0d
24 Nov	Gave Eliz. Shakespear	6d
28 Nov	Gave Eliz. Shakespear	1s 0d
5 Dec	Paid for shoes for Shakespears Girl	2s 4d
7 Dec	Gave Betty Shakespear	1s 0d
14 Dec	Gave Shakespear 6t of coals	5s 0d
2 Jan 1766	Gave Shakespears wife	1s 0d
5 Jan	Gave her	1s 0d
7 Jan	Gave Thomas Shakespear	6d
12 Jan	Gave Thomas Shakespear	6d
13 Jan	Gave Thomas Shakespear	6d
17 Jan	Gave Thomas Shakespear	1s 0d
19 Jan	Paid for 4t of Coals for Shakespear	3s 4d
21 Jan	Gave him	1s 0d
21 Jan	Gave him	6d
26 Jan	Gave Betty Shakespear	1s 0d
29 Jan	Gave Thos Shakespear	6d
4 Feb	Gave him	6d
6 Feb	Gave Thos Shakespear	6d
8 Feb	Gave Shakespear	1s 0d
13 Feb	Gave Shakespear	1s 0d
17 Feb	Gave Shakespear	1s 0d
19 Feb	Gave Shakespear	6d
22 Feb	Gave Shakespear	1s 0d
2 Mar	Gave Shakespear	1s 0d
3 Mar	For 11 yards of Cloth for Shakespear's	12s 7d
13 Nov 1766	For a pair of shoes for Shakespear's Child	2s 0d
Apr 1767	Gave Thomas Shakespear at several times in his need	£1 18s 2d
Apr 1770	Gave Thomas Shakespear when his Family had the Smallpox	8s 0d
Apr 1770	For a Coffin for Shakespear's Child	7s 0d
Mar 1774	Gave Elizabeth Shakespear at several times when her husband was in prison	£3 6s 6d

Source: WCRO, DRB0056/137 Overseers Accounts, Parish of Knowle, 1764–66.

5. *Payments to Bayliss family by Knowle Overseers, 1765–67*

Date	Record of payment	Amount
1765	Gave Jacob Bayliss	1s 0d
1765	Gave Bayliss's Children	6d
1765	Gave Jacob Bayliss	2s 0d
1765	Gave his children	6d
1765	Gave them	1s 6d
1765	Gave Bayliss's Children	1s 6d
1765	Gave Bayliss's Children	1s 0d
1765	Gave Bayliss's Children	1s 0d
1765	Gave Jacob Bayliss	2s 0d
1765	Gave his children	1s 0d
1765	Gave his children	1s 6d
1765	Gave his children	2s 0d
1765	Gave his children	1s 0d
1765	Gave his children	1s 0d
1765	Gave his children	1s 0d
1765	Paid for a Pair of Shoes for Bayliss's Son	3s 0d
1765	To Mr Boston for Clothes for Bayliss's Son	7s 4d
1767–68	To Isaac Bayliss 16 weeks at 3s 0d	£2 8s 0d
6 Aug 1767	For going to Birmingham to agree with a Master for Isaac Bayliss	2s 6d
6 Aug 1767	Spent when he was bound Apprentice	6d
6 Aug 1767	Paid for part of his Indentures	3s 0d
6 Aug 1767	For marking the register for his age	6d
6 Aug 1767	For 2 Shirts and Stockings for him	8s 4d
12 Dec 1767	For a Coffin for Bayliss's Child	2s 0d

Source: WCRO, DRB0056/137 Overseers Accounts, Parish of Knowle, 1764–66.

6a. Gender differences in employment (Birmingham New Meeting Sunday Schools, 1841)

Boys			Girls		
Type of employment	No.	Age of starting work	Type of employment	No.	Age of starting work
Brass foundry	42	8 yrs	Button-making	13	7 yrs
Button-making	7	7 yrs	Warehouse girls	6	8 yrs
Gun-making	12	9 yrs	Lacquering	4	10 yrs
Other metal	49	8 yrs	Other metal	16	10 yrs
Jewellery	5	10 yrs	Service/nurse	11	8 yrs
Other trades	24	9 yrs	Other trades	10	11 yrs
At school	23	–	At school	16	–
At home	6	–	At home	28	–
Total	168		Total	105	

Source: BPP, 1843, 431, XIV, Children's Employment Commission, Second Report, pp. 200–03.

6b. Boys in employment/or at school (Birmingham Educational Association Survey, 1857)

Boys (753)				
Age	No.	In employment	At school	At home
7–8	126	6%	62%	32%
8–9	147	13%	61%	26%
9–10	133	28%	45%	26%
10–11	116	44%	41%	14%
11–12	107	73%	17%	9%
12–13	114	82%	10%	7%

Source: BPP, 1864, 3414, Children's Employment Commission 1862, Third Report, App B.

6c. Girls in employment/or at school (Birmingham Educational Association Survey, 1857)

Girls (620)				
Age	No.	In employment	At school	At home
7–8	129	3%	53%	43%
8–9	112	9%	63%	27%
9–10	96	18%	46%	35%
10–11	84	27%	33%	39%
11–12	89	46%	36%	18%
12–13	110	60%	17%	22%

Source: BPP, 1864, 3414, Children's Employment Commission 1862, Third Report, App B.

7a. Details of 300 families interviewed in 1867

Families		%
Total no. of persons	1842	
Average income per head/per wk after rent	1s 1¼d	
Rent per head per week	5¼d	
Total no. of children of all ages	1322	100
No. of children at school	31	2
No. at work above 15 years	334	25
No. at work below 15 years	79	6
Neither at work or school above 15 yrs	28	2
Neither at work or school, 3 yrs to 15 yrs	440	33
Children under 3 years	410	31

Source: BAH, LB.48, *First Annual Report of Birmingham Education Society* (1868).

7b. Details of 80 families headed by women in 1867

Families		%
Total no. of persons	494	
Income per head per wk after rent	10¾d	
Rent per head per week	5½d	
Total no. of children	414	100
No. of children at school	4	1
No. at work under 15 years	90	18
No. at work above 15 years	64	15
Neither at work nor school above 15 yrs	18	4
Neither at work nor school 3 yrs to 15 yrs	174	42

Source: BAH, LB.48, *First Annual Report of Birmingham Education Society* (1868).

8. Requests to Boulton & Watt for Handsworth National School, 1813

Workman's name	Weekly wages	No. of children	Name of child wished to be recommended	Age of child
Wm Higginshaw	20s	2	Susannah Price	9
Jn Collingwood	30s	5	Wm Collingwood	8
John Tandry	24s	8	Jas & Wm Tandry	8 & 6
John Wells	24s	2	John Wells	9
Thos Galey	20s	6	Josh Galey	7
James Seager	40s	7	Ann Seager	8
"	"	"	Edward Seager	11
Benjamin Seager	18s	1	Benjamin Seager	7
Henry Molyneux	60s	6	Edward Molyneux	8
Wm Lucas	40s	5	Samuel Lucas	9
John Turner	34s	3	Wm Turner	9
"	"	"	Josh Turner	6
Thos Hands	10s	1	Mary Ann Hands	11
Wm White	18s	3	Joseph White	9
"	"	"	Hannah White	6

Source: BAH, MS 3147/9/29 Boulton and Watt, Collection, Note in Folder 3, 14 January 1813.

Bibliography

Archival sources

Birmingham Archives and Heritage (BAH)
660982 Minutes of the Birmingham Overseers of the Poor, 1803–13
EP 14/157 Northfield Parish Apprenticeship Certificates
EP 61/7/8 Harborne Parish Apprenticeship Certificates
GP B/2/1/1–5 Minutes of the Birmingham Board of Guardians, 1783–1852
HC GH/4/2/15 Birmingham General Hospital, Urgent Medical In-patients, 1839–48
LB.48 Birmingham Education Society First Annual Report, 1868
MS 466/253 Richard Bennett, A Few Extracts from Memory to the Association for the Suppression of Climbing Boys, 1858
MS 517/63 One Hundred Years of Child Care. The Middlemore Homes, 1872–1972
MS 517/93 & 93A Middlemore Homes Newspaper Cuttings Book, 1872–1929
MS 517/245 Middlemore Homes Application Book, 1877–78
MS 517/253 Letter from W. Hughes to J. Middlemore, 18 September 1899
MS 517/253 Middlemore Homes Settlement Reports, 1873–81
MS 517/463 Middlemore Homes Reports, 1873–79
MS 517/471 Middlemore Homes Entrance Books, Girls, 1875–78
MS 517/472 Middlemore Homes Entrance Books, Boys, 1875–78
MS 1010/8–9 Ralph Heaton & Son, Wages Books, 1840–73
MS 1622/2/1/1 Blue Coat School, Register of Pupils, 1724–83
MS 1683/1 Birmingham Statistical Society Report, 1837
MS 3147/8 Boulton and Watt Collection, Staff and Employment Records, 1784–1888
MS 3147/9/29 Boulton and Watt, Collection, Note, 14th January 1813
MS 4248 National Education League Leaflet, 1871

Staffordshire County Record Office (SCRO)
D3773/5/1059–1251 Tamworth Parish Apprenticeship Certificates
D4383/6/5 Wednesbury Parish Apprenticeship Certificates

Warwickshire County Record Office (WCRO)
DRB0019/83–89 Tanworth in Arden Parish Apprenticeship Certificates
DRB0056/137 Overseers Accounts, Parish of Knowle, 1705–1836
DRB0056/143–144 Knowle Parish Apprenticeship Certificates
DRB0100/107–109 Coleshill Parish Apprenticeship Certificates

Worcestershire County Record Office (WoCRO)
5498/9 Alvechurch Parish Apprenticeship Certificates
9135/38–41 Bromsgrove Parish Apprenticeship Certificates

Wolverhampton Archives and Local Studies (WALS)
D-COT/1/1 Wolverhampton Union Cottage Homes, School Log Book
D-COT/2/1 Wolverhampton Union Cottage Homes, Register of Children
D-EDS-168 Wolverhampton Day Industrial School

Official publications
BPP, 1812, III, *Minutes of Evidence for Petitions against the Orders in Council*
BPP, 1816, 397, *Report of the Minutes of Evidence to the Select Committee on the State of Children Employed in the Manufactories of the United Kingdom*
BPP, 1833, 450, XX.I, *Factories Inquiry Commission, First Report*
BPP, 1833, 519, *Factories Inquiry Commission, Second Report*
BPP, 1841, *Royal Commission on Hand-Loom Weavers*, Vol. II
BPP, 1842, 007, XXVII, Sanitary Inquiry England, Local Reports (Chadwick's Report, 1842)
BPP, 1842, 380, *Children's Employment Commission,1842, First Report*
BPP, 1843, 430, XIII, *Children's Employment Commission, Second Report*
BPP, 1843, 431, XIV, *Children's Employment Commission, Second Report*
BPP, 1843, 432, XV, *Children's Employment Commission,1842, Second Report*
BPP, 1855, XXVIII, *Eighth Annual Report of the Poor Law Board*
BPP, 1861, *Medical Officer of the Privy Council, Fourth Report*
BPP, 1861, *Report of Commissioners into the State of Popular Education in England*
BPP, 1863, 3170, *Children's Employment Commission 1862, First Report*
BPP, 1864, 3414, *Children's Employment Commission 1862, Second Report*
BPP, 1864, 3414, *Children's Employment Commission 1862, Third Report*
BPP, 1870, 91, LIV 265/54, *Return of Schools for Poorer Classes of Children in Municipal Boroughs of Birmingham, Leeds, Liverpool and Manchester: Report on Quality of Education which Schools Provide*
Canadian Census Reports, 1881 and 1891
Census Reports of England and Wales, 1841–91

Newspapers and journals
Aris's Birmingham Gazette
Birmingham Daily Post
Coventry Standard
The Examiner
The Guardian
Household Words
The Langham Magazine
Morning News
The Penny Magazine
Tamworth Herald
The Telegraph
The Times
The Washington Post
Westminster Review

Other printed primary sources

Bisse, Reverend Thomas, *Publick Education, Particularly in the Charity Schools*, pamphlet (London, 1725).

Bunce, John Thackray, *Josiah Mason: A Biography* (Birmingham, 1882).

Hill, Florence Davenport, *Children of the State* (London, 1889).

Holyoake, George Jacob, *Sixty Years of an Agitator's Life* (London, 1900).

Knight, Arnold, *Observations on the Grinder's Asthma*, Medical and Surgical Society of Sheffield (Sheffield, 1822).

Locke, John, *An Essay Concerning Human Understanding* (London, 1690).

Locke, John, *An Essay on the Poor Law* (London, 1697).

Locke, John, *Some Thoughts Concerning Education* (London, 1693).

Richardson, William, *The Chemical Principles of the Metallic Arts* (Birmingham, 1790).

Rousseau, Jean-Jacques, *Émile, ou De L'Éducation* (London, 1763).

Royal Statistical Society, 'Report on the State of Education in Birmingham', *Journal of the Statistical Society of London*, 3/1 (1840), pp. 25–49.

Shaw, Charles, *When I Was a Child: Autobiography of Charles Shaw* (London, 1903; reprinted 2013).

Thorne, Will, *My Life's Battles* (London, 1925).

Timmins, Samuel, *Birmingham and the Midland Hardware District* (London, 1866).

Tomlinson, Thomas, *The Medical Miscellany* (Birmingham, 1774).

Tucker, Josiah, *Collected Works of Josiah Tucker, Economics and Social Policy Volume III: Instructions for Travellers* (London, 1758; reprinted 1993).

Whitmore, William W., *A Memoir relating to the Industrial School at Quatt, addressed to the Rate-payers of the South East Shropshire District School*, LSE Selected Pamphlets (London, 1894).

Secondary sources

Bagnell, Kenneth, *The Little Immigrants: The Orphans Who Came to Canada* (Toronto, 2001).

Bailey, Joanne, *Parenting in England, 1760–1830: Emotion, Identity & Generation* (Oxford, 2012).

Bailey, Joanne, '"Think wot a mother must feel": Parenting in English Pauper Letters, c1760–1834', *Family and Community History*, 13/1 (2010), pp. 5–19.

Baird, Olga, 'His Excellency Count Woronzow the Russian Ambassador and the Hardware Man: The History of a Friendship', in Malcolm Dick (ed.), *Matthew Boulton: A Revolutionary Player* (Studley, 2009), pp. 92–106.

Bartley, Paula, 'Moral Regeneration: Women and the Civic Gospel in Birmingham, 1870–1914', *Midland History*, 25/1 (2000), pp. 143–61.

Bartrip, P.W.J., *The Home Office and the Dangerous Trades: Regulating Occupational Disease in Victorian and Edwardian Britain* (Amsterdam, 2002).

Behagg, Clive, 'Myths of Cohesion: Capital and Compromise in the Historiography of Nineteenth-Century Birmingham', *Social History*, 11 (1986), pp. 375–84.

Berg, Maxine, *The Age of Manufactures 1700–1820: Industry, Innovation and Work in Britain* (London, 1994).

Berg, Maxine and Hudson, Pat, 'Rehabilitating the Industrial Revolution', *Economic History Review*, 45 (1992), pp. 24–50.

Boucher, Ellen, *Empire's Children: Child Emigration, Welfare and the Decline of the British World, 1869–1967* (Cambridge, 2014).

Bowley, A.L., 'The Statistics of Wages in the United Kingdom. (Part V.) Wages in the Building Trades in English Towns', *Journal of the Royal Statistical Society*, 63/2 (1900), pp. 302–08.

Bowley, A.L., 'The Statistics of Wages in the United Kingdom During the Last Hundred Years. (Part IV.) Agricultural Wages', *Journal of the Royal Statistical Society*, 62/3 (1899), pp. 555–70.

Brogden, Anne, 'Clothing Provision by Liverpool's Other Poor Law Institution: Kirkdale Industrial Schools', *Costume*, 37/1 (2003), pp. 71–4.

Burnett, John (ed.), *Destiny Obscure: Autobiographies of Childhood, Education and Family from the 1820s to the 1920s* (London, 1994).

Burnette, Joyce, 'Child Day-labourers in Agriculture: Evidence from Farm Accounts, 1740–1850', *Economic History Review*, 65/3 (2012), pp. 1077–99.

Cale, Michelle, 'Saved from a Life of Vice and Crime: Reformatory and Industrial Schools for Girls, c1854–1901', DPhil thesis (University of Oxford, 1993).

Cawood, Ian, 'Middlemore, Sir John Throgmorton, first baronet (1844–1924)', *Oxford Dictionary of National Biography* (Oxford, 2013).

Cunningham, Hugh, *Children and Childhood in Western Society since 1500* (Harlow, 1995).

Cunningham, Hugh, 'The Employment and Unemployment of Children in England c1680–1851', *Past & Present*, 126 (1990), pp. 115–50.

Dando-Collins, Stephen, *Sir Henry Parkes: The Australian Colossus* (Sydney, 2013).

Davin, Anna, *Growing Up Poor: Home, School and Street in London, 1870–1914* (London, 1996).

Davin, Anna, 'When is a Child not a Child?', in H. Corr and L. Jamieson (eds), *Politics of Everyday Life: Continuity and Change in Work and the Family* (London, 1990), pp. 37–61.

de Vries, Jan, 'The Industrial Revolution and the Industrious Revolution', *The Journal of Economic History*, 54/2 (1994), pp. 249–70.

de Vries, Jan, *The Industrious Revolution, Consumer Behavior and the Household Economy, 1650 to the Present* (New York, 2008).

Dick, Malcolm, 'The City of a Thousand Trades, 1700–1945', in Carl Chinn and Malcolm Dick (eds), *Birmingham: The Workshop of the World* (Liverpool, 2016), pp. 125–57.

Dick, Malcolm, 'Discourses for the New Industrial World: Industrialisation and the Education of the Public in Late Eighteenth-century Britain', *History of Education*, 37/4 (2008), pp. 567–84.

Dick, Malcolm, 'English Conservatives and Schools for the Poor c1780–1833', PhD thesis (University of Leicester, 1979).

Dick, Malcolm (ed.), *Matthew Boulton: A Revolutionary Player* (Studley, 2009).

Fitzmaurice, Edmund, *Life of William, Earl of Shelburne* (London, 1912).

Floud, Roderick, and Harris, Bernard, 'Health, Height and Welfare: Britain, 1700–1980', *National Bureau of Economic Research*, 87 (1996), pp. 91–126.

Floud, R., Wachter K. and Gregory, A., *Height, Health and History: Nutritional Status in the United Kingdom 1750–1980* (Cambridge, 1990).

Franco, G., 'Ramazzini and Workers' Health', *The Lancet*, 354 (1999), pp. 858–61.

Frith, Simon, 'Socialization and Rational Schooling: Elementary Education in Leeds before 1870', in Phillip McCann (ed.), *Popular Education and Socialization in the Nineteenth Century* (London, 1977), pp. 67–92.

Frost, M.B., 'The Development of Provided Schooling for Working Class Children in Birmingham 1781–1851', MLitt thesis (University of Birmingham, 1978).

Gear, Gillian, 'Industrial Schools in England, 1857–1933', PhD thesis (University of London, Institute of Education, 1999).

Gleadle, Kathryn, 'We *Will* Have It. Children and Protest in the Ten Hours Movement', in Nigel Goose and Katrina Honeyman (eds), *Childhood and Child Labour in Industrial England: Diversity and Agency, 1750–1914* (Farnham, 2013), pp. 215–30.

Goose, Nigel, 'Employment Prospects in Nineteenth-Century Hertfordshire in Perspective: Varieties of Childhood?', in Nigel Goose and Katrina Honeyman (eds), *Childhood and Child Labour in Industrial England: Diversity and Agency, 1750–1914* (Farnham, 2013), pp. 157–214.

Goose, Nigel and Honeyman, Katrina (eds), *Childhood and Child Labour in Industrial England: Diversity and Agency, 1750–1914* (Farnham, 2013).

Harrison, Barbara, *Not only the 'Dangerous Trades': Women's Work and Health in Britain, 1880–1914* (London, 1996).

Higginbotham, Peter, *Children's Homes: A History of Institutional Care for Britain's Young* (Barnsley, 2017).

Holmes, Rachel, *Eleanor Marx: A Life* (London, 2014).

Honeyman, Katrina, *Child Workers in England, 1780–1820: Parish Apprentices and the Making of the Early Industrial Labour Force* (Farnham, 2007).

Hopkins, Eric, *Birmingham: The First Manufacturing Town in the World, 1760–1840* (London, 1989).

Hopkins, Eric, *Childhood Transformed: Working Class Children in Nineteenth-Century England* (Manchester, 1994).

Horn, Pamela, *The Victorian Town Child* (Stroud, 1997).

Horrell, Sara and Humphries, Jane, '"The exploitation of little children": Child Labour and the Family Economy in the Industrial Revolution', *Explorations in Economic History*, 32 (1995), pp. 485–516.

Horrell, Sara and Humphries, Jane, 'Old Questions, New Data, and Alternative Perspectives: Families' Living Standards in the Industrial Revolution', *The Journal of Economic History*, 52/4 (1992), pp. 849–80.

Horrell, Sara and Oxley, Deborah, 'Bringing Home the Bacon? Regional Nutrition, Stature and Gender in the Industrial Revolution', *The Economic History Review*, 65/4 (2012), pp. 1354–79.

Hudson, Pat, *The Industrial Revolution* (Sevenoaks, 1992).

Humphries, Jane, 'Care and Cruelty in the Workhouse: Children's Experiences of Residential Poor Relief in Eighteenth- and Nineteenth-Century England', in Nigel Goose and Katrina Honeyman (eds), *Childhood and Child Labour in Industrial England: Diversity and Agency, 1750–1914* (Farnham, 2013), pp. 115–34.

Humphries, Jane, *Childhood and Child Labour in the British Industrial Revolution* (Cambridge, 2010).

Jones, Peter, 'Birmingham and the West Midlands in the Eighteenth and Early Nineteenth Centuries', in Malcolm Dick (ed.), *Matthew Boulton: A Revolutionary Player* (Studley, 2009), pp. 3–29.

Jones, Peter, 'Clothing the Poor in Early-Nineteenth-Century England', *Textile History*, 37/1 (2006), pp. 17–37.

Jones, Peter D., '"I cannot keep my place without being deascent": Pauper Letters, Parish Clothing and Pragmatism in the South of England, 1750–1830', *Rural History*, 20/1 (2009), pp. 31–49.

Jones, Peter M., *Industrial Enlightenment: Science, Technology and Culture in Birmingham and the West Midlands, 1760–1820* (Manchester, 2009).

Kershaw, Roger and Sacks, Janet, *New Lives for Old: The Story of Britain's Child Migrants* (Kew, 2008).

Kirby, Peter, 'Causes of Short Stature among Coalmining Children, 1823–1850', *Economic History Review*, 48/4 (1995), pp. 687–99.

Kirby, Peter, *Child Labour in Britain, 1750–1870* (Basingstoke, 2003).

Kirby, Peter, *Child Workers and Industrial Health in Britain, 1780–1850* (Woodbridge, 2013).

Komolos, John, 'Shrinking in a Growing Economy? The Mystery of Physical Stature during the Industrial Revolution', *The Journal of Economic History*, 58/3 (1989), pp. 779–802.

Lane, Joan, *Apprenticeship in England 1600–1914* (London, 1996).

Lane, Joan, 'Apprenticeship in Warwickshire Cotton Mills, 1790–1830', *Textile History*, 10 (1979), pp. 161–74.

Laslett, Peter, *The World We Have Lost* (London, 1971).

Leland, John, *The Itinerary of John Leland in or About the Years 1535–1543* (London, 1907).

Levene, Alysa, 'Charity Apprenticeship and Social Capital in Eighteenth-Century England', in Nigel Goose and Katrina Honeyman (eds), *Childhood and Child Labour in Industrial England: Diversity and Agency, 1750–1914* (Farnham, 2013), pp. 45–70.

Levene, Alysa, *The Childhood of the Poor: Welfare in Eighteenth-Century London* (Basingstoke, 2012).

Levene, Alysa, 'Parish Apprenticeship and the Old Poor Law in London', *Economic History Review*, 63/4 (2010), pp. 915–41.

McCann, Phillip, 'Popular Education, Socialization and Social Control: Spitalfields 1812–1824', in Phillip McCann (ed.), *Popular Education and Socialization in the Nineteenth Century* (London, 1977), pp. 1–40.

McCrory, Patrick, 'Poor Law Education and the Urban Pauper Child: The Theory and Practice of the Urban District School, 1840–1896', in John Hurt (ed.), *Proceedings of the Annual Conference of the History of Education Society of Great Britain* (Leicester, 1980), pp. 83–100.

Madoc-Jones, Beryl, 'Patterns of Attendance and their Social Significance: Mitcham National School 1830–39', in Phillip McCann (ed.), *Popular Education and Socialization in the Nineteenth Century* (London, 1977), pp. 41–66.

Mainville, Curt, 'The Middlemore Boys: Immigration, Settlement and Great War Volunteerism in New Brunswick', *Acadiensis: Journal of the Atlantic Region*, 42/2 (2013), pp. 51–74.

Mark-Lawson, Jane and Witz, Anne, 'From Family Labour to Family Wage? The Case of Women's Labour in Nineteenth-Century Coalmining', *Social History, 13/2 (1988)*, pp. 151–74.

Marsh, Peter T., 'Chamberlain, Joseph (1836–1914)', in *Oxford Dictionary of National Biography* (Oxford, 2004).

Meiklejohn, A., 'John Darwall and "Diseases of Artisans"', *British Journal of Industrial Medicine*, 13/2 (1956), pp. 142–51.

Murdoch, Lydia, *Imagined Orphans: Poor Families, Child Welfare and Contested Citizenship in London* (New Jersey, 2006).

Nejedly, Mary, 'Earning their Keep: Child Workers at the Birmingham Asylum for the Infant Poor', *Family and Community History*, 20/3 (2017), pp. 206–17.

Nicholas, Stephen and Steckel, Richard H., 'Heights and Living Standards of English Workers During the Early Years of Industrialization, 1770–1815', *Journal of Economic History*, 51/4 (1991), pp. 937–57.

Parker, Roy, *Uprooted: The Shipment of Poor Children to Canada, 1867–1917* (Bristol, 2010).

Parr, Joy, *Labouring Children: British Immigrant Apprentices to Canada, 1869–1924* (Toronto, 1994).

Phillips, R.J., 'E.C. Tufnell: Inspector of Poor Law Schools, 1847–1874', *Journal of the History of Education Society*, 5/3 (1976), pp. 227–40.

Reinarz, Jonathan, 'Industry and Illness: Investing in Health and Medical Provision', in Carl Chinn and Malcolm Dick (eds), *Birmingham: The Workshop of the World* (Liverpool, 2016), pp. 239–60.

Sanderson, Michael, *Education, Economic Change and Society in England 1780–1870* (Cambridge, 1995).

Sharpe, Pamela, 'Explaining the Short Stature of the Poor: Chronic Childhood Disease and Growth in Nineteenth-century England', *Economic History Review*, 65/4 (2012), pp. 1475–94.

Sheldon, Nicola, '"Something in the place of home": Children in Institutional Care 1850–1918', in Nigel Goose and Katrina Honeyman (eds), *Childhood and Child Labour in Industrial England: Diversity and Agency, 1750–1914* (Farnham, 2013), pp. 255–76.

Smith, Dennis, *Conflict and Compromise: Class Formation in English Society 1830–1914: A Comparative Study of Birmingham and Sheffield* (London, 1982).

Smith, Harry, 'William Hutton and the Myths of Birmingham', *Midland History*, 40/1 (2015), pp. 53–73.

Snell, K.D.M., *Annals of the Labouring Poor: Social Change and Agrarian England, 1660–1900* (Cambridge, 1985).

Snell, K.D.M., 'The Sunday-School Movement in England and Wales: Child Labour, Denominational Control and Working-Class Culture', *Past and Present*, 164 (1999), pp. 122–68.

Speechley, Helen, 'Female and Child Agricultural Day Labourers in Somerset, c1685–1870', PhD thesis (University of Exeter, 1999).

Stephens, W.B., *Education in Britain 1750–1914* (Basingstoke, 1998).

Taylor, Steven, 'Poverty, Emigration and Family: Experiencing Childhood Poverty in Late Nineteenth-Century Manchester', *Family and Community History*, 18/2 (2015), pp. 89–103.

Thompson, E.P., *The Making of the English Working Class* (London, 1991).

Tosh, John, *The Pursuit of History* (Harlow, 2006).

Toulalan, Sarah, 'Child Sexual Abuse in Late Seventeenth and Eighteenth-Century London: Rape, Sexual Assault and the Denial of Agency', in Nigel Goose and Katrina Honeyman (eds), *Childhood and Child Labour in Industrial England: Diversity and Agency, 1750–1914* (Farnham, 2013), pp. 23–44.

Verdon, Nicola, 'The Rural Labour Market in the Early Nineteenth Century: Women's and Children's Employment, Family Income, and the 1834 Poor Law Report', *Economic History Review*, 55/2 (2002), pp. 299–323.

Voth, Hans-Joachim, 'Living Standards and the Urban Environment', in R. Floud and P. Johnson (eds), *The Cambridge Economic History of Modern Britain* (Cambridge, 2008), pp. 268–94.

Walvin, James, *A Child's World: A Social History of English Childhood, 1800–1914* (Harmondsworth, 1982).

Wohl, Anthony S., *Endangered Lives: Public Health in Victorian Britain* (London, 1983).

Websites

Oxford Dictionary of National Biography (Oxford, 2004); online edn 2013 <http://www.oxforddnb.com/view/article/32350>, accessed 22 August 2017.

Victoria County History, *A History of the County of Warwick, the City of Birmingham*, Vol. 7, ed. W.B. Stephens (London, 1964) <http://www.british-history.ac.uk/vch/warks/vol7>, accessed 31 May 2016.

Index